ALPHA BRAVO DELTA
GUIDE TO
THE U.S.
NAVY

JOHN HELFERS

SERIES EDITOR
WALTER J. BOYNE, USAF (RET.)

ALPHA
A member of Penguin Group (USA) Inc.

Dedicated to the men and women of the United States Navy, past, present and future, who guard the liberty of America and the world.

Publisher: *Marie Butler-Knight*
Product Manager: *Phil Kitchel*
Senior Managing Editor: *Jennifer Chisholm*
Acquisitions Editor: *Gary Goldstein*
Development Editor: *Tom Stevens*
Production Editor: *Billy Fields*
Copy Editor: *Krista Hansing*
Cover Designer: *Doug Wilkins*
Book Designer: *Trina Wurst*
Creative Director: *Robin Lasek*
Indexer: *Julie Bess*
Layout/Proofreading: *Becky Harmon, Mary Hunt*

CONTENTS

FOREWORD

The history of the United States Navy is the history of American freedom. It is the history of a Navy built upon the tradition of wooden ships and iron men, a Navy shaped by grit and determination, and the realization by a visionary few that the projection of power on the high seas is perhaps the most effective way to demonstrate the will and resolve of a nation. After all, a world-class Navy provides not only tangible, visceral evidence of a nation's will to defend itself, but also enhances the conduct of diplomacy. There's nothing like the implied threat presented by a battleship's 16-inch guns to let a president speak softly but still carry that big stick. Or as King Frederick II of Prussia once put it: "Diplomacy without arms is like music without instruments."

In the beginning, however, some argued against the creation of a federal navy altogether. During the earliest days of the Revolution, despite the advice of pro-navy advocates like John Adams of Massachusetts, the Continental Congress shied away from the concept of a navy. In those first weeks and months of rebellion, the individual states were encouraged to raise and maintain separate mini-fleets to fight the British. Finally, a handful of ships, including armed schooners such as the *Hannah* and the *Lee*, were mustered by the Congress (and by General George Washington).

In March, 1777, Congress even authorized the posting of broadsides encouraging "all GENTLEMEN SEAMEN and able-bodied LANDSMEN who have a Mind to distinguish themselves in the GLORIOUS CAUSE of their Country, and make their Fortune, an Opportunity now offers on board the Ship RANGER … commanded by JOHN PAUL JONES."

In 1794, Congress finally approved funds to build the first truly American "fleet," six armed frigates. But it was not until 1798—when John Adams himself was president—that Congress actually created the United States Department of the Navy.

The Navy Congress did finally create was as unique as the United States itself. Unlike the navies of France, Britain, Spain, the Netherlands, and other European nations, our Navy was never developed primarily as a means for expanding national empire. *We* did not sail to colonize. Our

Navy might—and did—protect American trading routes, as it did defeating the Barbary pirates. It would deploy to guard our borders, as was the case with the Battle of Lake Erie. But our Navy was conceived from the very first as a bulwark—"our proper and natural means of defense," as President Woodrow Wilson once described it, protecting American interests and defending America's shores.

Wilson spoke those words in 1914, eighteen years after the Navy had launched its first modern battleship, and twenty-eight months before America's entry into what would become known as the First World War. His thinking was archetypal nineteenth century: that America would always be protected from its enemies by the broad expanses of the Atlantic and Pacific oceans. Wilson was wrong, of course. Pearl Harbor proved that, just the way 9/11 shattered any complacency about America's imperviousness to Islamist terrorism from within its borders.

Indeed, the events of September 11, 2001 are what make this book mandatory reading. History, after all, comes down to lessons from the past that will help us to live more wisely in the present. The history of the United States Navy—its ebbs and its flows, its victories and its debacles, parallel the growth of the United States from provincial nation to superpower. The ability of our Navy to move with the times, to adapt to the age of UAVs, netcentric warfare, and WBOM (War By Other Means) is crucial to America's twenty-first century survival. After all, today's gunboat diplomacy isn't done with battleships, but with nuclear submarines and Tomahawk missiles or carrier battle groups. Teddy Roosevelt's "big stick" has gone from analog to digital.

The real key to victory, however, lies not in technology, but in the motivation of people: turning raw recruits and junior officers into dedicated men o'warsmen. To do that, you need to know about the examples set by heroes like John Paul Jones, who wrote in 1778, "I wish to have no connection with any ship that does not sail fast; for I intend to go in harm's way."

You will discover John Paul Jones in these pages. And also many of our other great Naval leaders: Stephen Decatur and Oliver Hazard Perry; or legendary, pugnacious Warriors like Adm. William F. "Bull" Halsey Jr., who ordered his sailors "Hit hard, hit fast, hit often!" and John Bulkeley, the audacious young officer in the John Paul Jones mold whose flotilla of four battle-scarred PT boats extracted Gen. Douglas MacArthur from the Philippines on March 11, 1942. It is *their* stories—and many others—all told herein, that make this history such a fascinating, inspiring, motivational, and page-turning book.

John Weisman wrote eight *New York Times* best-selling Rogue Warrior novels. His latest book, the Black-Ops novel *SOAR*, will be released in August 2003 by William Morrow.

INTRODUCTION

"A powerful Navy we have always regarded as our proper and natural means of defense; and it has always been of defense that we have thought, never of aggression or conquest. But who shall tell us now what sort of Navy to build? We shall take leave to be strong on the seas, in the future as in the past, and there will be no thought of offense or provocation in that. Our ships are the natural bulwarks."

—President Woodrow Wilson in an address to Congress, December 8, 1914

The rise of the United States Navy has followed the rise of America itself. Ever since the beginning, when the country was a fractious collection of squabbling territories that weren't even sure *they* wanted to ally together. It took the injustices imposed by America's parent nation, Great Britain, to help solidify the original 13 colonies into one organized nation, and even then, they still had their differences, as evidenced by the Civil War in the nineteenth century. But the country survived to prosper and grow, and has taken its place at the forefront of the world, leading the way into the twenty-first century.

Since the beginning of our country, the Navy has proven instrumental in defending our shores and people. Even in its early days, when a navy was often constructed from the water up only to be dismantled when the current conflict was over, the men and ships of the United States Navy stayed their course, performing their duties with skill and valor that is still demanded to this day. Over the past two centuries, the Navy has risen from a motley collection of converted ships to the most powerful fleet in the world, much like America has risen from a collection of colonies to the most powerful nation in the world. Much like their forefathers, today's Navy has used the American spirit of hard work and perseverance to build the mightiest, most advanced ships sailing the oceans.

With the end of the Cold War in the early 1990s, it was thought that the role of the U.S. Navy would diminish in this new age of satellite spying and airplanes that can circle the globe. But as the last two decades have shown, this is definitely not the case. Navy vessels continue to serve as the spearhead of patrolling forces and, when necessary, an invading force as well. In a sense, the task forces of the Navy serve as an all-too-tangible reminder of America's worldwide presence, ready to intervene at a moment's notice with whatever forces are needed, and often delivered to their destination by Navy ships.

The following chapters chronicle the history of the U.S. Navy, from its humble incarnation as the Continental navy during the Revolutionary War, to the strife as American fought against American in the Civil War, to the bloody hell of the Pacific theater during World War II, to the modern military operations of Operations Desert Storm and Enduring Freedom. Naturally, with more than two hundred years of history to cover, not every action of the Navy can be examined in detail, but it is hoped that the salient points of the fleet's history have been presented in an educational, informative, and useful manner.

Although the Navy is often referred to in the following pages as a collective branch of the U.S. armed forces, rather than a proud group of millions of individuals who have earned the right to call themselves U.S. Navy sailors and officers, this in no way diminishes the strength, devotion to duty, and pride of every man and woman in the service, from the Chief of Naval Operations to the thousands of engineers, cooks, and others who keep the fleet running strong every single day. The Navy serves as a perfect example of how thousands of people come together and become much, much more than just the sum of their parts. They become a unified force, capable of going anywhere, at any time, to complete their mission, determined, focused, and unstoppable. Without that vital human element, all of the Navy's technology and power becomes inert and useless. And while this is the story of the U.S. Navy, in reality it is the story of every single man and woman who has sailed into harm's way without a thought for their own safety, only looking to protect the welfare of others, whether that be for America or the rest of the world. This is their history. This is their story.

ACKNOWLEDGMENTS

Thanks to Marty Greenberg for offering the opportunity and the challenge.

Thanks also to Barrett Tillman, whose keen eye and knowledge of military history helped tremendously in the shaping of this book. Any errors or omissions are mine alone.

Finally, thanks to my wife Kerrie Hughes, for her endless patience and support.

CHAPTER 1

MEET TODAY'S NAVY

The U.S. Navy's primary purpose is to "maintain, train, and equip combat-ready naval forces capable of winning wars, deterring aggression, and maintaining freedom of the seas." This mission has grown and evolved from America's first years as a new country to the U.S.'s emergence as the only world superpower in the twenty-first century. Along the way, the naval fleet has grown as well, from small sloops and brigs to thick-hulled frigates, to the battleships of World War II, to the nuclear-powered carriers and submarines that make up today's U.S. Navy.

The United States Navy currently consists of a fleet of roughly 310 ships and 53 submarines; with 384,300 active personnel consisting of 54,600 officers, 4,300 midshipmen (officer trainees), and 325,400 enlisted men. There are 44 active Navy stations, submarine bases, and air bases. Ships are homeported in 16 cities around the nation and Guam. In addition, several vessels are forward-deployed in Italy and Japan.

THE MAKING OF A SAILOR

Navy recruits follow two main paths: enlisted personnel training or officer training. All Navy recruits must have the following qualifications:

- Be between 18 and 34 years old
- Possess a high school diploma or equivalent
- Pass the Armed Services Vocational Aptitude Battery (ASVAB), a test indicating what career path a candidate might be suitable for in a branch of the armed forces

After enlistment, a new recruit goes to the Military Processing Station, where his or her medical history and fitness level is checked, possible careers are discussed, a final interview is conducted, and the recruit is fingerprinted and takes the oath of enlistment.

Then it's on to the Naval Training Center in Great Lakes, Illinois, where all Navy recruits go through an eight-week basic training course, which combines physical fitness with instruction on the structure of the Navy, its core values, and rules and regulations.

Afterward, the recruit goes on to intermediate training as well as classroom and hands-on instruction in several basic skill fields, including mechanical skills, electronics, and computers. From here the recruit may go directly to his or her duty assignment. Or, the recruit might go on to advanced training, consisting of specialized, in-depth education in a particular area of Navy operations. Advanced training can also be picked up during a sailor's Navy career.

After intermediate or advanced training, a sailor is assigned duty depending on skills and training. A typical term of duty is four years, although some fields, such as submarine duty, may require a longer enlistment term. Enlisted men also have the opportunity to volunteer for other assignments, such as nuclear submarine duty or the Navy Sea, Air, and Land (SEAL) special operations unit.

NAVY RANK—ENLISTED PERSONNEL:

E-1 Seaman Recruit	E-6 Petty Officer 1st Class
E-2 Seaman Apprentice	E-7 Chief Petty Officer
E-3 Seaman	E-8 Senior Chief Petty Officer
E-4 Petty Officer 3rd Class	E-9 Master Chief Petty Officer
E-5 Petty Officer 2nd Class	E-10 Master Chief Petty Officer of the Navy

NAVY OFFICERS

Officer candidates, or midshipmen, can begin their Navy careers as early as high school. In addition to the basic Navy requirements, officer candidates must have the following qualifications:

- Be a U.S. citizen
- Be between 19 and 35 years old
- Possess a four-year college degree
- Achieve a qualifying score on the Officer Aptitude Rating Exam

There are several ways to become a Navy officer. If enlisted already, a sailor may enter Officer Candidate School (OCS), a 13-week program in Pensacola, Florida. Candidates are educated in academic and military coursework as well as the obligatory physical fitness.

The second method is by direct appointment, primarily open to professionals with several years of experience in their chosen fields. Appointees undergo a six-week course at Officer Indoctrination School at Newport, Rhode Island, where they are schooled in naval officer protocol and command. Professional fields in demand include dentistry, engineering, law, medicine, and religion.

For students who want to start their Navy careers as soon as possible, there's the Naval Reserve Officers Training Corps (NROTC). This program is for college-bound high school students and first- and second-year college students. NROTC students take naval courses and curriculum, as well as officer, management, and leadership training. They also have the chance to participate in midshipman cruises, where they sail and receive hands-on training as part of a ship's crew. To enroll in NROTC, an applicant must …

- Be a U.S. citizen.
- Be between 17 and 27 years of age.
- Have a high school diploma or equivalent.
- Not have any moral or personal convictions against bearing arms and defending the United States.
- Physically qualify for service.
- Gain acceptance into a certified NROTC university.

The following scores on either college entrance exam are required:
- **SAT:** Verbal: 530; Math: 520
- **ACT:** English: 22; Math: 22

For those who know they want to make the Navy their career, attending the U.S. Naval Academy is a good first step. The Naval Academy gives men and women the most intensive possible preparation, education, and training for an officer position. The requirements for admission to the Naval Academy are a bit more stringent than the rest of the Navy. An applicant must …

- Be a U.S. citizen.
- Be between 17 and 23 years old.
- Possess good moral character.
- Be unmarried.
- Not be pregnant or have any dependents.
- Obtain a nomination letter to the Naval Academy from an official course, which could include the following:

    A member of the U.S. House of Representatives

    A member of the U.S. Senate

    The vice president of the United States

    The president of the United States

NAVY RANK—OFFICERS:

O-1	Ensign	O-7	Rear Admiral (lower half)
O-2	Lieutenant Junior Grade	O-8	Rear Admiral (upper half)
O-3	Lieutenant	O-9	Vice Admiral
O-4	Lieutenant Commander	O-10	Admiral
O-5	Commander	O-11	Fleet Admiral*
O-6	Captain		

The rank of fleet admiral is bestowed only during a time of war. There are currently no fleet admirals in the U.S. Navy.

The Navy's core values are summed up in three words: honor, courage, commitment. Navy enlisted men and officers are expected to conduct themselves in a highly ethical manner in all their relationships; possess the conviction to do what is right for the nation and their Navy, regardless of possible personal sacrifice; and always remain dedicated to the principles of the Navy, to the officers above them and the sailors around them, and to the team of Navy personnel who work together every day safeguarding the waters of the world.

THE STRUCTURE OF TODAY'S NAVY

The Navy's command structure is as follows:

- Secretary of the Navy
- Chief of Naval Operations
- Commanders-in-Chief of the Pacific and Atlantic Forces
- Operating Forces Commanders in the Pacific and Atlantic (a Naval Air Force, Submarine Force, and Naval Surface Force for each theater)

The secretary of the Navy (SECNAV), a civilian position, is responsible for conducting the Navy's day-to-day operations, including recruiting, organizing, supplying and equipping, training, and mobilizing and demobilizing. The secretary works to create programs and policies consistent with America's national security policy and objectives, which are established by the president and the secretary of defense of the United States. He is assisted by the undersecretary of the Navy, among others. (For a complete list of the secretaries of the Navy, see Appendix A.)

The Chief of Naval Operations (CNO) is a four-star admiral and the senior military officer of the Navy. He answers to the secretary of the Navy and is responsible for commanding and operating the forces of the U.S. Navy. A member of the Joint Chiefs of Staff, the CNO is the principal naval advisor to the president and the secretary of the Navy on the conduct of war, and the primary executive to the secretary of the Navy on the conduct of the Navy itself. (For a complete list of the Chiefs of Naval Operations, see Appendix B.)

THE PURPOSE OF THE NAVY

Today, the Navy plays a vital role in the defense of America and the free world. With its "forward deployment" strategy, the Navy is always close by possible trouble spots around the planet, ready to assist whenever and wherever necessary.

Forward deployment, the stationing of vessels in key areas around the world, constantly achieves four goals of the Navy and the U.S. government:

- Providing the reassurance of a strong military presence to allied and friendly nations
- Dissuading current and future military competition
- Deterring threats against U.S. interests
- Defeating an adversary if deterrence fails

With the advent and rise of the aircraft carrier in tactical operations, the Navy has become the most multifunctional of the military branches, able to patrol and guard coastlines of both friends and foes while naval aircraft and ballistic ship- and submarine-launched missiles strike deep in an enemy country. The Navy is also best equipped to support all other branches of the military, whether amphibious landings of Army and Marines forces, work with land-based Air Force units on bombing missions, or fire support for all three forces. The Navy has become the point force in today's military arena.

The Navy is currently divided into five fleets:

- The Second Fleet, deployed in the Atlantic Ocean
- The Third and Seventh Fleets, both stationed in the Pacific Ocean
- The Fifth Fleet, assigned to the United States
- The Sixth Fleet, headquartered in Europe

THE CARRIER BATTLE GROUP (CVBG)

While a task force is assembled out of whatever ships are needed to accomplish the task at hand, the main force used since World War II has been the carrier battle group, which contains the following:

- One *Nimitz*-class fleet carrier, armed with fighters (the F-14A/B Tomcat, F/A-18E/F Super Hornet) and reconnaissance planes (the E-2C Hawkeye and EA-6B Prowler). In addition to its air wing, the latest carriers also armed with Sea Sparrow surface-to-air missiles, the Phalanx Close-In Weapons System (CIWS), and an electronic warfare system.

- Two guided missile cruisers. Fast and powerful, these *Ticonderoga*-class ships provide offensive support with the guided Tomahawk cruise missile. The cruiser can also attack enemy ships or planes, as well with surface-to-air missiles or torpedoes.

- One guided missile destroyer. Smaller than a cruiser, the missile destroyer also provides fire support for land or water targets. It is armed with the Tomahawk and the Harpoon guided antiship missile.

- One destroyer, designated for antisubmarine warfare. It has the option of launching a torpedo at an enemy or a torpedo-armed helicopter to extend the ship's offensive range.

- One frigate, also for antisubmarine warfare.

- Two attack submarines, to support the surface ships by targeting enemy surface vessels and submarines or to provide reconnaissance of an enemy's coastline or forces.

- A combined ammunition, oiler, and supply ship for logistics support.

With this combination, a task force is protected from attack by land, sea, and air, and can strike back with deadly force no matter where an assault comes from.

NAVY PLANES

If the backbone of the modern Navy is its carrier, then its primary weapons are the planes it carries, from the fast, deadly fighters to the intelligence-gathering reconnaissance planes. Here are brief overviews of the main airplanes used by the Navy today:

- The F-14 Tomcat is the Navy's primary fighter plane, a multirole air-to-air or air-to-ground strike fighter. Armed with the Phoenix, Sidewinder, and Sparrow antiaircraft missiles as well as the M-61 Vulcan 20mm cannon, the F-14 is a top line of defense for a Navy carrier.

- The F/A-18 Hornet, a supreme air-to-air combat plane, is the Navy's all-weather jet fighter and attack aircraft. It has the ability to carry more kinds of ordinance than the Tomcat, including the AIM-120 AMRAAM, the successor to the Sparrow, and the Harpoon antiship missile, as well as a wide array of mines, bombs, and rockets for use against enemy ground forces. In 2002, the F/A-18 E/F Super Hornet was introduced, with its first operational sortie on November 6. It can fly 40 percent farther than its predecessor, has more weapons points, and can bring back three times the payload a normal Hornet can (instead of jettisoning it for a safe landing).

- The E-2C Hawkeye is the Navy's early-warning aircraft, performing surveillance duties, fighter control, and communications relay. Working with the Aegis guided missile cruisers, the Hawkeye, known as "the eyes of the fleet" has total reconnaissance superiority over whatever area it's in.

- The EA-6B Prowler's purpose is to jam enemy communications and radar, providing an umbrella of protection for U.S. Navy planes. The Prowler also gathers intelligence on an enemy force in a combat area.

IN THE BEGINNING ...

Over the course of 228 years, the Navy has undergone its share of change, expansion, contraction, victories, and defeats. Along the way it has been led by officers both good and bad and has played a part in the expansion of America, carrying out foreign policy and defending the United States and other countries throughout the past two centuries. But before there was a Navy, there had to be a nation to defend. In 1775, the first steps were taken to create a United States of America. At the same time, a national force of ships was requested to help protect it.

CHAPTER 2

THE REVOLUTIONARY WAR

The origin of what is now the mightiest seagoing fleet in the world, the United States Navy, was inauspicious, at best. After years of putting up with British-imposed taxes, including tariffs on imported sugar, lead, paper, glass, tea, and legal documents, and forcing American colonists to feed and house British soldiers, all with no apparent means to redress the colonies' grievance in Parliament, the settlers of the New World had had enough. After suffering the Boston Massacre in 1770 and protesting the English taxes with the Boston Tea Party in 1774, the first Continental Congress met that year to discuss what to do about British rule.

The British were also causing problems at sea. The first proposal for an American fleet, presented by Stephen Hopkins and Samuel Ward of Rhode Island on October 3, 1775, was in response to British frigates disrupting trade on the New England coast. Unfortunately, the Continental Congress tabled the motion for further consideration, with naysayers in the new legislature claiming that a fleet would bankrupt the struggling nation.

But when news arrived that two munitions ships had sailed unescorted from Great Britain in early August, Congress appointed John Adams, John Langdon, and Silas Deane to investigate capturing the ships and getting their supplies to Gen. George Washington and his army. The three-man committee sent orders to General Washington to outfit a schooner and sloop to capture the two British ships.

A brig is an efficient two-masted ship that used square-set sails.

A schooner is a sailing ship with anywhere from two to six masts. The most common type had two masts, a foremast and a taller mainmast. Schooners are always fore-and-aft rigged, with the sails set parallel to the keel of the boat; this is different than the larger, square-set sailing vessels, in which the sails are set along yardarms, or beams, at right angles to the boat's hull.

A sloop is a single-masted ship, also fore-and-aft rigged. Smaller and more agile than schooners, sloops were popular among privateers.

FIRST ACTION AGAINST THE BRITISH

On his own initiative in early September 1775, General Washington had ordered the *Hannah*, a fishing schooner out of Marblehead, Massachusetts, to be converted into an armed raiding ship and to "intercept the supplies of the Enemy." As a duly appointed (if not completely official) government vessel, the *Hannah's* record was not exemplary. A lack of suitable targets caused her crew to mutiny, and the British supply ships slipped through America's fingers, leaving Washington fuming about the unreliability of private vessels working for the new government.

However, some men got results. John Manley, also of Marblehead, commanded the schooner *Lee*, which captured nine British ships near Massachusetts in November and December of 1775, including the munitions brig *Nancy*, whose cargo of arms and ammunition was welcomed by Washington's army.

Back in Philadelphia, Adams, Deane, and Langdon were just getting warmed up. On October 13, 1775, the three-man committee advocated the commission of two small ships to search the North Atlantic for British supply vessels. At the end of the month, they requested a budget for 10 warships, signaling the start of a new era in America's fight for independence.

Congress was not persuaded so easily, allowing funds for only four ships. The committee purchased four vessels for refitting: two ships, the 30-gun *Alfred* and the 28-gun *Columbus*, and two brigs, the 16-gun *Andrea Dorea* and the 14-gun *Cabot*. These ships would form the backbone of the American Navy until more could be purchased.

THE START OF THE WAR AGAINST GREAT BRITAIN ON THE HIGH SEAS

On November 9, America received the news that plunged the country into war with Britain: King George III had denied Congress's Olive Branch Petition and declared the colonies to be in open rebellion. Conflict was inevitable; now it was a race against time and the British navy, which would step up its harassment of the colonies' coastline. The news spurred Congress to approve the construction of 13 frigates at an estimated cost of $66,500 each, a serious expenditure for the cash-strapped new government.

> At this time, ships were rated by the number of cannons and crew they carried:
>
> 1st rate: 100 or more cannons/850 to 875 men
>
> 2nd rate: 90 to 98 cannons/700 to 750 men
>
> 3rd rate: 64 to 88 cannons/500 to 650 men
>
> 4th rate: 50 to 62 cannons/320 to 420 men
>
> 5th rate: 32 to 48 cannons/200 to 300 men
>
> 6th rate: 20 to 30 cannons/140 to 200 men
>
> Sloop: 16 to 18 cannons/90 to 120 men
>
> Gun brig and cutters: 6 to 14 cannons/5 to 25 men
>
> A post captain commanded any of the six rated classes of ship. A commander was the top man on a sloop, fire-ship, or warship *en flute,* which was used primarily for transport, with some of its cannon removed. A lieutenant commanded a schooner or cutter. A very small vessel or supply boat could be commanded by a master's mate or a midshipman. These last two ranks could also be placed in charge of a prize until they reached port.

The transformation of the first four ships was proceeding well, but they still needed officers, crews, weapons, supplies—everything to make them into men-of-war. Rhode Island's governor, Stephen Hopkins, "persuaded" the committee to appoint men he knew; his younger brother Esek was promoted to the position of commander in chief of the Fleet of the United Colonies. Esek's son, John Burroughs Hopkins, was placed in command of the *Cabot*. Silas Deane's brother-in-law, Dudley Saltonstall, was given command of the *Alfred*, with his first lieutenant a Scottish immigrant named John Paul Jones. The *Andrea Dorea* was captained by Nicholas Biddle. A former midshipman in the Royal Navy before settling in Philadelphia, he was the only one among them with military naval experience. Armed, equipped, and provisioned at last, the fleet set sail in early January 1776.

> The primary ship's weapon since the mid-1500s, the cannon, was defined by the weight of the shot fired, from as little as 2 pounds, to 3-, 4-, 6-, 8-, 9-, 12-, and 18-pound guns.
>
> A cannon could fire several types of ammunition. The most common was round shot, a solid iron projectile used to smash a ship's hull. There was also chain shot, two small weights attached to each other by a length of chain, which was used at close range to slash through sails and rigging, hampering a ship's maneuverability. Cannons could fire antipersonnel charges as well. Canister or case shot was like a huge shotgun shell: When fired, the metal container disintegrated, scattering the shot in all directions. Grapeshot worked on a similar principle and consisted of small balls loaded into a canvas bag. When the cannon was fired, the bag burned up, leaving just the deadly hail of shot to shred sails or sailors.
>
> To fire the cannon, a charge of gunpowder (contained in a canvas bag) was rammed down the barrel, followed by whatever ammunition was chosen, which was held in place by a wad of cloth. Then a spike was inserted into the "touch-hole" on the top rear end of the cannon, piercing the powder bag. A bit of powder was poured into the hole, and the whole thing was touched off. The cannon roared and recoiled backward, held in place by breeching ropes attached to the hull of the ship. The barrel was swabbed out with water to extinguish any flaming residue, and the cycle began again.
>
> The main problem the colonies had was finding enough cannons to arm their ships. Although American smiths could make just about anything, the casting of cannons had been forbidden, because if the colonies revolted they would already have weapons for their ships. While American metal-smiths figured out how to make cannons, they were almost always behind the British in terms of the number available. Thus, they had to rely on capturing enemy ships to supply arms or, in the case of Esek Hopkins, steal them, as we'll soon see.

One of the main difficulties facing the Continental navy was deciding what kind of administrative body should lead this new military branch. From 1775 to 1781, various kinds of committees and Boards of Admiralty were formed, each failing in inexperience, inefficiency, and a basic lack of understanding about how a navy should be run. Order didn't arrive until 1781, when Robert Morris became the sole marine agent responsible for the organization and oversight of the Continental navy.

The Continental Congress commanded Hopkins to take his ships to Chesapeake Bay and attack any British ships he found. Hopkins, however, came from the privateering tradition, where men-of-war went after unarmed merchant ships, disrupting supply lines and bringing valuable equipment and munitions back to the country they were working for. Knowing his own abilities and those of his eager but undisciplined force of nonmilitary sailors, Captain Hopkins did the exact opposite of what Congress had asked: He headed south.

> A privateer is a ship whose captain has been given letters of marque and reprisal by the country he's working for, authorizing him to capture merchant vessels of an enemy country. An expedient, less violent, and popular method of fighting against a superior foe by hitting them where it hurt (in the treasury), American privateers captured around 2,200 prizes with an estimated value of $66 million (in 1780s dollars) during the Revolutionary War.

He sailed to the Bahamas, where his fleet, now six ships strong with the addition of the small sloops the *Providence* and the *Fly*, attacked the port of Nassau on New Providence Island. Seizing cannons, muskets, and powder, he and his crew then set sail for Rhode Island in early March of 1776. They were almost home when they encountered a lone British frigate, the 24-gun *Glasgow*, commanded by experienced Captain Tyringham Howe.

At last, the Continental navy sailed into combat on the high seas. And six American ships against one British vessel ..., the outcome would be inevitable, right? Well, not exactly.

When the smoke and confusion cleared, Captain Howe's experienced crew had sailed and fought rings around the Americans. Unused to operating together, the American ships had relied on the standard privateer rule when a group was attacked: Every craft for itself. The fight ended with the *Cabot* and the *Alfred* disabled, the *Andrea Dorea* and the *Columbus* outsailed and outmaneuvered, and the damaged *Glasgow* escaping. The *Providence*'s captain hadn't even entered the fight and was later relieved of his command for his cowardice. Hopkins's battered fleet limped to Providence, Rhode Island, where he tried unsuccessfully to repair his ships and get them out to sea.

Esek Hopkins was eventually censured by Congress and dismissed from his post in 1778 for what was then considered insubordination. In reality, he had utilized his tiny force for maximum effect, striking where the Royal Navy wasn't and getting desperately needed supplies for the Army. Congress had expected him to single-handedly (and miraculously) clear American waters of the Royal Navy, the best fleet in the world at the time, an impossible task under the best conditions.

Thus went the first maritime action of the Continental navy, inconsequential and ultimately embarrassing for the new nation.

> The frigate class was created in the late seventeenth century by the British Navy, who wanted a vessel fast enough to capture merchantmen and escape heavier warships. The frigate was a three-masted, square-set sailing ship with two decks, the main deck, or gundeck, and an upper deck, which, ironically, had no name until U.S. Navy sailors began calling it the spar deck. American frigates were typically larger than British models and were often employed for scouting and escort duty.

ONE IF BY LAND, TWO IF BY ... LAKE? THE BATTLE OF LAKE CHAMPLAIN

During the summer and fall of 1776, a contest developed between the British and Americans that had severe consequences for the War for Independence. In the thick forests of New York, a rising hero saved his fledgling country, only to betray it later.

In the latter half of 1775, both sides were launching offensives. Two small elements of the Continental army invaded Canada, taking Montreal and combining to lay siege to Quebec over the winter, only to be driven off when a British ship sailed down the thawed St. Lawrence River in the spring. The army, under the command of Gen. Benedict Arnold (yes, *that* Benedict Arnold), pulled up stakes and retreated to the southern end of Lake Champlain.

Meanwhile, the British were trying to cut off New England from the rest of the colonies, figuring that with the country divided, it would be easier to finish off each part. To do this, they had to control Lake Champlain, which, once firmly in British hands, would be the primary corridor to transport redcoats from Canada into the United States to reinforce Gen. William Howe's army. The only colonial force in their way was Arnold's motley crew.

During the summer of 1776, both sides built fleets using the natural resources at hand. When the sawdust settled, Arnold had pulled together one sloop (the 10-gun *Enterprise*), two schooners (the 12-gun *Royal Savage* and the 8-gun *Revenge*), four galleys (the 8-gun ships the *Trumbull*, the *Congress* [Arnold's command vessel], and the *Washington*, and the six-gun craft the *Lee*), eight gondolas (two with 5 guns, the *Connecticut* and the *Spitfire*, and five 3-gun vessels, the *Providence*, the *Philadelphia*, the *Jersey*, the *New York*, and the *Boston*). The eighth gondola, the *Liberty*, wasn't in the battle, having sailed for supplies before it started). Forced to man his ships with inexperienced crewmen (only 10 percent of the roughly 700 men had any maritime experience), Arnold resolved to do everything in his power to stop the British from seizing Lake Champlain.

> The gondolas built by Arnold's men were rough-hewn, flat-bottomed boats approximately 50 feet long, powered by a single fore-and-aft sail and oarsmen. Their armament consisted of a 12-pound gun on the bow, two or three 9-pound cannons, and a swivel gun, which was basically a pellet-firing deck sweeper used to clear an enemy ship of a crewman or two.
>
> In 1935, the gondola the *Philadelphia* was recovered from the bottom of Lake Champlain, amazingly intact—and with a British cannonball still lodged in its hull! It is currently on display in the Smithsonian Institution, a relic of the humble beginnings of the United States Navy.

The British forces, led by Maj. Gen. Sir Guy Carleton, also the governor of Quebec at the time, were a bit better off. Their fleet consisted of the 18-gun, three-masted *Inflexible*; the 14-gun schooner *Lady Maria*; the 12-gun schooner *Carleton*; the 18-gun scow *Thunderer*; the 7-gun gondola *Loyal Convert*; and 20 flat-bottomed, 30-foot–long rivers boats known as bateaux, each carrying one gun.

Carleton was so confident of his victory that he had ordered both the *Carleton* and the *Inflexible* to be dismantled and transported over land to be rebuilt at the port of St. John. The delay gave the American forces badly needed time to construct their ships. Ironically, if Carleton had attacked the U.S. forces when he had first arrived at Lake Champlain, he probably would have defeated them, gained control of the lake, and cut the colonies in half as originally planned. But poor weather delayed the ships' arrival, so the British fleet didn't get underway until October 11, heading south toward where they thought the Americans were.

General Arnold hid most of his fleet between Valcour Island and the mainland, and sent the *Royal Savage* and the *Enterprise* out as decoys. The British main force, including their lead ship, the *Lady Maria*, cruised past the rebel fleet and was at a disadvantage because they had to come around into the wind to attack the Americans.

The *Carleton* was the first large ship to sail out past the struggling British line, where it was immediately exposed to cannon fire from the *Congress*, the *Royal Savage*, the *Enterprise*, and one other gondola. The American ships pounded the British schooner, severely wounding its commander, and first mate, leaving the youngest officer, a teenager named Edward Pellew, in charge. After half the crew was injured and with 2 feet of water in the hold, two other British ships came by to tow the *Carleton* out of harm's way.

Meanwhile, the *Inflexible* had managed to get the drop on the *Royal Savage*, which was trying to join the fight, and broadsided her. The inexperienced crew ran the ship aground on Valcour Island. The *Loyal Convert*'s captain, not wanting to lose such a prize, boarded the grounded vessel with his crew and captured 20 men who hadn't fled, commanding them to turn their cannons on the American fleet. However, once the rest of the American ships turned their own cannons on the grounded ship, he lost half of his boarding party and had to abandon the vessel.

> A broadside is a naval tactic in which one ship positions itself so that all of the cannons on one side of the vessel can fire at one target in quick succession. The destruction from a successful broadside attack was incredible, and when properly used, often resulted in the surrender of the broadsided vessel.

General Arnold and the rest of his fleet were also taking fire from the other British ships, which had finally gotten in position. His flagship, the *Congress*, was set upon by the two British schooners and another boat firing 18-pound cannons. During the battle, the galley was rammed 12 times and took several shots below the waterline. Arnold's sailors just patched up the holes and kept fighting.

But the rebels were also inflicting damage of their own. An American cannonball hit the powder magazine of a British ship, with the resulting explosion killing most of the crew. The survivors crowded into another boat, nearly swamping it.

The battle raged until around 5 P.M., when the British discovered that the Continentals were out of ammunition. They retreated to a distance of about 700 yards, out of range of the American fleet's grapeshot blasts, and regrouped without taking further damage. The British fleet, wanting to trap the Americans in the southern part of the lake, spread out in a line across the water. But inclement weather allowed the battered American ships to slip through a large hole in the British line.

> A local legend around Lake Champlain tells of a rock that was bombarded by the British forces in the early morning hours of October 13, 1776, when they mistook it for a rebel ship. More than 225 years later, the rock is still called "Carleton's Prize."

When the British discovered what had happened, almost a full day had passed before they gave chase. The Americans had holed up near Schuyler's Island and spent most of October 12 making repairs. They had lost three gondolas, including the *Philadelphia*, and almost every other ship had sustained damage.

The British spotted the Americans on the morning of October 13 and engaged them again seven hours later. This time the battle was shorter and more one-sided. The *Congress* and the *Washington* took on the enemy to give the rest of the fleet time to escape, but the British turned their guns on one and then the other. Although the *Congress* fought valiantly, battling three British ships at once, in the end General Arnold and his surviving men set their remaining boats on fire and fled through the forest to Fort Amherst at Crown Point, New York, just ahead of the pursuing British. All that remained of the American fleet was the *Enterprise*, the *Revenge*, the *Trumbull*, and a lone gondola, all of which escaped to Fort Ticonderoga.

With the lake secure, all Sir Carleton and his men had to do was march over and join General Howe's army. But by the time the fighting was over, winter had set in and Sir Carleton was forced to halt his advance and wait for spring. Although the American naval forces lost the battle of Lake

Champlain, they had blunted the British long enough to prevent the dissolution of the colonies, allowing the United States to continue fighting for her freedom.

ASSAULT OF THE TURTLE

The only other maritime operation that year was the underwater assault of the *Turtle*, America's first submersible, against a flagship of the Royal Navy.

The *Turtle* was a 7-foot-high shell of oak timbers joined, caulked, bound in iron, and sealed with a coating of pitch over the entire outside. Operated by hand and foot cranks, it descended by the pilot opening a valve to let water into the ballast tank, and ascended by using pumps to force the water out. There was a snorkel breathing device on it, the first of its kind, and it moved through the water by a two-bladed propeller attached to a set of pedals the pilot cranked with his feet, also an innovation.

After testing and working out the craft's bugs during 1775, inventor David Bushnell and his brother Ezra, the *Turtle*'s pilot, offered their services to General Washington, who requested that they try the submersible against the enemy. When Lord Richard Howe, commander of the British naval forces, anchored the 64-gun frigate *Eagle* off Staten Island, they had found their target.

On the night of September 6, 1776, Ezra Lee (Ezra Bushnell was unable to pilot the submarine due to fever) took the submarine into the harbor and headed toward the British ship. The plan was to drill a hole in the hull of the *Eagle*, attach the bomb, and leave.

Lee reached the hull of the ship undetected. But with no way to hold the *Turtle* in place while he set the drill, he couldn't produce enough force to get the bit started in the timbers. After two unsuccessful tries and with dawn approaching, he gave up and began moving away from the ship. Worried that he would be swept out to sea with the outgoing tide, he jettisoned his ballast water and began pedaling, knowing that part of the submarine was now sticking out of the water.

He wasn't the only one aware of this. Two British soldiers noticed the odd shape in the harbor and set out in a skiff to investigate. Spotting them, Lee released a 250-pound mine, also timer-activated, in his wake and headed back to the Battery. Later that morning, the mine exploded, causing the British fleet to move into the comparative safety of lower New York Bay.

While the *Turtle*'s mission could be seen as a failure, it so unnerved the British that they were unable to keep up their blockade of New York City. Also, the sheer audacity of the plan had to have demoralized the British on some level, to know that one of their flagships had almost been lost, with them powerless to prevent the attack.

Although several more attempts to use the *Turtle* were made, none was successful. Her ultimate fate remains a mystery, with the British claiming they sank a sloop that had been trying to sneak the submarine out of the harbor, and the Americans saying she was dismantled to keep her from falling into enemy hands. Whichever story is true, the *Turtle* was America's first submarine, beginning the long and glorious history of the underwater Navy.

THE LEAN YEARS

The years of 1777–1778 were hard for the infant Continental navy. Although individual captains and ships distinguished themselves, particularly by taking America's war with England to the enemy's shores, the overall state of the U.S. Navy limped along much like Esek Hopkins's fleet, still stuck at port in Providence.

With Congress still not getting its act together and centralizing a U.S. Navy, 11 of the 13 states equipped and provisioned their own fleets, comprised mainly of shallow-water vessels, galleys, half-galleys, barges, and fire-ships. The new government was still relying primarily on privateers, issuing hundreds of letters of marque during the Revolutionary War.

But some captains were bringing in prizes, even if that meant doing it all by themselves. At the end of 1776, Capt. Lambert Wickes, commander of the *Reprisal*, led a mission to transport Benjamin Franklin to France. The elder statesman had been charged with convincing France to come to America's aid against the British. His negotiations with King Louis XVI were partially successful: The monarch granted American privateers the use of French ports and also arranged to loan ships and money to the United States. But he refused to commit further, having just destroyed much of his own country's navy battling England during the Seven Years' War.

Franklin decided to bring France in by provoking a war between Great Britain and France. Having France's ports open for American ships to use was a good start, and Captain Wickes took the next step.

After delivering Franklin, the *Reprisal* sailed over to England to see what havoc it could raise. The waters around the British Isles were a rich hunting ground, and Wickes's crew took five prizes in January alone—bringing them all back to France. Great Britain protested, wanting the *Reprisal* forced out of port. But by this time Franklin had enlisted the help of the Comte de Vergennes, Louis XVI's foreign minister, who blocked the request, allowing Captain Wickes to repair his ship.

Ready to sail again, and supported by the 14-gun brigantine the *Lexington* and the 10-gun cutter the *Dolphin*, the *Reprisal* set out for the English seas again. On their one-month voyage, they captured 18 English vessels, panicking the kingdom's merchants, who petitioned the government for help. The British put the 74-gun ship the *Burford* on Wickes's trail, causing him to retreat to France again.

> Similar to a sloop, a cutter is a single-masted ship with a fore-and-aft sail. The only difference is that the mast of a cutter is positioned farther back on the boat.
>
> A man-of-war is any combat vessel serving in a recognized navy.

The French were still not quite ready to commit to the war (the government even ordered Wickes to stop using France's ports in the fall of 1777), so the *Reprisal* and the *Lexington* were sent home. The *Lexington* was captured by the British off the coast of France. In an effort to escape the still-pursuing *Burford*, the *Reprisal*'s cannons were thrown overboard, Wickes apparently sawed through some of the ship's hull beams to gain more flexibility. It was a fatal decision. As they sailed back to North America, the *Reprisal* foundered off the coast of Newfoundland, taking Captain Wickes and all of his crew (except one lucky man) with her.

Fortunately, another American captain had risen through the ranks to take up the mantle where Captain Wickes left off, and he earned a place in history by doing so. Capt. John Paul Jones hatched an even more audacious plan. In his own words, "When an enemy thinks a design against them is improbable, they can always be surprised and attacked with advantage."

Jones's plan was to do the unthinkable: attack villages and ports along the English coast.

When John Paul Jones first arrived in France, the Gallic people were firmly allied with the Americans. Upon sailing into Quiberon Bay, Jones ran up his colors while sailing past the French flagship. As was the custom of the day, he gave the ship a salute with 13 of his cannons. The French man-of-war responded with nine of its own guns, as befitting the *Ranger*'s lower status. That was unimportant, however; this incident was the first time a United States Navy ship was recognized and acknowledged by a foreign power. Not being a modest man, Jones ensured that he was the first American captain to claim this honor by doing the same thing the next day.

As daring as this idea sounds in theory, it was much less glorious in practice. The *Ranger*'s first raid in mid-April 1778 against the fishing village of Whitehaven was a complete failure. In fact, some of the crew even tried to warn the villagers of what was going to happen. Jones ordered the fishing boats burned, but a sudden rainstorm quenched the smoldering fires. In the end, he had accomplished nothing.

It wasn't a particularly brave or daring raid because the village boats weren't used for any kind of military purpose. However, it did stir the local populace's ire against their own government. Coastal towns and villages besieged their representatives for protection. So as propaganda, the attack served its purpose, which is good because it didn't accomplish much else.

Jones's next idea was, if anything, even more ill conceived. He planned to land at St. Mary's Island and kidnap the local lord, the fourth Earl of Selkirk. On this raid, everything that could have gone wrong did, starting with the fact that the good earl was not home to be stolen. Even if Jones had snatched him, he was such a minor lord that the London Parliament probably wouldn't have taken much action upon receiving news of his abduction. Finally, the man Jones had targeted for ransom was actually on the colonies' side, so the captain would have been holding someone loyal to the rebels.

By now his crew was growing surly at this second raid with no appreciable spoils of war, so they took Lady Selkirk's collection of silver plate. Jones redeemed himself at this point by buying the silver from his crew and sending it back to the family with a gracious note of apology. Now the British populace began to think of him as a Robin Hood type of free-booter, which helped improve his tarnished image after the embarrassing debacle at Whitehaven.

It was on the way back from St. Mary's Island that Jones's legend began. Encountering the 20-gun sloop the *Drake*, Jones readied his crew and engaged the enemy vessel. After a fierce hour-long battle in which the *Drake*'s captain was killed and its rigging was torn to pieces, the crew surrendered. Jones returned to France with the ship and 133 prisoners who were later exchanged for Americans held by the British. This was another first for America: Before this incident, Great Britain had not allowed any prisoner exchanges.

All of this was leading up to the battle that immortalized John Paul Jones in the annals of U.S. Navy history forever. Using his capture of the *Drake* as proof that he deserved a more powerful ship, after several months, Jones received the 900-ton, 42-gun *Duc de Duras* from the French. An older but still sound vessel, he rechristened it the *Bonhomme Richard* in honor of Benjamin Franklin's *Poor Richard's Almanac*, which was also popular in France at the time.

THE *BONHOMME RICHARD* VS. THE *SERAPIS*

The seas were set for conflict on the evening of September 23, 1779. Jones had been roaming the Irish Sea for the past several weeks, along with the 32-gun frigate *Alliance*, commanded by a Frenchman, Pierre Landais. The two captains had already clashed over where and how to capture prizes, an argument that would have severe consequences later. They were accompanied by three French navy ships, the 32-gun frigate the *Pallas*, the 18-gun cutter the *Le Cerf*, and the 12-gun brigantine the *La Vengeance*, and two French privateers who had deserted the fleet at the first opportunity.

Jones had already taken several prizes when he encountered a convoy of 41 ships escorted by the 44-gun *Serapis* and the 20-gun sloop the *Countess of Scarborough* off Flamborough Head near Scarborough, England. Jones wanted to capture some of the merchant ships and their rich cargo, but the *Serapis* interposed itself between his ship and the English merchantmen. Jones signaled his fleet to attack immediately, but the *Alliance* withdrew and the *Pallas* moved to engage the *Countess of Scarborough*, leaving the *Bonhomme Richard* to tackle the *Serapis* alone.

Both ships tried to get into position for raking fire. Jones had just gotten a broadside off, which was answered in kind by Captain Pearson's crew, when a thunderous explosion shook the *Bonhomme Richard*. Two of her 18-pound cannons had exploded, killing both crews and blowing a hole in the upper deck.

> Also known as "crossing the T," raking fire occurred when one ship sailed in front of or behind its enemy and fired a broadside at the bow or stern, the weakest parts of a ship. In the days of wooden vessels, not only was the targeted ship unable to return fire, but the attack also often caused a deadly hail of wooden splinters, shredding the deck and any unlucky crewmen caught in the blast.

Trying to maneuver his ship into better position so his crew could board the *Serapis*, Jones watched as the *Richard* became entangled with the British ship, leaving his own guns unable to fire while being subjected to the enemy's after guns. At this point, when asked by Captain Pearson whether he would strike his colors, Jones gave the famous reply that forever marked him in history: "I have not yet begun to fight!"

He followed those words with immediate action. Disengaging from the *Serapis*, Jones brought the *Richard* around and tried to rake his enemy, but instead the two ships became entangled again. They stayed that way for the next two hours, each blasting away at the other with whatever guns could be brought to bear. The *Richard* was down to three 9-pound cannons, and before Jones could order the third one brought to starboard, the ship was rocked by another broadside—not from the *Serapis*, but from the *Alliance!*

Crewmen on the *Richard* tried to signal Captain Landais that he was firing on the wrong vessel, only to be blasted again by the frigate's cannons. Once Jones raised the proper recognition signal, the *Alliance* ceased firing, but Jones was convinced that the attack had been deliberate. He later brought official charges against Landais, causing him to be cashiered from the French navy.

By now both ships looked like they had sailed through hell, with casualties everywhere and water (the *Richard* had taken on 5 feet of ocean and was on fire, to boot) in both holds, yet the crews fought on. Now Jones's topsmen were turning the tide of battle, their accurate musket fire making it hard for the British to man their weapons.

> Marines and sailors stationed in a ship's rigging armed with muskets were known as topsmen. Their job was to shoot anyone they could see on the enemy vessel, which, of course, would be very distracting to anyone trying to sail the ship or fire the deck cannons.

The final blow came when one of Jones's crew was able to scatter a sack of hand grenades on the deck of the *Serapis*. One of them landed in a powder magazine, and the resulting explosion destroyed the gundeck and killed 20 men. Meanwhile, Jones' three 9-pound cannons had been battering the *Serapis*'s mainmast, which was almost ready to give way. Unable to subdue the *Richard*, Captain Pearson struck his colors and surrendered.

The Americans had won the fight, although at a terrible cost, with each side having lost about half its crew. But there was one more casualty before it was all over. Though the crew worked hard to save her, the *Bonhomme Richard* had been hulled below the water line and, two days after the battle, slipped beneath the waves.

> When a ship took damage from cannon or mines that had breached the hull of the vessel, allowing water in, it was said to have been hulled. Unless it was quickly repaired, the ship usually sank soon afterward.

It was the high-water mark of Jones's career, and he returned first to France and then to America as a hero. The Continental Congress gave him command of the brand-new man-of-war the *America*, but the war ended before Jones could put to sea and she was given to the French navy in 1783. It was just as well: In their haste, American builders had resorted to using green, unseasoned wood, which rotted quickly when exposed to seawater. The *America* was already falling apart by the time she was sent to France, and the ship never saw action.

Other notable naval action in the colonies continued the ignoble tradition begun by Esek Hopkins. Men such as Capt. Nicholas Biddle, who traded up from the *Andrea Dorea* to the 32-gun frigate the *Randolph*, the first ship built from the keel up and launched for the United States Navy, continued sailing single ships against the British fleet. In a brave yet foolhardy decision, he decided to take on the 64-gun man-of-war the *Yarmouth* and was blown out of the water.

The American string of bad luck and bad decisions continued in the waning years of the War. In late July 1779, a fleet of more than 30 ships sailed for Penobscot Bay, Maine, to break the British hold on the Bagaduce—today called Castine—peninsula, where the redcoats were guarding their timber supplies. The entire fleet of Massachusetts and New Hampshire (all of three ships), along with three Continental navy vessels, the 32-gun frigate the *Warren*, the 12-gun sloop the *Providence*, and the brig the *Diligent*, led 16 privateer vessels and 20 transports carrying 3,000 militia up the coast.

On August 13, the British were ready with a line of 10 ships led by the 64-gun *Raisonable*. Even with a two-to-one advantage, the Americans couldn't do anything right. Sticking to their tried-and-failed "every ship for itself" strategy, they surrendered 28 vessels and destroyed 14 others, including the *Warren*. The leader of this abject failure, Capt. Dudley Saltonstall, who had also accompanied Esek Hopkins to Barbados and lost the six-against-one battle versus the *Glasgow* in 1776, was court-martialed and drummed out of the Navy in 1780.

Also in 1780, the Continental navy embarrassed itself again when it sent a sloop and three frigates to South Carolina to stop Gen. Sir Henry Clinton from capturing the port city of Charleston. They beat the British to the city, so when the redcoats arrived, they simply blockaded the harbor, trapping the American fleet, and sent troops ashore. Unable to maneuver, the ships surrendered when Charleston did on May 12.

Fortunately for America, Gen. George Washington, with a combination of skill, surprise, and luck, had been pulling off a miracle with his army (see *Alpha Bravo Delta Guide to the U.S. Army*). By 1781, Washington had Lord Charles Cornwallis on the run to Yorktown, where he faced his final defeat. By this time, the Continental navy was all but gone, its ships captured or destroyed, often by the men that crewed them, with no sense of organization or direction. Thus, the United States Navy's first sortie into battle ended much like it had begun: with no standing Navy to speak of, no organized department, and no official recognition, either in America or abroad.

CHAPTER 3

THE QUASI-WAR WITH FRANCE AND THE BARBARY COAST PIRATES

After the Revolutionary War, America struggled to establish itself as a rightful nation of the world. But foreign powers from Europe to the coast of North Africa tried to take advantage of the new country, especially on the high seas.

No longer protected by the Royal Navy, American merchant ships were fair game for pirates, particularly from the Barbary Coast countries—Algiers, Morocco, Tripoli, and Tunis. As the last American man-of-war was sold in 1785, two vessels, the merchant ship the *Dolphin* and the schooner the *Maria*, were captured by ships belonging to the dey (king) of Algiers, who demanded a ransom of $59,496 for the crews. The impoverished American government could barely scrape up $4,200 (they hadn't passed the Constitution yet and, therefore, could not levy taxes to finance the government). The men languished for more than eight years while factions in Congress argued over their fate.

John Adams, a long-time proponent of an official American fleet, strangely advocated paying whatever was necessary to free the sailors. Thomas Jefferson, who would almost scrap the Navy during his term as president, claimed that building a fleet of ships would be cheaper than paying the ransom and annual tributes.

In 1789, the Constitution of the United States was passed, including the following language in Section 8 of its first article: "To define and punish Piracies and Felonies committed on the high seas, and Offences against the Law of Nations; To declare War, grant Letters of Marque and Reprisal, and make Rules concerning Captures on Land and Water," and perhaps the most important clause, "to provide and maintain a Navy."

Now that the official order was approved, it was time to build ships. But Congress delayed again until 1794, while the Barbary States continued raiding Yankee shipping. When Portugal lifted its blockade of the Strait of Gibraltar, pirate ships flooded the Atlantic, targeting unprotected U.S. vessels. On January 20, Congress reviewed a proposal to build six ships, four 44-gun and two 20-gun vessels, later modified to be 36-gun craft, at a cost of $600,000.

The plan was opposed by a group in Congress led by James Madison and William Giles of Virginia, who questioned the ability of an American fleet to patrol the far Atlantic Ocean without inviting conflict from European powers, and also the financial strain it would put on the new government. Their arguments were refuted, and on March 27, Congress passed the bill with a provision that the shipbuilding would cease if a peaceful settlement were reached with Algiers.

The new Secretary of War, Henry Knox, quickly appointed six captains, with three of them—John Barry, Richard Dale, and Thomas Truxton—to oversee construction of the fleet. Using the expertise of shipbuilders Joshua Humphreys and Josiah Fox, they began building the best sailing ships in the world.

Shipbuilders Joshua Humphreys and Josiah Fox created a vessel that could take on virtually any ship it encountered—and if it couldn't overpower its opponent, then it could outsail it. Longer, wider, and heavier than any previous vessels built in America, the three frigates the USS *Constitution,* the USS *Constellation,* and the USS *United States* were constructed of durable Georgia live oak, ensuring that each ship's average life would be at least 50 years, 4 times longer than a regular ship built during that time. Each hull was sheathed in copper, increasing the ships' speed and extending their lives by eliminating the need to scrape barnacles from the bottoms every six months. The frigates were well armed, carrying either thirty-six or forty-four 24-pound guns to batter an opponent into surrender. Although small by modern standards, these three vessels, two of which (the *Constellation* and the *Constitution*) are still on the seas today, were truly mighty vessels when they were first launched—agile, quick, and capable of launching devastating broadsides. The action they would see in the years to come would secure their reputation and America's as a premier shipbuilding and fighting country. (For a more detailed look at the USS *Constitution,* see Appendix E.)

The three three-masted, square-set frigates almost weren't completed, due to the government's treaty with Algiers (achieved at the exorbitant price of $525,000 in ransom and bribes, and a custom-built frigate for the dey as well). Although the ships were under construction when the treaty was signed, work on them stopped in 1795. After President George Washington dressed down Congress for its incredible shortsightedness, the three ships were finished two years later. But it still took a new enemy to force America to provide a military defense for its merchant ships at sea.

THE QUASI-WAR WITH FRANCE

Near the end of the eighteenth century, England and France had gone to war again and drew an unwilling America into the conflict as well. Special envoy John Jay tried to negotiate a treaty with Great Britain to stop its depredation of U.S. merchant ships trading with the French. Although he got favored nation status and opened the British East Indies to American trade, the British refused to stop seizing cargo on American ships bound for the France.

The treaty terms caused an uproar in America and also angered France, which felt insulted after supporting America in the Revolutionary War. Paris' reaction was swift: In the summer and fall of 1796, French privateers seized more than 300 American ships.

Newly-elected President John Adams addressed Congress on May 16, 1797, advocating immediate expansion of the Navy. He also demanded that the three frigates be completed and deployed as soon as possible.

(Naval Historical Center)

Commodore John Barry, the first leader of the United States Navy.

Capt. John Barry was already hard at work. Six days earlier, the USS *United States* had been launched, and Barry was outfitting her while Congress debated America's role at sea. The USS *Constitution* was also coming along nicely, with a planned launch date of mid-August, but the *Constellation* was still being built and would not be completed for several weeks.

Then the French emissaries to the United States demanded a large bribe and personal loan from the government before beginning negotiations to stop the privateers. When the French government passed a resolution empowering its ships to seize goods bound for England from American ships, the United States had taken enough.

Congress authorized funds to purchase 24 more ships on April 30, 1798. Along with the funds came eight cutters from the United States Treasury. Even more important, the United States Navy was finally established as a separate military department, complete with its own secretary, Benjamin Stoddert.

President John Adams's first choice for the first Secretary of the Navy was a retired Boston shipbuilder, George Cabot. Cabot gracefully turned down the post, citing his "invincible indolence of disposition." As it was, Cabot's refusal was the Navy's gain. Benjamin Stoddert (1751–1813), born in Charles County, Maryland, was the perfect man to fill the post.

Having served in the Pennsylvania cavalry during the Revolutionary War, Stoddert understood the logistics of the military. His time as a merchant and partner in a shipping company in Georgetown, Maryland, after the war meant he knew how to run a merchant fleet. The combination proved invaluable for setting policy and standards during the first years of the Department of the Navy.

Stoddert was quickly allocated funds for the six new frigates and recommended that the United States procure 12 ships of the line, 74-gun vessels, as soon as possible. Congress agreed—but gave him half the number he'd requested. Those ships weren't begun until after the end of the Quasi-War. During Stoddert's time in office, however, the Navy swelled to 54 vessels (most of which were sold after the war, but it was a start). He helped draft legislation that would keep 13 frigates in service as a permanent peacetime fleet, ensuring that the Navy would finally survive beyond the most current conflict.

By 1801, there were 5,600 men in the United States Navy, including 354 midshipmen and 28 captains. Stoddert raised the base pay for seamen from $8 to $17, ensuring a steady stream of recruits. He also founded shipyards in Boston, New York, Norfolk, Philadelphia, and Portsmouth, some of which are still in operation today.

Benjamin Stoddard left his post in March 1801 to return to his commercial interests. He died on December 13, 1813, secure in the knowledge that his role in forming the United States Navy was no less important than any captain or military leader.

For naval officers, the course of action was clear, and on July 7, 1798, the first blow was struck. Capt. Stephen Decatur, commanding the 20-gun sloop the *Delaware*, captured the 12-gun French schooner the *La Croyable* near Egg Island, New Jersey. The prize was renamed the *Retaliation*, and it sailed in the Navy until recaptured by another French ship, the *L'Insurgente*.

American privateers captured around 80 French vessels, mostly privateers like themselves, before the hostilities between the two countries trailed off, for lack of a better term. The treaty ratified in February 1800 to halt the conflict was designed to soothe insulted pride on both sides. It nullified the military alliance between France and the United States, and affirmed America's stance of neutrality in exchange for the government not demanding any kind of reparations for the losses incurred by French privateers. But before this came about, there were two naval battles of note during the Quasi-War, both won by the same captain: Thomas Truxton.

On February 9, 1799, Truxton's the *Constellation* encountered another ship that ran up American colors when hailed. But when the ship didn't respond to the Americans' signal of the day, a private recognition sign ensuring that a ship claiming to be American actually was, the *Constellation* opened fire. After a long battle lasting more than an hour and 15 minutes, during which the *Constellation* raked the *L'Insurgent* several times, the French ship struck her colors.

Only 1 American sailor was killed, and 2 of the 440 crewmen were wounded, due to the French habit of firing at an enemy ship's rigging. The British and Americans had no such compunction, and they aimed their cannons at a ship's hull and deck, inflicting much higher casualties. The *L'Insurgent* suffered 29 men killed and 44 wounded, out of a crew of 340 men. Captain Truxton took his damaged prize to St. Kitt's, where it was repaired and sailed in the American Navy as the *Insurgent*.

Truxton's next engagement with the enemy was not as successful. On February 2, 1800, he spotted and pursued a large French frigate, the 54-gun *La Vengeance* off Guadeloupe. After chasing the enemy ship for most of the day, Truxton got close enough to demand its surrender. The French answered with a hail of grapeshot at the *Constellation*'s rigging, and the battle commenced.

The two ships exchanged broadsides for five hours, until *La Vengeance* stopped firing. Truxton prepared to take possession of the enemy warship but discovered that his mainmast was about to collapse. He disengaged to brace the mast, but soon afterward it fell overboard, taking with it several men who subsequently drowned, including James Jervis, who went with the mast into the ocean rather than leave his post without orders.

Meanwhile, *La Vengeance* slipped away in the darkness and confusion. In his report, the French captain claimed he had been attacked by a two-deck ship of the line, overestimating the *Constellation*'s size but not her abilities.

> As fighting with cannons became more prevalent in the sixteenth and seventeenth centuries, tactics were developed to take advantage of the increased firepower. The naval line of battle, in which vessels formed a straight line to better attack their enemies, was formed. A ship of the line was any vessel of the first (100-plus guns), second (90-plus guns), or third (64-plus guns) rank, the only ones that carried enough weaponry to engage in this kind of fleet-to-fleet combat and survive.

Although the Quasi-War with France was just that—an undeclared conflict fought mostly to salve national pride on both sides, it did impress on Congress the need to have at the very least a fleet of ships ready to protect America's maritime interests, particularly trade across the Atlantic. As the next section illustrates, that need became even more apparent when trying to quell the Barbary Coast.

CONFLICT IN THE MEDITERRANEAN—THE WAR AGAINST THE PIRATES

Although the Navy had proved its usefulness as a deterrent against other countries, when the Quasi-War was over, the legislature enacted by John Adams and Benjamin Stoddert was put into effect. All but 13 ships (the *Adams, Boston, Chesapeake, Congress, Constellation, Constitution, Essex, General Greene, John Adams, New York, Philadelphia, President,* and *United States*) were sold in 1801. Of those ships kept, six remained on active duty; the rest were laid up at port. The new Secretary of the Navy, Robert Smith, followed President Thomas Jefferson's antinaval lead, reducing the Navy's size and effectiveness until something else came along to distract him.

Fortunately (for the Navy, at least), the pasha of Tripoli, Yusef Karamanli, demanded higher tribute payments in May 1801, or he would declare war on the United States. President Jefferson's response was to send a small fleet to defend American merchant ships traveling near the Barbary Coast.

On July 1, 1801, under the command of Commodore Richard Dale, the American fleet, consisting of his flagship, the 44-gun frigate *President;* two frigates, the 36-gun *Philadelphia* and the 32-gun *Essex;* and the 12-gun schooner the *Enterprise,* arrived at Gibraltar. Dale had been instructed to pay part of the annual tributes if the leaders of Algiers, Tripoli, and Tunis were peaceful, and to attack their vessels if they weren't. Intelligence sources had led the Navy to believe that only Algiers had any kind of fleet or defenses worth mentioning. It was one of several underestimations that proved costly later.

Commodore Dale immediately set to work from a position of strength by blockading the harbor at Tripoli, attempting to intimidate Algiers and Tunis with a show of force, keeping an eye on Tripolitan cruisers stationed at Gibraltar and escorting American merchant ships in and out of the Mediterranean. It was an ambitious set of goals for a man with only four ships trying to cover thousands of square miles of ocean.

Although the American presence was mostly passive, some incidents proved the Navy's skill in maritime combat. On August 1, the 12-gun schooner the *Enterprise,* captained by Lt. Andrew Sterrett, fought and defeated the 14-gun corsair the *Tripoli,* killing 60 out of 80 enemy crewmen without taking a single casualty itself. But because the United States hadn't officially declared war on Tripoli, he was not able to claim the ship. Instead, he sent it off after having its cannons thrown overboard.

Dale soon realized that he had overextended his small fleet. He requested more ships to patrol the Tripoli harbor and asked for permission to attack and capture armed Tripolitan cruisers as prizes of war. On February 6, 1802, the Congress acknowledged that a state of war existed between Tripoli and America (the pasha had already declared open hostilities).

Dale was replaced by Commodore Richard Morris, who continued his predecessor's policy, blockading Tripoli and escorting American merchant ships in and out of the Mediterranean. While this protected U.S. merchants' interests, it did nothing to stop the Barbary States' aggression toward America. Morris was recalled home in June 1803 and was censured for "inactive and dilatory conduct," even though he had followed the orders he was given. He was dismissed from the service that same year.

MEN OF ACTION IN THE MEDITERRANEAN

The next captain to take up the task was Commodore Edward Preble, who upheld the running tradition of prickly Navy commanders. Preble was described by one sailor who resigned rather than serve under him as "cross, peevish and ill-tempered, surly and proud." And maybe just the right man for the job of pacifying the arrogant Barbary Nations. Commodore Preble was quite willing to fight the pirate states, claiming in a letter to Naval Secretary Robert Smith, "The Moors are a deep designing artful treacherous set of villains, and nothing will keep them so quiet as a respectable naval force near them."

First he had to survive the ineptness of his own men. On October 31, the USS *Philadelphia*, commanded by Capt. William Bainbridge, ran aground in shallow water while chasing a blockade-runner from Tripoli. Despite trying everything to lighten her, including throwing cannons overboard and cutting off the foremast, in the end the crew surrendered the ship without firing a shot. Now the pasha of Tripoli held 307 American officers and sailors hostage—and the 36-gun frigate, to boot, which was freed two days later and stationed in Tripoli harbor.

Both the U.S. government and Preble were livid. The commodore took the winter to consider his options. Negotiation with the pasha was unthinkable—the despot would demand an enormous ransom. The harbor at Tripoli was the most heavily fortified in the region, and an American ship would be blown out of the water before it could even find the *Philadelphia*, much less take her over and escape. Something had to be done, and early in February 1804, something was.

The plan was audacious, simple, and suicidal: Sail a captured ketch into Tripoli harbor past 115 cannons mounted on the walls and 23 well-armed ships, including a 10-gun brig, a pair of 8-gun schooners, and 2 galleys carrying 100 men apiece. Locate the captured USS *Philadelphia*, board and destroy her, and escape in the confusion afterward.

> A ketch is a two-masted, fore-and-aft rigged ship with a secondary mast located between the mainmast and the rudder of the vessel.

Led by Lt. Stephen Decatur Jr., 75 men set sail on February 3, 1804. Renaming their captured prize the *Intrepid*, they had packed it full of powder and explosives. Their pilot was a Sicilian who spoke Arabic and hated Tripoli. The mission became one of the most famous operations in the history of the United States Navy.

Although the ship and crew reached Tripoli harbor with little incident, a sudden gale kept them at sea for nine days with little food. Tossed about on the open ocean, crowded into inadequate living quarters (Decatur and four officers shared the only cabin, and conditions were worse for the rest of the men) and living only on bread and water, the crew was ready for action by the time the storm blew itself out.

On the night of February 16, the bedraggled ship sailed into the arms of the enemy. Spotting the *Philadelphia*, the pilot steered over to the ship and hailed the guards on deck. Claiming his anchor had been lost in the storm, he asked permission to moor alongside. The guards agreed. Before they knew what was happening, the frigate was swarming with armed intruders.

The rest of the mission was accomplished in less than 20 minutes. After a brief but vicious battle in which several guards were killed, the Tripolitans' morale broke and they jumped overboard. Decatur and his men then set fire to the ship. The munitions burned faster than expected and almost caught several crewmen and the *Intrepid* in the flames.

The ketch now had just one more obstacle: the gauntlet of cannons surrounding the harbor. The Tripolitans opened fire but didn't have a clear target. Add to that the *Philadelphia*'s own exploding guns, and the *Intrepid* was being shelled on all sides. Despite this barrage of cannon fire, the ketch was only hit once, in the sail.

Decatur and his men pulled off this incredible mission without losing a single man. For his heroism, Decatur was promoted to captain at age 25—and is still the youngest man in the history of the Navy to achieve that rank.

With morale raised after Decatur's unqualified success, Preble continued his blockade of the harbor and assembled a force of 15 vessels and over 1,000 men to attack Tripoli five separate times, shelling the harbor on several occasions. Having been stationed in the area for more than a year, he had a firm grasp of the political and military situation, and in time he might have been able to force the pasha to the bargaining table in good faith. But before that could happen, he was replaced on September 9 by Commodore Samuel Barron, who was already in ill health when he accepted the post. Continuing the line of ineffective leadership in the Mediterranean, Barron contented himself with blockading the main ports of the Barbary nations, sitting back, and waiting.

This doesn't mean, however, that alternate plans weren't tried. On September 14, 1804, the *Intrepid*, the same ketch used in the daring raid on the *Philadelphia*, was loaded with 100 barrels of gunpowder, one hundred 9-inch shells, and fifty 13.5-inch shells, and sailed as a floating bomb back into Tripoli harbor. Although there were boats for the volunteer crew to escape in, something went horribly wrong—the vessel ran aground, and, whether to escape capture or by accident, the ketch's cargo was set off in a tremendous explosion, killing all aboard.

In another even more unorthodox plan, Navy agent William Eaton hatched an idea to stage a coup, remove the pasha from the throne, and install his brother, Hamet Karamanli. Eaton persuaded Karamanli to go along with his scheme and assembled a mercenary army of Arabs, Christians, and a handful of Navy personnel. In April 1805, he marched them 450 miles across the desert to the Gulf of Bomba, where he met with the brig the *Argus* and the sloop the *Hornet*. From there he headed for Derna, where the rag-tag army captured the city with the assistance of three Navy ships (they were joined by the schooner *Nautilus*) and raised the Stars and Stripes over the town—the first time the American flag had ever been raised in conquest anywhere in the world.

While this brave action impressed Pasha Karamanli, he saw no reason for alarm. He still had the 307 hostages taken from the *Philadelphia*, including Captain Bainbridge, and he had repulsed Commodore Eaton from Tripoli harbor several times. He was also holding members of his brother's family hostage, so he was unconcerned about an attack from that quarter. He still felt himself to be in a position of strength, and apparently so did the United States. When Commodore Barron was relieved of duty on May 22, 1805, the new commodore, John Rodgers, had been instructed by the United States consul general in Algiers, Col. Tobias Lear, to negotiate with Tripoli, no matter what.

By June 10, the treaty was ratified and signed. America paid Tripoli $60,000 for the return of its men, but there was no payment for the treaty itself or tribute. For its part, Tripoli recognized the sovereignty of America and agreed to leave its merchant ships alone. Eaton was ordered to leave Derna, and poor Hamet was left high and dry, with his family still being held prisoner by his own brother (although the United States government later gave him a lump-sum settlement and pension, and he was reunited with his family after the conflict ended).

The men of the Navy were outraged at this meek concession by their government. Colonel Lear, having discovered that his solution to the Barbary Coast problem had made him a pariah in America, later committed suicide. As unconventional as William Eaton's tactics had been, they had also been effective. Given a little more time, the United States might have checked the aggressive Barbary States once and for all, rather than allowing them to harass American shipping on and off for the next two decades.

CHAPTER 4

THE WAR OF 1812

The War of 1812 has been called "the war nobody wanted." However, the causes of this seemingly minor conflict actually stemmed from America's willingness to go to war not only to protect itself, but also to remove the British presence in the burgeoning United States once and for all.

At the beginning of the nineteenth century, the English still had interests in North America, particularly in Canadian forts and outposts. They also wanted to stay involved in the rich fur trade by claiming territories in the Ohio Valley, Kentucky, and frontier regions. To maintain their holdings, the British fostered alliances with the Indian Tribes of the Great Lakes region, particularly with the Shawnee chief Tecumseh. The Native Americans were promised protection and retention of their lands in exchange for their allegiance.

When a state of war broke out, the British did not take another conflict with the United States seriously. They disregarded the American Navy as small and unskilled, the Army as a ragtag bunch of farmers, and the U.S. Congress as upstart, ill-bred landowners. In many ways they were correct, but they underestimated America's resolve to succeed as an independent country.

Preoccupied with their long-running war against France, Great Britain didn't allocate enough resources to the dispute. Instead, the British planned to fight the war with terrorism and by proxy, using Native Americans to attack settlers in the newly purchased Louisiana territory. They also fostered an alliance with several New England states, hoping to persuade them to secede from the United States and join Canada.

The British strategy of control and harassment began long before war was declared. The Royal Navy seized more than 250 American ships from 1803 to 1812, impressing approximately 10,000 American sailors into serving on British vessels.

> Because the hard life of a sailor in the Royal Navy caused many to "jump ship" and sign on elsewhere, the British used the pretense of looking for deserters to forcibly search American merchant vessels. Once on board, they often took anyone deemed fit for duty, regardless of whether they had actually deserted, as well as anything they deemed valuable.

Britain was also determined to limit America's expanding sea trade, harassing merchant ships by blockading American ports and trying to enforce control over established trade routes. To further limit trade between America and Europe, Great Britain passed Orders-in-Council in 1807 preventing any neutral nation from trading with French-held European ports without first going through a British port and paying British tax. When Napoleon Bonaparte heard of the British edict, he said that the United States was free to obey the new rules, but the French would consider any American ship that did so to be non-neutral and a lawful target. Now America couldn't trade with one country without incurring the wrath of the other. The Royal Navy also confiscated goods on ships that violated the Orders-in-Council while ignoring an American smuggling ring trading with English merchants off the coast of New England at the same time. Naturally, these incidents were met with outrage by the American people.

ADDING INSULT TO INJURY: THE *CHESAPEAKE* AND THE *LEOPARD*

In 1807, the British 56-gun frigate the *Leopard* approached the American 36-gun frigate the *Chesapeake* and asked its captain, James Barron, to carry dispatches to the Mediterranean. This was a common request for nations not at war, but the real reason the *Leopard* wanted to come alongside the *Chesapeake* was to search for deserters from the Royal Navy.

This was the first time that the British had attempted to board a Navy ship. Barron refused, knowing the rules stating that the captain of a U.S. Navy vessel must not give up his men without surrendering his ship. But the *Chesapeake* was not ready for a fight, so Captain Barron told his second-in-command, Master Commandant Charles Gordon, to get the men and decks ready for battle while he tried to stall the British.

The *Leopard* fired across the *Chesapeake*'s bow and then bombarded her with 22 shots that hulled the ship and shattered her main and fore masts. After 3 sailors were killed and 18 were wounded, including Captain Barron himself, he struck his colors, whereupon the British searched the ship and took 4 men. Although Barron begged British Capt. S. P. Humphreys to take the shattered *Chesapeake* as a prize, Humphreys refused, leaving the Americans to limp back to Hampton Roads, Virginia. Barron was later court-martialed when it was revealed that he had not prepared his ship properly for battle. He was removed from service without pay for five years.

Fearing further conflict with England, President Thomas Jefferson recalled all American ships from the Mediterranean. As further retaliation, but mostly to avoid the appearance of American partisanship with England or France, he created the Embargo Act, which went into effect on December 22, 1807. It forbade U.S. ships from trading with any foreign country. Jefferson decided that stopping trade would be one way to hit England and France where it hurt: in the treasury. England needed supplies to fight France, and he thought the act would send a message that America wouldn't trade with any country that tried to forbid free trade.

Unfortunately, instead of punishing England, discord was sown through-out the United States as exports plummeted from $108 million in 1807 to $22 million in 1808. The nation soon felt the pinch of reduced trade, increased unemployment, and economic depression. Smuggling sprang up all along the coast, with whaling ships going out to sea and bringing back successful "catches" that consisted of bales of English textiles.

Before the Navy's limited success in the Barbary conflict, Jefferson had planned to put the fleet, consisting of one cutter (the 10-gun *Viper*), two schooners (the *Enterprise* and the *Vixen*, both 12-gun ships) two sloops (the 18-gun *Wasp* and the 16-gun brig-sloop *Argus*), three brigs (the 18-gun ships the *Hornet* and the *Siren* and the 14-gun *Nautilus*), nine frigates (the 44-gun ships *President, United States*, and *Constitution*, the 36-gun ships *Chesapeake, Constellation*, and *Congress*, the 32-gun *Essex*, the 28-gun *John Adams* and the 24-gun *Adams*) and 69 gunboats, in dry dock until needed. Even though the fleet had proved its necessity as protection for American commerce and coastal safety, it was still small, with limited leadership, and it was unproven against the more experienced and much larger Royal Navy.

With Jefferson's approval, the current Secretary of the Navy, Robert Smith, requested $852,500 for 188 gunboats to supplement the completed 69 (in 1806, Congress had voted to appropriate $250,000 for these boats rather than spend more than twice that amount to complete the six 74-gun ships still under construction) and bolster coastal defenses. Citing their relative low cost and practicality in defending ports and harbors, Smith claimed that every "modern maritime nation" used these agile vessels to protect their own coastlines. Congress agreed, and gunboats became the answer to guarding America's coast, rivers, and ports.

A gunboat is a small, shallow-water vessel powered by sails or oars and mounting one or two guns. Unable to tackle a frigate or ship-of-the-line, a gunboat's primary purpose was to harass the crew of enemy ships in swarms, spraying the deck with small-arms fire and the occasional cannon blast.

In 1809, James Madison took office and continued Jefferson's maritime policy, building gunboats to patrol ports in the Gulf of Mexico and on the Atlantic Coast. However, he did not start or complete any larger ships. Instead, Congress reactivated four frigates—the *John Adams, Essex, United States*, and *President*—despite fears that it would be seen as a show of strength by the British and provoke them into attacking. Congress's fear was well founded: The British fleet at the time numbered some 600 vessels, many of them prizes from France and Spain. America did not want to see its own ships captured and impressed, like its sailors, into the Royal Navy.

The antagonism between Britain and America reached the boiling point in 1811. On May 1, the British 38-gun frigate the *Guerrière* impressed an American sailor from the brig the *Spitfire* outside New York Harbor. In response, the frigate the *President*, captained by John Rodgers, was ordered to sail to Sandy Hook, New York, to guard against further maritime assaults. The afternoon of May 16 the *President* was 50 miles off Cape Henry when it encountered and fought the 20-gun sloop-of-war *Little Belt*. When the brief battle was over, the Americans had one wounded sailor and light damage to their rigging. The British had 13 killed and 19 wounded, and their vessel had been reduced to a floating wreck.

The U.S. administration was overjoyed at this long-overdue payback. When the British complained about the attack, Monroe took great pains to remind the minister that his government had not made any reparations for the unprovoked attack on the *Chesapeake* four years earlier. The English government was quick to reply, releasing the two surviving sailors from the *Chesapeake* and providing compensation as well.

At the same time, British-backed Indian attacks were heating up the western frontier. In 1811, Tenskwatawa, the brother of Shawnee war chief Tecumseh, led more than 2,000 warriors against the camp of William Henry Harrison in the Battle of Tippecanoe (see *Alpha Bravo Delta Guide to the U.S. Army*). Knowing that Britain had armed the Shawnee, and still outraged by the *Chesapeake* incident and continued impressments of U.S. sailors, American voters elected 40 new Congressional representatives aligned with a prowar group known as the "War Hawks."

Tired of British injustice on land and at sea, the War Hawks wanted to fight and were backed by a large contingent of frontiersman and merchants. Kentucky representative Henry Clay was also elected as Speaker of the House, and he appointed many War Hawks to important posts in foreign relations, military affairs, and the Navy. Soon after the Hawks took office, they persuaded President James Madison to go along with their demands. On June 1, 1812, the declaration of war against Great Britain went to Congress for vote. The House of Representatives passed the decree 79 to 49; the Senate passed it 19 to 14. Thus began the War of 1812. What role the United States Navy would play in this conflict, however, was still undecided. During the winter of 1811–1812, Secretary of the Navy Paul Hamilton had tried to acquire 20 more frigates immediately and 12 more ships-of-the-line in the future. The House Naval Affairs Committee turned down his request, recommending adding only 10 more frigates and leaving the Navy outmatched in every way against the British.

AMERICAN VS. GREAT BRITAIN, ROUND TWO

Three areas of America needed protection from British invasion: the Atlantic Coast, the Great Lakes, and the western frontier. Each presented its own set of problems, but Congress thought its best chance for victory lay in invading Canada to cut off British supply lines and invasion-launching sites. Simultaneously, the small U.S. Navy would patrol the coastline and prevent supplies from getting to Canada. Outnumbered, outgunned, and inexperienced, no one seriously expected the U.S. Navy to fight the Royal Navy.

Secretary of the Navy Paul Hamilton consulted with his top-ranking officers, Capts. John Rodgers and Stephen Decatur, on how to best utilize America's meager forces. Decatur thought keeping the fleet together increased the risk of having America's entire Navy captured or destroyed at once. He advocated sending the frigates out, singly or in pairs, with no set sailing plan. The idea would be that one or two frigates could easily handle a convoy and take on one or two British ships, but be able to elude a larger force. This plan would also limit the Royal Navy's ability to blockade American ports because they would have to send their own ships out to chase down the Americans.

Apparently Decatur's plan was voted down. On June 21, 1812, the frigates the *President*, under Rodgers; the *United States*, captained by Decatur; and the *Congress*, along with the sloop the *Hornet* and the brig the *Argus*, sailed out to find and confront the British.

Rodgers immediately found the 36-gun *Belvidera*, one of a pair of British warships lurking around Sandy Point, New York. Giving chase with his *entire fleet*, they sailed for 10 hours before drawing within cannon range. The battle was apparently between the *President* and the *Belvidera*, whose sailors jettisoned whatever they could to lighten the ship. The *President* was bigger and faster and had more cannons, but one of her bow guns exploded early in the running fight, breaking Captain Rodgers's leg. The chase continued, however, and he tried to bring his heavier cannons to bear by sailing at an angle to the enemy warship. This enabled the *Belvidera* to pull away faster, while its stern guns plinked at the *President's* sails and riggings, slowing it even further. At midnight, Rodgers called off the pursuit and rejoined his ships. The rest of the voyage was just as unsuccessful; the fleet missed several opportunities to capture merchant vessels and suffered a scurvy outbreak that forced the crew to return to port empty-handed on August 31.

(Naval Historical Center)

Capt. Stephen Decatur Jr., hero of the Barbary Coast and the War of 1812.

Rodgers claimed his fleet had forced the British to keep their vessels together rather than blockading ports and protecting British merchant ships, but the tactic had not been successful. His claim was further weakened by the exploits of David Porter, whose frigate the *Essex* snatched a ship carrying British soldiers from its own convoy in a daring night raid. Porter captured nine more prizes in the next two months, proving more effective than Rodgers's entire fleet.

THE CHASE OF THE *CONSTITUTION*

Meanwhile, Isaac Hull and the *Constitution* were given orders to patrol without provocation by Secretary Hamilton. Hamilton wanted Hull to keep a low profile to keep America from losing any ships. Hull had other ideas, however, and worked tirelessly to ready his inexperienced crew of 450 for battle by the time they sailed on July 4, 1812.

Twelve days into the voyage, the *Constitution* sighted unidentified sails on the horizon. They belonged to five Royal Navy warships, the *Belvidera*, the 52-gun *Shannon*, the *Aeolus*, the 38-gun *Guerrière*, and the 64-gun *Africa*. Before the U.S. frigate could elude the British squadron, the *Constitution* was sighted and the pursuit began.

Hull ordered his ship's back railing cut away and placed a cannon there. An hour into the chase, the wind died and Hull deployed his cutters to pull the *Constitution* to safety. The *Belvidera* and the *Shannon* also dropped their cutters, and the pursuit continued. The British ships had more cutters and closed to a half mile. At this point, Captain Hull switched to kedging to increase the distance between his ship and the enemy.

> Kedging was a method of propelling a becalmed ship that involved rowing an anchor out on a cutter, dropping it, and then using the capstan, which normally hauled the anchor up, to pull the boat to the anchor as another cutter took a second anchor ahead. This backbreaking task amounted to dragging a ship forward, with sweat and muscle replacing wind power.

Half an hour later, the distance was close enough that Captain Hull hoisted the American flag and fired his rear cannon at the *Belvidera*, making the rowers on the British ship's cutters back off.

Meanwhile, the *Shannon* kept coming, while the *Guerrière* attempted to attack the *Constitution* from the side. The *Africa* was still pursuing, but was farther behind due to its great weight. Ninety minutes later, the *Belvidera* drew within range and fired its bow cannon, barely missing the *Constitution*. The U.S. man-of-war answered with a shot that struck the *Belvidera*'s main deck. The *Guerrière* also opened fire on the *Constitution* and missed.

For two more hours, the chase continued. Then the wind freshened and the *Constitution* raised sail. To gain more speed, Captain Hull ordered the entire ration of drinking water thrown overboard. With the ship lightened by more than 9 tons, the gap widened to 2 miles. The pursuit continued for another 18 hours, through the rest of the day and into the night. At dawn, two and a half days after the *Constitution* first sighted the British ships, the American coast was within sight and the British fleet fell behind for good. Captain Hull, his tireless crew, and the *Constitution* had escaped what had first looked like certain capture.

Over the next few weeks, the *Constitution* captured three British cargo ships. The rest of the American navy, the frigates the *President*, the *United States*, and the *Congress*, and the smaller warships the *Hornet*, the *Argus*, and the *Essex*, were also capturing merchant ships and preventing supplies from reaching Canada. Claiming that the *Constitution* had escaped him only by luck, Capt. James Dacres of the *Guerrière* issued a challenge to the American ships to meet him in battle. On August 19, 1812, Capt. Isaac Hull accepted that challenge.

THE *CONSTITUTION* VS. THE *GUERRIÈRE*

Captain Hull sighted the *Guerrière* off the coast of Newfoundland as it tried to reach Halifax for resupply. The *Constitution* came up from behind, and the two vessels circled each other for almost an hour in an attempt to use the wind to their advantage and unleash a broadside. The *Guerrière* fired first but missed. Then the *Constitution* turned and bore down on the British ship. Hull told his men to wait until he gave the order to fire, wanting to save his cannons until he was alongside the *Guerrière* so his marines could also shoot with the broadside. As the ships closed to within 50 feet, Hull gave the order, and cannonballs poured into the doomed *Guerrière*. At one point, the bowsprit of the British ship became tangled in the *Constitution*'s rigging, and boarding parties clashed on both decks. The *Constitution* pulled away, taking the *Guerrière*'s fore and main masts with it. In less than two hours, Captain Dacres surrendered. The British had suffered 23 men killed and 57 wounded, including the captain. The *Constitution* had lost 7 men and had 23 wounded.

During the battle, American and British sailors were stunned to see cannonballs from the *Guerrière* actually bounce off the live oak sides of the *Constitution.* "Her sides are made of iron!" an unknown sailor said, and the nickname has stuck to the warship ever since.

The next day, the wounded British sailors were escorted onto the *Constitution.* At first Hull wanted to tow the *Guerrière* to port, but she was so damaged that he ordered her set on fire. The *Guerrière* slipped beneath the waves of the Atlantic Ocean at 3:15 P.M.

Britain now had something to fear from the American navy, and the continued string of U.S. victories over British men of war proved it. In the year 1812 alone, the *Wasp* defeated the *Frolic,* the *Essex* triumphed over the *Albert,* the *Constitution* destroyed the *Java,* and the *United States* captured the *Macedonian.* During the next three years, the Americans captured scores of British ships and any allied vessels that made hostile actions toward the United States.

The flow of captured ships restored the Navy's luster to Congress. Morale was riding high, and after getting rid of the well-meaning but alcoholic and incompetent Secretary Hamilton, Congress reserved $2.5 million to build six more 44-gun frigates and four 74-gun ships-of-the-line. At last the Navy would have a fleet to call its own.

The United States didn't just rely on its military vessels to fight the British. Privateers were also actively used throughout the war. Privately owned and often secretly financed by wealthy Americans, privateers were responsible for more captures of British merchant ships and goods than the Navy itself. They also didn't tarnish the reputations of the American officers and government, who didn't want to be accused of making war on civilians. Privateering was an accepted means of profiting during a war while supporting one's country. It also kept the United States from going bankrupt; payment on prizes and cargo to the U.S. Customs Department was a major source of revenue.

THE BATTLE FOR THE GREAT LAKES

Inside the United States, all was not going as well on the Canadian border. Fort Detroit was the major supply line for British troops occupying Canada and backing the Indian attacks. Two major blows to American defense of the area came when Gen. William Hull (the uncle of Isaac Hull) surrendered his army to British Gen. Isaac Brock. The Army also sustained severe losses in the massacre on Raisin River (see *Alpha Bravo Delta Guide to the U.S. Army* for more details).

At sea, the Americans were dealt a severe blow when the unlucky *Chesapeake*, repaired after her 1807 battering by the *Leopard*, engaged the *Shannon* and was overwhelmed.

THE *CHESAPEAKE* VS. THE *SHANNON*

There are few instances of one ship doing everything it possibly could to prepare for a battle and its opponent blundering unprepared into the fight. But those were the roles of the *Shannon* and the *Chesapeake*, respectively, when the two met on June 1, 1813.

Captain Lawrence had not wanted to command the *Chesapeake*, not from lack of courage, but because his wife was seriously ill. He requested a position on the *Constitution*, which was being overhauled, but was ordered to the *Chesapeake*. He had been in command of the ship for just 10 days before the battle, and his crew had never worked together. The fact that the *Leopard* had mauled the ship six years earlier also didn't help morale.

Lawrence was overconfident as well; during his previous command on the *Hornet* just three months earlier, he had subdued the *Peacock* in a brief 10-minute fight. He felt the officers of Her Majesty's Navy were resting on their laurels, as the recent string of American victories had proven.

British Capt. Philip Broke, however, had learned from the defeats of other Royal Navy captains. Knowing the durability of American vessels, he concluded that cannons alone would not win a fight. His strategy depended on luring the *Chesapeake* close so that his trained marines and sharpshooters couldn't miss. His martial philosophy was simple: Take out the enemy officers, and the battle was theirs. During the fight, he utilized this gambit to devastating effect, with his men killing Lawrence and shooting every officer on deck but one at least twice.

When the two ships found each other, Broke let Lawrence come to him while he prepared a hot reception for the American frigate. His rigging was filled with deadly topsmen, and two cannons had been moved to the front of the ship. One was a 32-pound shot-filled carronade to sweep the *Chesapeake*'s deck; the other was a 9-pound gun that could be elevated to take out the enemy's headsails, which were used for steering the vessel. A matching 9-pound gun was at the rear of the *Shannon* to destroy the spanker, or rear steering sail.

Lawrence, whose only real plan of action was to approach to about 40 yards and then "cross the T" to broadside the British ship, played right into his enemy's hands. The ships met at noon and sailed away from shore until 4 P.M., when Lawrence fired a single shot to announce the commencement of hostilities. He sailed alongside the *Shannon* and began pounding away with his cannons.

The British ship and crew suffered more damage than the *Chesapeake* early on, but then Broke's excellent battle plan began to see results. The fore and aft guns decimated the foresails and spanker of the *Chesapeake*, while the topsmen took out the helmsman and any relief men. Other sharpshooters targeted any officer on deck. Within minutes, the *Chesapeake* was totally out of control and, with her steering sails destroyed and helmsmen dead, had no way of getting under way again either. Lawrence, who had been shot twice as he had tried to restore order, was carried below, all the while repeating what would be known as his famous last words: "Don't give up the ship!"

The unguided *Chesapeake* lurched around until it hit the *Shannon*. This time, Broke let his cannonades do the work for him, and hails of lead shot swept the U.S. frigate's deck. The British boarded immediately afterward and secured the ship 15 minutes after the battle started.

Casualties were heavy for both sides. The *Chesapeake* lost 48 men out of a crew of 340, including almost every officer (Third Lt. William Cox had been in command by default when the battle had ended), and 98 were wounded. The *Shannon* suffered 30 dead and 56 wounded, including Captain Broke himself, who sustained a nearly fatal saber cut to the head that eventually forced him to retire. The *Shannon* took the *Chesapeake* in tow to Halifax, where Lawrence and the other slain officers were interred with full military honors.

Although the decisive battles shook American morale while bolstering the enemy, in the end it only reinforced the U.S. Navy's desire to drive the British from American soil. Despite Lawrence's obvious lack of preparedness, his last command became the battle cry for the War of 1812, and he was accorded a hero for his gallant attempt to rally his crew.

THE BATTLE FOR LAKE ERIE

The Great Lakes had to be under American control if the war was to be won. President Madison placed Isaac Chauncey in charge of creating a fleet on the Great Lakes. Chauncey had previously been in charge of the New York Navy Yard and was the perfect man for the job. He had completed his holding defense of Lake Ontario by moving men and equipment to Sackets Harbor, New York. Instead of sailing out and challenging the British ships on the lake, he maintained a strong line of defense, content to keep the British where they were. Although his strategy wasn't aggressive, Chauncey accomplished his purpose; keeping the redcoats from using the Great Lakes to pour men and supplies into the United States. Chauncey prevented the British from gaining any ground, and he helped set up Master Commandant Oliver Hazard Perry for his decisive battle the year after.

Sent directly by Chauncey to handle the defense of Lake Erie, 28-year-old Perry assembled a crew of lumbermen, carpenters, and a remarkable shipwright, Noah Brown. Five months later, they had six new ships to support the three that were already in use. The fleet consisted of the 20-gun brig the *Niagara*, the 20-gun brig the *Lawrence*, the 4-gun schooner the *Ariel*, the 3-gun brig the *Caledonia*, the 2-gun *Scorpion*, the 4-gun schooner the *Somers*, the 1-gun sloop the *Trippe*, the 1-gun schooner the *Tygress*, and the 1-gun *Porcupine*.

The British had the 17-gun *Queen Charlotte*, the 13-gun schooner the *Lady Prevost*, the 10-gun brig the *Hunter*, the 3-gun schooner the *Little Belt*, and the 1-gun schooner the *Chippeway*. The 24-gun ship the *Detroit* was almost completed, but there almost weren't enough guns and sailors to equip it. With British supply lines dwindling due to the U.S. Navy's success in the Atlantic, it was imperative that the British maintain control of the lakes as a supply corridor.

Lt. Robert Barclay, in charge of the British force on the Great Lakes, had trouble from the start. His superiors gave less credence to the defense of Lake Erie in favor of their forces on Lake Ontario. Barclay was ordered to resupply by defeating the Americans and capturing their resources. He decided to seize the initiative and take the ships he had, including the *Detroit*, armed with 20 guns, to the American base. He hoped to destroy the ships there and get some much-needed supplies at the same time.

The ships built by the Americans were located on Presque Isle, where Erie, Pennsylvania, is today. The shipyard was protected by a large sandbar that kept enemy ships from getting close enough to shell the construction area. Barclay settled for blockading the harbor, but his lack of provisions forced him to leave in the night to resupply. Perry immediately hauled his ships over the sandbar and out onto the lake.

On September 10, 1813, Perry met the British just outside Put-in-Bay. He had decided to pit the *Lawrence*, named after his fallen friend Capt. James Lawrence, against the *Detroit* while the *Niagara* was supposed to engage the *Lady Charlotte*. It didn't take long for the *Detroit* to open fire on the *Lawrence*. The *Niagara* tried to engage the *Lady Charlotte*, which avoided combat and maneuvered around the Americans to join the *Detroit* against the *Lawrence*. Instead of moving to engage any other British vessel, the *Niagara* inexplicably stayed out of the battle.

The entire British fleet poured shells into the *Lawrence* until she was ruined, although somehow still afloat. Although the American vessel gave as good as she got, at the end of 2 hours, only 19 crewmen were still able to fight. Perry, who escaped James Lawrence's fate by dressing as an ordinary sailor, did not give up and signaled for one of the gunboats to take him to the *Niagara*. The *Scorpion*, the *Porcupine*, and the *Tigress* kept crossing in front of the British ships to protect Perry until he could get on board.

By the time Perry arrived, most of the British officers were dead or wounded. Barclay himself was seriously injured and hoped that the Americans would take this opportunity to flee. Instead, Perry ordered his fresh ship into the fight and shelled the British fleet until it surrendered. When the battle was over, the British had lost 145 men to America's 123 dead, with the *Lawrence* accounting for 22 casualties alone. Both the *Detroit* and the *Lawrence* were lost, but Lake Erie was now won. The British evacuated Fort Malden before the U.S. Army could get there.

THE BATTLE OF LAKE CHAMPLAIN, THE SEQUEL

The second lake action was on Lake Champlain, where Benedict Arnold had saved the United States in 1776. The battle was similar to the *Chesapeake–Shannon* encounter, only this time the roles were reversed, with the British blundering into the well-prepared Americans.

Lt. Thomas Macdonough had requested men and supplies for the conflict he knew was coming. Navy Secretary William Jones gave him everything he needed, along with an ace: shipwright Noah Brown. Answering Macdonough's request for a powerful lake cruiser, Brown created the *Saratoga*, a 26-gun 3-masted sloop-of-war with only 1 deck of guns. In an amazing feat of shipbuilding, it was launched 40 days after construction was begun. Afterward, the Americans learned the British were finishing a frigate at Ile aux Noix, so they turned out the 20-gun brig the *Eagle* in a stunning 17 days!

The British were also building, with Capt. George Downie overseeing the construction of the 36-gun frigate the *Confiance*. Although the British had an 11,000-man army nearby, their commander, Sir George Prevost, would not move until Lake Champlain was secure. Downie had to beat the oncoming winter and the Americans, in that order. By September he had 4 ships (the *Confiance*, the 16-gun brig the *Linnet*, and the 11-gun sloops the *Chubb* and the *Finch*) and 12 gunboats, all manned by green crews.

Macdonough, however, had been training his men for the past six months, just one of many preparations he had made for battle. He ascertained the best spot to cover not only the approach the Royal Navy would have to take to engage his ships, but also the land route the army would use to bypass the lake. At the bay off the town of Plattsburgh, he anchored his ships and waited. His battle plan used a trick borrowed from Admiral Horatio Nelson, who had used the method known as "winding" ships to defeat the French Navy at the battle of Trafalgar.

> To wind (rhymes with bind) a vessel means to anchor it and then run extra ropes from the anchor lines back onto the ship. These lines were manned by sailors who, working in concert, could actually spin the ship around without using the sails. If one side became too heavily damaged, the vessel could be turned and a fresh side of cannons could enter combat. Winding ships also provided a more accurate gun platform, since the ship itself was restrained by the anchor ropes and, therefore, was not subject to the effects of recoiling cannons.

The British army and the Royal Navy set out together on September 11, 1814. When Provost sighted the four American ships (the *Saratoga*, the *Eagle*, the 17-gun converted steamship the *Ticonderoga*, and the 7-gun sloop *Preble*) and 10 small 1-gun galleys, he waited for Downie's fleet to engage them.

Captain Downie decided the best way to fight the anchored ships would be to anchor and wind his own fleet. However, he first had to get within range of the Americans. Sailing in a line abreast, they approached, taking fire all the way. They dropped their lines and the battle began. Here Macdonough's preparations made all the difference. The British had no chance to wind their ships because they were already taking heavy fire from the U.S. fleet. Then one of the *Saratoga's* shots struck a cannon in front of Captain Downie. The blast shifted the weapon off its mount and back onto the British captain, crushing him to death.

> The cannon that killed Captain Downie, still bearing the evidence of the *Saratoga's* accurate shot, can be seen to this day at the U.S. Naval Academy in Annapolis, Maryland.

In less than two hours, the battered British fleet struck its colors. Like Benedict Arnold's fleet had done 38 years earlier, the Americans had parried a British advance into their heartland and foiled another attempt to split the country in two. This time, however, the United States Navy also won the contest. Prevost was later court-martialed for his mistakes at Lake Champlain, but he died before sentencing could be handed down.

THE END OF THE WAR

By early 1814, the British had settled their war with France and moved to end the conflict with the United States once and for all. They launched a three-pronged invasion designed to cut off New England from the rest of the States while an army attacked from the Atlantic and another force came up through New Orleans.

The attempt to split the country was a good strategy. Many New Englanders were so against the war that their delegates had already met to discuss the possibility of seceding from the Union. Fortunately for America, the measure was voted down.

The British planned to use Lake Champlain to take New York and come from the Atlantic to invade Washington, Baltimore, Charleston, and Savannah. The first assault was led by Adm. Alexander Cochrane in early

August 1814. He sailed into Chesapeake Bay with 4 ships of the line, 20 frigates and sloops, and 22 troop-transport ships carrying an army of 4,000. The coastal defense at the time consisted of 15 gunboats with 500 sailors under Commodore Joshua Barney. When the invasion began, the 7,000 Army troops stationed in Washington, D.C., fled. Knowing he had no chance against the British, Barney blew up his boats rather than see them used against America. This allowed the British Army to disembark and attack Washington, D.C. (see *Alpha Bravo Delta Guide to the U.S. Army* for more details).

America was now warned of the invasion, and Baltimore began making preparations for battle. In early September, Admiral Cochrane planned to sail in and take Fort McHenry as easily as Washington. He found the harbor blocked by sunken ships and more than 16,000 troops ready for battle. The artillery of the fort fell short of the ships, giving the British some advantage. The British fleet had to settle for bombarding Fort McHenry the entire night, hitting the defenseless ramparts with more than 1,800 cannonballs.

> During the shelling of Fort Henry, 35-year-old poet-lawyer Francis Scott Key, detained on a British vessel after securing the release of a friend, watched the bombardment 8 miles away. Throughout the night he caught glimpses of the Stars and Stripes proudly waving, despite the battering of the fort by the Royal Navy. The sight so moved him that he composed "The Star-Spangled Banner," which was officially adopted as America's national anthem in 1931.

Support from nearby naval Fort Covington, and the Navy flotilla provided firepower when the British army tried to land during the night. Gen. Robert Ross was killed during the attempted invasion, and his troops were driven back, causing Admiral Cochrane to beat a hasty retreat.

December came, and Admiral Cochrane sailed south to invade America by way of New Orleans. With 50 warships and an army of 10,000, it seemed there was little that would stand in his way.

Gen. Andrew Jackson was rounding up an army to defend New Orleans because the American fleet was scattered at sea. Fortunately, a privateer ship, the 14-gun *General Armstrong*, commanded by Capt. Samuel Reid, distracted 3 British ships (including a 74-gun ship-of-the-line!) from joining

Cochrane's fleet for a month. The extra time allowed Jackson to gather together a motley crew of recruits and volunteers known as "dirty shirts," including Native Americans, free blacks, and pirates, to fight for the United States (see *Alpha Bravo Delta Guide to the U.S. Army*).

When he discovered that a 2,000-man British force was encamped just 7 miles from New Orleans, Jackson took a raiding party, and the American gunboat *Carolina* and ambushed the invading force, shaking British morale while raising the spirits of his dirty shirts.

On January 1, 1815, with what can only be described as guerilla fighting vs. British protocol, Jackson's force routed the redcoats, killing 291 with 1,262 wounded while suffering only 13 killed and 39 wounded. Admiral Cochrane's invasion force retreated, this time for good.

In this age of unreliable, slow communication, peace had actually been declared with the signing of the Treaty of Ghent on Christmas Eve. Word did not reach America until mid-February and was announced by President Madison on February 17, 1815. The Battle of New Orleans was fought after the treaty was negotiated, as were battles on the seas. The *President*, now commanded by Stephen Decatur, was captured in January after running aground trying to escape the British blockade. She was towed to England, where the British marveled at how well built she was. On February 20, the *Constitution* took both the British frigate the *Cyane* and the corvette *Levant* in a spectacular two-against-one duel. Later still, on March 23, the American 18-gun *Hornet* captured the 18-gun brig-sloop the *Penguin*.

But Great Britain would strike the last (unofficial) blow on the seas in this war. On March 27, 1814, the 46-gun frigate the *Essex*, commanded by David Porter, ran into two British ships, the 36-gun frigate the *Phoebe* and the 18-gun sloop the *Cherub*. Because of a refit in 1812, the *Essex*'s 12-pound long guns had been replaced with short-range 32-pound carronades. Any ship with long-range cannons could stay out of range of the American vessel while still hitting it, which is exactly what happened.

Although the *Essex* tried to outrun her enemies, a squall toppled its main topmast. Porter took cover in a Chilean bay, hoping the British wouldn't violate neutral waters. After a two-and-a half hour target practice session for the enemy ships, the American frigate surrendered with 58 men killed, 65 wounded, and 31 missing, totaling nearly 60 percent of the 255-man crew on the ship. The British had lost only 5 men, with 10 wounded. Porter and his crew were allowed to return to America with letters of parole on the converted brig the *Little Essex*, to be exchanged for British prisoners.

It was realized afterward that the war could have been shorter and less costly if America had been prepared with standing peacetime forces both on land and at sea. Congress agreed, and the Navy was ordered to construct 21 new warships that would be continuously manned and prepared. Decades after a Constitutional provision established the United States Navy, it finally had a permanent fleet to sail.

CHAPTER 5

PEACETIME AND THE WAR WITH MEXICO

America's victory over Great Britain in the War of 1812 proved that the U.S. was equal to any other nation and would defend itself with tenacity and courage. Following that conflict, America had one more foreign disagreement to resolve before enjoying 32 years of peace.

While the United States had been concentrating on the English threat, Ali V, the dey of Algiers, declared open season against U.S. merchant ships. On February 25, 1815—just a few days after the treaty ending the War of 1812 was signed—President James Madison sent Congress a request for America to send two naval squadrons against Algiers immediately.

Capt. Stephen Decatur, already experienced in fighting the pirate nations, was itching to get back to the Mediterranean. He beat Capt. William Bainbridge (the man who had surrendered the *Philadelphia* at Algiers) to the punch, having his squadron of three frigates and seven smaller warships out to sea by May 20.

Decatur sailed to the Mediterranean and instantly captured the 46-gun *Mashuda* and its 400-man crew. From there he sailed straight to Algiers, with the new American consul general, William Shaler, to brace the astonished dey.

Decatur and Shaler demanded a most-favored-nation clause and the renouncing of any tribute payment to Algiers. The commodore insisted that negotiations be held on his flagship, saying that if any of the dey's vessels even showed up, he would capture them. Caught between the Navy and a hard place, the dey signed the treaty on June 30, 1815. America's fleet had proven decisive in stopping the aggression of Algiers, while simultaneously inventing the art of "gunboat diplomacy," or negotiating terms from a position of superior naval strength.

WHAT TO DO DURING PEACETIME?

Once that brief show of force was over, the United States was free to concentrate on development, exploration, and expansion. With no foes threatening U.S. borders, the armed forces had to adjust to a prolonged period of peace. The next three decades allowed for some attempts at technological innovation, but they also meant the fleet had to survive various attempts to trim the department.

The first change was the development of a three-man Board of Navy Commissioners. Staffed by senior captains (the first three were John Rodgers, David Porter, and Stephen Decatur), they assisted the secretary in developing policy, the first time professional officers had a say in Navy administration.

The other major occurrence was a general act passed in April 1816, allowing for the "gradual increase of the Navy." To this end, Congress allocated $1 million per year for the next six years to the fleet. The Navy ramped up its shipbuilding program, planning a dozen 44-gun frigates, nine 74-gun ships of the line, and three new steam vessels for harbor defense.

The increased production meshed well with newly elected President James Monroe's general policy for the Navy. Attempting to strengthen America's official neutrality position, he advocated strong coastal defenses to deter foreign powers that might attempt to blockade U.S. harbors. This increased state of readiness also meant that the Navy would be ready in the event of war. While ships of the line would be useful primarily as blockade breakers, they were of secondary importance compared to swifter frigates, sloops, and schooners that could capture enemy merchant vessels. Monroe also wanted American ships in areas of increased commerce, including the Mediterranean, the southern Atlantic Coast (including the Caribbean Sea and the Spanish-held islands there), and the Pacific and Indian Oceans, where more American merchants were traveling every year.

PIRATE HUNTING IN THE CARIBBEAN

These new policies were implemented at the right time. American trade was booming, with new markets opening up in the East (China, the Philippines, and soon Japan), West (the West Indies), and South (South America and the Caribbean). As the seas became more crowded with slow-moving, rich cargo vessels, pirate fleets in these new markets became the primary threat. From 1816 to 1822, there were more than 3,000 cases of piracy (averaging 9 a week) in the Caribbean Sea alone.

The raiders also moved up the coast into the Gulf of Mexico, where New Orleans had become the second-busiest port in the nation after New York City. When Spain and the countries of South America couldn't police their coasts, the United States took it upon itself to rid international waters of the pirate menace.

In 1821, a squadron was created and deployed to stop commerce raiding in the Caribbean Sea. Consisting of the 36-gun flagship frigate the *Macedonian*, an 18-gun sloop, two 18-gun brigs, and four 12-gun schooners, it mustered 1,300 men and was the Navy's largest command. Later Congress increased it even further with the addition of a shallow-water fleet consisting of 10 schooners, 5 cutters, and the *Sea Gull*, a converted river steamer, the first time a steam-powered vessel was used by the U.S. Navy. To command this mighty fleet, the Secretary of the Navy chose two of the best captains in the fleet: James Biddle and then David Porter.

The West India Squadron cleared the Spanish-held Caribbean islands, including Cuba and Puerto Rico, of buccaneers in two years. With the help of the Royal Navy, the pirates had been eradicated by 1826, ending three centuries of attacks on merchant ships of the world.

THE NAVY IN DECLINE

After this high-water mark, the U.S. Navy experienced a gradual decline in funds, ships, and officers. Of these, the loss of experienced captains was the most telling, both for future generations of sailors and for the continued course of the fleet itself.

First, Oliver Hazard Perry, the hero of Lake Erie and the War of 1812, died in 1819 of yellow fever contracted during a trip to negotiate American maritime trade and security with Venezuela. Next, Stephen Decatur, arguably the most renowned naval hero of his generation, died on March 22, 1820, wounded in a duel versus James Barron, the former commander of the *Chesapeake*.

The third captain to go was David Porter, another hero of the War of 1812, who pursued America's policy against the Caribbean pirates a bit too zealously. When he landed 200 men on Puerto Rico in 1824 to free one of his officers who had been arrested and imprisoned while chasing thieves there, the officer was quickly freed and an official apology was tendered. All of this would probably have been fine, except for President Monroe's famous Monroe Doctrine issued the year before. Because Puerto Rico was a Spanish holding, Captain Porter had violated Monroe's edict, despite the fact that he had gone there to rescue one of his own.

When James Monroe announced his now famous Monroe Doctrine to Congress in 1823, he announced America's commitment to democracy, stating that North and South America would not be "considered as subjects to further colonization by any European powers" and declared that the United States "should consider any attempt on their [the European continent's] part to extend their system to any portion of this hemisphere as dangerous to our peace and safety."

President Monroe went even further, saying aggression by foreign powers against any independent nation in North and South America would be viewed unfavorably: "But with the Governments who have declared their independence and maintain it, and whose independent we have, on great consideration and on just principles, acknowledged, we could not view any interposition for the purpose of oppressing them, or controlling in any other manner their destiny, by any European power in any other light than as the manifestation of an unfriendly disposition toward the United States."

In effect, the U.S. established itself as the Western Hemisphere's big brother, extending the offer of assistance to any country that might need help against aggressive European nations.

Congress didn't agree with Porter's assessment of the situation and court-martialed him on the charge of disobeying orders, eventually suspending him for six months. The verdict disgusted Porter, and he resigned, the third of the Navy's most famous and effective officers gone in five years.

CHAPTER 5: PEACETIME AND THE WAR WITH MEXICO

As new trade routes opened up on both coasts, the Navy was called upon not only to navigate unpredictable ocean waters, but also to handle international politics and commerce. On March 27, 1824, Commodore Isaac Hull brought Herman Allen, the first United States minister to Chile (and Hull's brother-in-law), to Valparaiso to open relations with the nation and protect American maritime interests. It proved difficult at best, for while Hull and Allen had the right to protest any action against U.S. commerce by newly emerging (and often embroiled in civil war) South American nations, Congress had forbidden the pair to follow up any formal complaint with any show of force. Even when four Peruvian vessels were illegally boarding and taxing vessels in the area, the United States could do nothing about it. But when the *United States* left Valparaiso in 1827, the Pacific Squadron, as it came to be known, had sent ships out to the Galapagos Islands, Hawaii, and Tahiti, and maintained patrols on the western coasts of both American continents.

In 1829, the sloop *Vincennes* set off on what would be a two-year journey around the world, the first circumnavigation of the globe by a United States Navy vessel. When it returned, Monroe was out of office and "Old Hickory," Andrew Jackson, was in. The Hero of New Orleans was anti-Army, feeling that the national militia was the key to America's defense. This did not make him anti-Navy, however, although not much growth occurred during his term. Jackson scrapped the partially completed ships of the line sitting in various Navy docks since 1821 because the skyrocketing cost versus their effective return would be unacceptable. Instead, he advocated stockpiling timber and ship-building supplies in the event of confrontation with one of the European nations. The 5,000 man-Navy—roughly the crew of one of today's supercarriers—was plenty to handle whatever might come up at home.

This is not to say that Jackson wasn't averse to rattling his Navy cutlass when necessary. In 1831, a small group of islands off Argentina, the Falklands, had been declared off-limits to American seal hunters, to prevent overhunting. When the American vessel the *Harriet* was found killing seals there, the ship was seized and taken to Buenos Aires.

When the news reached Montevideo, Capt. Silas M. Duncan took his ship, the 24-gun sloop the *Lexington*, down to Buenos Aires and demanded a trial of Louis Vernet, the Argentine governor general of the islands.

When the Argentinian government refused to hand him over, Duncan landed on the islands and arrested several colonists. This time the American government fully backed Duncan's actions, claiming that Vernet and his colonists were no better than pirates (despite the fact that it was an American ship breaking Argentinean law). Great Britain annexed the islands in 1833, and Buenos Aires severed diplomatic relations with America for more than 10 years.

On the other side of the world, when armed natives attacked an American vessel, the *Friendship*, at Sumatra, Jackson and his Secretary of the Navy Levi Woodbury sent the 50-gun frigate the *Potomac*, captained by John Downes, to investigate. Downes had been ordered to verify the attack before responding to it, but on February 6, 1832, he landed marines and sailors at the port of Quallah Battoo and killed more than 100 Sumatrans in combat; then he shelled the remaining defenders. Although his diplomacy-by-cannon-fire approach extracted promises of future good conduct from Sumatra, it caused an uproar in Washington. While President Jackson publicly praised Downes, his reception at home was much cooler, and Downes never commanded a warship again.

Not all of America's diplomatic treaties were gained over the barrel of a cannon. From 1832 to 1834, Secretary Woodbury sent the sloop-of-war the *Peacock* and the schooner the *Boxer* to the Pacific Rim to obtain trade treaties with Asian nations. The ships were led by Master-Commandant David Geisinger and also carried a New Hampshire businessman named Edmund Roberts to handle the negotiations. They visited the Philippines, Cuba, Bangkok, Singapore, Yemen, and Mozambique. The two men obtained treaties with Thailand and the Sultan of Muscat, and Roberts was sent out again to contact the still-isolationist Japanese. On the way, however, he fell victim to cholera *and* dysentery in Macao. Without Roberts's silver tongue, Geisinger returned to America—circumnavigating the globe in the process.

A NEW TECHNOLOGY ON THE HORIZON—THE POWER OF STEAM

While America protected its borders, expanded its trade routes, and tried to decide what kind of ships to build, the rest of the world embraced a new technology: steam power. Great Britain was already using steamships, using an unarmed, powered vessel in 1824 in Burma and assembling armed steamers in 1828. In 1827, the steamship was first used in combat by Greece. In 1830, France joined the steam power movement, sending six armed steamers into battle against Algeria.

But while it was clear to the rest of the world that steam was the next big advancement in ship technology, the United States Navy wasn't as quick to explore this new development. Even though a steam-powered vessel had traveling on the Hudson River since 1807, when Robert Fulton introduced the *Clermont,* steam power was still fighting an upstream battle for acceptance. Except for David Porter's use of the steamboat the *Sea Gull* to chase pirates in the Gulf of Mexico in 1822–1823, the Navy had been resistant to the invention. Despite the passage of a bill apportioning $500,000 to develop a steam-powered vessel for the Navy in 1814, the first real steamship was several years away.

But when Mahlon Dickerson replaced Levi Woodbury as secretary of the Navy at the beginning of Andrew Jackson's second term as president, things began to change. Dickerson knew he had to convince the Board of Navy Commissioners, now headed by decorated war veteran John Rodgers and men who had fought in the War of 1812. Although they had America's best interests at heart, they were conservative and not inclined to support steam power.

A revolt by the Seminole tribe in Florida and the Creek tribe in Georgia and South Alabama in 1835 led to an eight-year guerilla war and also revealed the need for more versatile vessels that could execute both shallow and deepwater operations, an ideal situation for steamships. But this new technology had problems, including extending its supply lines. The USS *President's* tour of duty during the War of 1812 had covered more than 30,000 miles, relying only on manpower and sail. A steamship could not have gone even a hundredth of that distance without needing to resupply.

The term "blue water navy" refers to all deep draft ships designed to sail on the ocean, mostly ships-of-the-line and large frigates. The "brown water navy" consists of shallow draft vessels that could patrol coastlines and sail on rivers and smaller lakes, and were often flat-bottomed steam vessels. Both aspects of the Navy were named for the color of the water the respective ships sailed on.

When Martin Van Buren succeeded Andrew Jackson in 1836, he kept Dickerson as Secretary of the Navy. In Jackson's last speech, he urged Congress to expand the fleet as quickly as possible, saying that a well-equipped Navy could not only protect America, but also take a war to an enemy country, if necessary.

But the only practical American steam vessel in existence, the *Sea Gull*, had been rotting in Philadelphia for the past decade. Robert Fulton's 1814 creation, the *Demologos*, later renamed the *Fulton* in honor of her creator, had been in service since the end of the War of 1812 but was completely unsuitable for the Navy's purposes. The ship was originally designed for harbor defense, but its shortcomings did not bode well for the future of steam in the military. Although the *Fulton* was steam-powered and supposedly propelled by a paddlewheel flanked on either side by two hulls, it had no steering apparatus. In fact, with no masts or sails, the steam engine was designed as a secondary method of power, with the primary means to have the vessel kedged or towed by other boats. It remained in New York harbor until its destruction by fire in 1829.

Undaunted, Dickerson asked Rodgers to go back to the drawing board. Having accepted the advantages of steam power at last, the 63-year-old Rodgers recommended 25 steamships in his report on the status and future of the Navy. But while he had no problem recommending them, knowing how to build one was another matter entirely. The Navy had to purchase a tugboat, the 142-ton *Engineer*, and hired noted engineer Charles H. Haswell to convert it to steam. When Haswell was done, the 180-foot tug, renamed the *Fulton II*, reached a more-than-respectable speed of 12 knots during her trials.

In 1837, the Navy Board's response to the *Fulton II* trials was to authorize the building of the 120-gun *Philadelphia*, the largest ship-of-the-line the Navy would ever build—and also the last. Rather than accept the possibilities of steam, the keel of the 210-foot sailing white elephant was laid while Great Britain and France expanded their respective steam fleets.

But everything Dickerson and Haswell had accomplished stopped dead with the appointment of James Paulding as Secretary of the Navy in June 1838. Paulding, a writer, had been associated with the Navy since 1815, when he was given the post of secretary to the Navy Board. Spending more than 20 years at the side of men like Rodgers, Porter, and Decatur (all fine men in their own right, but not as forward-thinking as one might hope) didn't help Paulding understand that by the late 1830s, the sailing ship was dying out.

This was not to say that Paulding did nothing to advance the Navy. In 1838, he signed the orders sending Lt. Charles Wilkes on a four-year journey to survey and study the South Pacific Ocean, Australia, Fiji, Antarctica, and dozens of points of interest along the way. During his voyage, Wilkes explored the western coast of North America, mapping the shoreline of what would later become Washington, Oregon, and northern California. From there he visited Hawaii and the Philippines, and came home in 1842 by way of Singapore and the Cape of Good Hope. Wilkes's voyage proved valuable not only in the wealth of maps and information he brought back; he also proved that the U.S. Navy could be an important peacetime asset. His voyage, which covered 87,000 nautical miles, was accomplished by sail power alone.

Steam soon gained a valuable ally in Matthew Calbraith Perry. The younger brother of Lake Erie hero Oliver Hazard Perry, he was part of the next generation of naval officers. Perry realized that the Navy must change with the times if it were to stay at the forefront of maritime technology. After traveling in Europe and meeting like-minded people, including Sir Charles Wood, the Secretary of the British Admiralty, Perry returned to America and persuaded Congress to pass a bill authorizing the construction of two steam frigates, the *Mississippi* and the *Missouri*, in 1839. Perry risked the ire of Secretary Paulding and the current Navy Board, but his tactics were necessary to modernize the fleet, which was already trailing Great Britain and France in the naval race.

> The U.S. Navy's general unwillingness to adopt steam power was so apparent by this time that when the steam frigates the *Mississippi* and the *Missouri* were launched in 1842, they were accompanied out of the yards by the now-obsolete sail-powered frigates the *Cumberland* and the *Savannah,* both of which had been started after the War of 1812, almost 30 years earlier!

In 1841, Abel P. Upshur replaced Paulding as secretary of the navy and was the exact opposite of his predecessor: innovative, aggressive, and looking to upgrade and expand the Navy as much as possible. His main accomplishment was to replace the Navy Board with an administrational system that lasted for the next century: the naval bureaus. Upshur's plan sectioned the Navy into five departments: Provisions and Clothing, Medicine and Surgery, Ordnance and Hydrography, the Navy Docks and Yards, and the Bureau of Construction, Equipment, and Repair. Although the new departments had their problems in transition (the last department gained the nickname "the Bureau of Destruction and Despair" during this time), it was still a great step forward from the Navy Board.

Arguing that America needed more ships to protect its foreign merchant interests, President John Tyler advocated increasing the standing fleet to 41 vessels, up from 25, and also building 12 "smaller ships."

The next step in steam power came from Capt. Robert F. Stockton. In 1843, he gained support for and commissioned the *Princeton*, a 1,043-ton steamship armed with two heavy 12-inch cannons. Stockton and the ship's designer, noted engineer John Ericsson, had also been experimenting with new cannon designs that used self-encased shell ammunition. On February 28, 1844, Stockton alone was demonstrating the *Princeton*'s abilities, including her two huge cannons. While sailing on the Potomac River, at the request by Navy Secretary Thomas W. Gilmer, Stockton ordered one last round fired from one of the 12-inch guns, named the *Peacemaker*. The cannon exploded, wounding more than 20 guests and killing 8, including Secretary Gilmer, who had held his position for 9 days, and the current Secretary of State, Abel P. Upshur. Stockton blamed Ericsson for the defective cannon, when it was his own rush to cast and demonstrate the weapon that caused the explosion. The accident held back steam power in America until the Civil War.

After the *Princeton* was repaired, President Polk ordered Stockton to cross the Atlantic Ocean in late February, 1845, while the U.S. was finalizing the annexation of Texas. Stockton knew Mexico would not let Texas go without a fight, so he delayed his departure until new orders were received: to sail to the Gulf of Mexico.

MANIFEST DESTINY ACHIEVED, ONE WAY OR ANOTHER

The United States was now aggressively expanding its borders, and there was a role for the U.S. Navy as well. After negotiating the Webster-Ashburton

Treaty, which codified the border between Maine and Canada and increased U.S. land by 7,000 square miles, Congress turned its attention westward.

Lieutenant Wilkes's report on the Pacific Northwest highlighted the rich timber and hunting grounds in the Oregon Territory. Along with the San Francisco harbor and the commerce potential of Puget Sound, the entire area would enrich America, allowing increased communication and trade with Pacific Rim countries as well as the West Coast of South America.

Fearful that Wilkes's findings would influence negotiations with Great Britain, the report was kept secret until 1911. The final border was drawn in 1846 along the north forty-ninth latitude, with Vancouver Island staying with Canada, and adding 285,000 square miles to the United States of America.

THE DIRTY WAR: THE MEXICAN-AMERICAN WAR: 1846–1847

After the East and West had been secured, America looked to the area containing what would eventually become Texas, New Mexico, Arizona, and California. The U.S. government had coveted the Texas territory for more than two decades, ever since President John Quincy Adams had offered to buy it from Mexico and been turned down in 1825. A repeated offer by Andrew Jackson during his term in office had been refused as well, although Jackson was able to officially recognize the Republic of Texas on his last day in office, March 3, 1837. If the United States was going to gain control of Texas and the surrounding territories, more drastic measures would be called for.

Although Mexico claimed control of a large part of what is now the southwestern United States, the reality was a bit different. Texas dissolved its bonds with Mexico in 1836, declaring itself an independent republic and winning national recognition from the United States, France, and Great Britain, but not from Mexico. The republic would have let the United States annex it immediately, but slavery was becoming a divisive issue in America. The Missouri Compromise of 1820 had kept an uneasy balance of slave and free states in the Union. It was feared that letting in the pro-slavery Texas territory, which could be divided into several states, would upset the delicate balance that had been maintained so far.

> The Missouri Compromise was an agreement reached by the House of Representatives and the Senate that let Maine into the Union as a free state and admitted the Missouri Territory in as a slave state, thereby keeping the balance of slave states to free states equal. Although the bill initially banned slavery in the rest of the Louisiana Purchase, that condition did not survive debate, and an amended version of the bill with no restriction on slavery in Missouri, but also no restriction on the rights of American citizens (including free African Americans), passed both houses of Congress in August 1821.

Without support from the United States, the Lone Star Republic (as Texas was now called) had to fend for itself against Mexican plans to reacquire it. In 1836, the bloody Battle of the Alamo was fought, and Sam Houston's later defeat of the Mexican forces kept Texas out of Mexican hands for the time.

Meanwhile, California followed Texas's lead in 1842. Although Mexico recognized the new government, it maintained that it still owned the land. The Spanish watched, seemingly inactive or unable to respond as territory after territory broke free of their grasp.

On October 20, 1842, in a foreshadowing of things to come, Commodore Thomas ap Catesby Jones, commander of the Pacific Fleet, bloodlessly captured Monterey, the Spanish capital in Upper California. He had taken action after hearing false news that Mexico and the United States were at war. As the Oregon Territory negotiations were still ongoing at the time, the possibility had existed that Great Britain was mobilizing a fleet to claim Upper Cali-fornia, possibly by signing a secret accord with Mexico. When the error was corrected two days later, Jones gave the town back to the Spanish, with no ill will on either side (although Jones did lose his command for sailing to a conclusion). That would not be the case four years later.

MUTINY ON THE *SOMERS*

Although instances of mutiny in the Navy were extremely rare, one case that deserves mention is the supposed planned mutiny on the brig the *Somers* in 1842.

Used to teach new ensigns basic seamanship, the *Somers* was a poor choice: it was oversensitive, small, and unwieldy. On this training cruise, it was also overloaded with more than 120 men, most of them trainees.

During the voyage, a truculent midshipman, Philip Spencer, was accused of planning a mutiny. Supposedly he and his accomplices were going to kill anyone who resisted, turn the *Somers* into a pirate vessel, and sail south to international waters. The captain, a suspicious man named Alexander Slidell Mackenzie, immediately put Spencer in irons along with several of his supposed conspirators. When a list written in Greek was found that allegedly showed who would be killed, it was enough for Mackenzie. After conferring with his officers (who put forth several other plans of action that the captain rejected), Spencer and two other sailors, including a master boatswain, were hanged without a trial or the chance to defend themselves. The *Somers* then returned to New York harbor, where the rest of the "conspirators" were eventually released.

The fact that Mackenzie didn't even call a court-martial speaks about the impropriety of his act. Although ships' captains could convene a lesser court-martial for minor offenses, they've never had the power to execute sailors under their command.

Although Mackenzie requested a court of inquiry, where he was cleared of any wrongdoing, he was called again to a general court-martial, where he was found not guilty of murder and other charges against him. The news and handling of the incident put a cloud over the Navy in general, with particular scrutiny on its training methods and the officer class in general. Owing to Mackenzie's overreaction, the American public thought the officers of the Navy considered themselves above the law.

When Robert Stockton arrived at Galveston on May 12, 1845, he sent his secretary, Dr. Wright, to propose a plan for the head of the Texas militia, Maj. Gen. Sidney Jones, and the current president of the republic, Anson Jones, to provoke a war with Mexico by raising an army and attacking the town of Matamoros across the Mexican border. Wright told them that Stockton's ships would provide transport, supplies, and assistance as needed. He also claimed that President Polk secretly approved of Stockton's plan but did not want his approbation known publicly. Jones delayed his answer until he had confirmation that Mexico had acknowledged Texas's independence to the British minister to Texas, whereupon he turned down Dr. Wright and Stockton. Stockton then sailed for the Pacific Ocean, where California and presumed greatness awaited him.

Before President James K. Polk sent Gen. Zachary Taylor across the Texas-Mexico border to instigate the Mexican War in January 1846, he had already prepared the U.S. Navy. In the Gulf of Mexico, Commodore

David Connor, commanding what was known as the Home Squadron (consisting of the steamer the *Mississippi,* two frigates, three sloops, and three brigs), received orders to blockade Mexican ports, protect American merchant ships from capture by privateers, and assist the U.S. Army whenever and wherever possible.

With no standing Mexican Navy and few ships willing to take the letters of marque and reprisal that Mexico offered, the deadliest enemies the Navy faced were boredom and disease. While the port blockade was easily enforced, scurvy, malaria, and yellow fever ran rampant among the sailors. With the newly created naval bureaus still disorganized, supplies of food, medicine, and ammunition to the Gulf were intermittent, to say the least.

Connor's men weathered illness, quick-rising Gulf storms, and no enemy to fight for nine months before seeing any action. Acting on an officially approved plan from President Polk, Maj. Gen. Winfield Scott proposed putting an army of 14,000 men ashore and taking Veracruz, a coast town only 220 miles from Mexico City. The task facing Connor and his squadron was a daunting one; such a large-scale amphibious invasion had never been attempted. Scott wanted enough boats to land 2,500 men at a time, so the first vessels designed specifically for putting men ashore were created. They were wide, flat-bottomed, and double-ended, and they could carry 40 men with a crew of 8. After reconnaissance and selection of the landing sites by Connor, the operation began on March 9, 1847. Within 5 hours, 8,600 American soldiers had been shuttled onto the deserted beach without a single man lost. The rest of the army followed, and just before General Scott was to begin his assault on Veracruz, Connor was replaced by Commodore Matthew C. Perry.

Perry wasn't content to sit back and blockade Mexico; he wanted to go where the action was. With his large fleet, consisting of Connor's ships as well as the ship-of-the-line the *Ohio;* three more sloops; six shallow-draft, small steamships; seven lightly armed schooners; four bomb barges; and a parade of supply vessels, he had more than enough power at his command.

A bomb barge is a relatively flat vessel holding several mortars, which can lob explosive charges in a high arc onto a target. Because these ships require very calm water to accurately fire their ordnance, they were rarely used outside of bays or harbors.

With 13,000 soldiers landed and ready to take Veracruz, the siege was a foregone conclusion. Ten days after he arrived, Perry was in the castle, with Connor's fleet and his own ships helping in the most successful troop landing in history to date.

Perry was just getting started. In April, he turned his attention toward the port of Tuxpan, halfway between Veracruz and Tampico. The Mexican town was more of a challenge because its inhabitants had armed themselves with scavenged cannons and ammunition from the brig the *Truxtun*, which had foundered in a storm the year before. None of their preparations helped against the American forces, which, led by Commander Franklin Buchanan, stormed ashore and charged the high ground containing the cannons. Within hours, Tuxpan was in American hands.

In June 1847, the commodore set his sights on Tabasco, the last major Gulf port still controlled by Mexico. In a three-day engagement, Perry himself led 1,000 men ashore. While his assault was successful and provided valuable practice for future captains like David Porter (see Chapter 6), the occupying troops fell victim to an enemy they couldn't see, much less fight. Yellow fever and malaria hit the Navy squadron hard, even incapacitating Perry himself, who contracted yellow fever with one of his sons. In July, the weakened fleet withdrew from Tabasco, but the diseases remained, with clouds of mosquitoes breeding in the stagnant water of the *Mississippi*'s bilges. By this time, the action had ended in the Gulf of Mexico, leaving just a very chaotic and confused squadron milling about in the Pacific.

SAILING IN CIRCLES: THE PACIFIC SQUADRON

While men like Connor and Perry were achieving their goals in the Gulf of Mexico, the Pacific Squadron, commanded by John D. Sloat, was not doing nearly as well. Sloat's orders instructed him to gather his fleet off the coast of what was then the coast of Mexico and Oregon, but forbade him to attack unless he was positive that Mexico had declared war against the United States.

It wasn't until July 7, 1846, almost two months after the Mexican War began, that Sloat took action. On July 9, he sailed into Monterey and captured both it and San Francisco. He then immediately overstepped his authority by declaring California part of the United States.

Although concerned by the possibility of Great Britain interfering in his mission, Sloat was surprised when he saw no English response at all. Nevertheless, he was relieved when his replacement arrived—none other than Robert F. Stockton on the frigate *Congress* along with the sloop-of-war *Cyane*.

Stockton, like Perry, was a man of action. He teamed up with John C. Fremont, a lieutenant in the U.S. Army Topographical Engineers who had organized a successful American rebellion in Northern California. Then he sailed south, pausing to proclaim American control of Santa Barbara, and then marshalling a 368-man unit of sailors and marines to take Los Angeles, which was completely undefended when they arrived.

Once there, Stockton, like Sloat before him, immediately exceeded his authority, organizing a local government for California and making plans to blockade the entire west coast of Mexico, neither of which were in his orders. His grandiose plan was to take Acapulco, which he claimed was a haven for nonexistent Mexican privateers; from there it would be on to Mexico City and victory.

Secretary of the Navy George Bancroft was incensed as word reached him of U.S. Navy commanders sailing pell-mell up and down the Pacific Coast. Bancroft didn't help matters by first ordering Sloat to step down from his command in favor of Stockton or Commodore James Biddle, who was arriving from the Far East after trying (and failing) to begin negotiations with Japan. Three weeks later, the Navy secretary sent instructions for Sloat to assume command of the squadron again. By the time the second set of orders had arrived, it was too late; Stockton was in charge.

But things did not go as Stockton had planned. Mexico mounted a defense of the contested lands, driving his small garrison from Los Angeles and ambushing Brig. Gen. Stephen Watts Kearny's army as it came into California through New Mexico. The remains of his once-proud "Army of the West" limped into Los Angeles in January 1847 and helped Stockton and Fremont retake the city, securing what was then Upper California.

Afterward, both Stockton and Kearny laid claim to governorship of the territory. Fortunately, Commodore Branford Shubrick landed in Monterey on January 22 and put an end to the bickering. Kearny retained the governor's seat of California. James Biddle, while technically in command during

Stockton's foray up and down the coast, was in the twilight of his career and relinquished the Pacific Squadron to Shubrick. Stockton was relieved of his command; he headed back east in June 1847.

Shubrick continued blockading Mexican ports for the next six months. Lacking enough men to take and hold any ports, he conducted quick raids on coastal towns and chased Mexican merchant ships when he found them. While he occupied La Paz, the capital of Baja, California, and Mazatlán, Mexico's largest west coast port, he was marking time until General Scott could take Mexico City. (See *Alpha Bravo Delta Guide to the U.S. Army*.)

THE END OF THE WAR

With Mexico defeated in a conflict it didn't want against a superior foe, all that remained was to divide up the spoils. Although a powerful "All-Mexico" contingent, including Secretary of State James Buchanan, Vice President George Dallas, and Robert F. Stockton, recommended annexing the entire nation, wiser heads prevailed. Gen. Winfield Scott and U.S. diplomat Nicholas Trist both spoke out against the idea, citing the difficulty of governing a culture and people so different from America's. Even more important, President Polk was wise enough to realize that America should not impose its will on other cultures and nations (despite starting the war to gain land in the first place, apparently there were limits beyond which even he wouldn't go); otherwise it would be going against the very ideals that led its people to fight for freedom in the first place (Storm clouds of the Civil War, already building on the horizon, would severely test this theory).

In the end, under the Treaty of Guadalupe Hidalgo signed on February 2, 1848, America gained what are today the states of Arizona, California, Nevada, New Mexico, and Utah, along with parts of Colorado and Wyoming. The United States had grown by more than half a million acres, at the bargain price of $15 million paid to Mexico, or roughly 48 cents an acre. The cost of the war itself came to about $58 million.

Afterward, men such as Abraham Lincoln and Frederick Douglass criticized America's bullying tactics in provoking the conflict with Mexico for no other motive than land greed. The American Anti-Slavery Society accused the government of creating the war to perpetuate slavery through the Mexico territory, which would have its own repercussions in less than 20 years.

CHAPTER 6

FOREIGN INTERVENTIONS

After America's swift victory over hapless Mexico, the young country's thoughts turned toward overseas trade. With the nation still expanding, Congress and naval officers alike realized the value of San Francisco Bay as an access point to the Far East. However, conventional men such as Stephen R. Mallory, later the Confederate Secretary of the Navy, still pressed for a primarily brown water navy for coastal defense, and frigates and sloops for blue water missions. Mallory was basing the nation's needs on the War of 1812, which consisted mainly of single ship vs. single ship actions (except for the battles of Lakes Erie and Champlain), a now obsolete defensive concept.

Five naval secretaries served during the 1850s, and while the desperately needed steamships were eventually pushed through by James C. Dobbin, reforms on the manpower side took longer. Three secretaries tried to reform the officer promotion system and abolish the practice of flogging sailors for punishment, but they couldn't get Congressional approval. Secretary Dobbin, however, created a review board that evaluated every officer in the service and then recommended dismissing or placing on leave 201 officers judged unfit for duty. Dobbin also created a system of courts martial and finally banned flogging as punishment. But his crowning accomplishment came in 1854, with the approval for six first-class steam frigates, the first of which was launched in 1856. Secretary Dobbin was one of the few men of the time who understood that a powerful Navy was needed to keep up with the rest of the world powers.

It was just as well that Dobbin had gotten his ships built quickly, for the next secretary, Isacc Toucey, was committed to coastal defense and urged limiting the Navy in power and scope, no matter how large foreign navies became. While he did urge that all Navy ships be steam-powered, the Civil War broke out before his recommendation could be enforced.

THE NAVY AROUND THE WORLD

During the 1850s, six Navy squadrons patrolled various areas of the world. The African Squadron swept the Atlantic for slave traders; the small Brazil Squadron escorted merchant ships around the Cape of Good Hope; the East India Squadron sailed between the coast of China and Hawaii; the Home Squadron guarded the Gulf of Mexico, the Mediterranean Squadron covered the sea of the same name; and the Pacific Squadron patrolled the west coast of North and South America.

The Mediterranean Squadron was the plum assigment of the six. Matthew C. Perry, among others, lobbied for it because of its high profile but no real action potential. The North African states had been subjugated by France in the 1830s, and the region had been quiet ever since. In 1851, Lajos Kossuth and Martin Kostza, two Hungarian nationalists who spoke out in favor of Hungary's secession from Austria, were picked up at Constantinople along with 50 allies by the steamship the *Mississippi* and were taken to America. In 1853, Kostzka was rescued by the Navy again, this time from an Austrian brig where he was being held prisoner. The sloop that picked him up, the *St. Louis,* stared down several armed Austrian vessels during the incident.

The Pacific Squadron was charged with keeping watch over the entire west coasts of North and South America. While guarding American merchant interests, which had exploded in the Pacific during the past two decades, the squadron also had to keep an eye on overzealous Americans taking the idea of "manifest destiny" a bit too far. In 1854, a ship named the *Portsmouth* was called in to rescue comrades of armed expansionist William J. Walker, who had tried to "liberate" Baja, California and Sonora from Mexico. The year afterward, Walker decided to take over Nicaragua and tangled with local soldiers of fortune hired by steamship tycoon Cornelius Vanderbilt. The Navy ship the *St. Mary* was sent down to broker a truce and remove him in 1857. Walker's habit of being bailed out by the Navy came to an end in 1860, when he was shot by a firing squad as he once again prepared to invade Nicaragua.

On the other side of the Pacific, the East India Squadron, composed of the frigate the *Brandywine*, the sloop-of-war the *St. Louis*, and the brig the *Perry*, all sail-powered vessels, received grand reinforcement in 1851 with the arrival of the steamship *Susquehanna*, despite the scarcity of U.S. coal stations in the region. The next year brought an even greater addition, Commodore Matthew C. Perry.

With a shrewd blend of genuine respect, unforced politeness, and amazing technology, Perry cracked the self-imposed isolation of Japan. It was the East India Squadron's most glorious achievement of the decade. All relations with Asian countries would not be so polite, however.

On April 4, 1854, a skirmish between Chinese soldiers and a British-American landing party left three Americans dead and seven wounded. Commodore Perry used the strong relationship between Great Britain and America to authorize a bilateral response in September of that year. In 1855–1856, American and British vessels fought both Chinese pirates and imperial soldiers. The incident culminated in two warships, the *Portsmouth* and the *Levane*, engaging and destroying Chinese barrier forts on the Pearl River while a British force attacked Chinese positions in the beginning of a second Anglo-Chinese war.

Allied with France, Britain declared war on China under questionable circumstances, and a joint force captured Canton in early 1858. President James Buchanan dispatched the screw propeller-driven *Minnesota* to oversee American interests in the region. While a treaty was reached in 1858 granting western access to 11 more Chinese ports, imperial soldiers reinforced forts on the Pei Ho River. They then dealt a vicious blow to the returning British in 1859, killing and injuring more than 450 sailors. The ratified peace treaties were exchanged two months later. The following year a fleet of 30 British ships returned to the Pei Ho River and stormed the forts, enforcing the end of the Chinese aggression.

With relations with China calm again, the East India Squadron returned to chasing pirates, sailing up shallow Asian waterways with the *Saginaw*, a side-wheel steamship built especially for the squadron. The *Saginaw* showed off its special abilities in 1861, when it traveled 700 miles up the Yangtze Kiang River, accompanied for part of the way by the shallow-draft sloop the *Hartford*. During the voyage, however, the squadron commodore, Flag Officer Cornelius K. Stribling, was replaced by order from Navy Secretary Gideon Welles. With Captain Frederick Engle in charge, the East India Squadron languished, ending its reign of gunboat diplomacy.

In the Atlantic, events remarkably like those that had helped begin the War of 1812 were happening between the British and American navies. Far from the pleasant relationship enjoyed with Great Britain by the East India Squadron, tensions were rising in the Gulf of Mexico and South Atlantic.

After the Crimean War of 1854–1856, Great Britain, in accordance with many other European countries, began cracking down on the African slave trade, including searching any ships suspected of slave trafficking—even American vessels. Of course, the American government, remembering all too well the impressments of the early 1800s, replied that any ship flying the Stars and Stripes was exempt from boarding by foreign naval officers.

While President Buchanan did want to fight the slave trade, he was caught between two intractable forces. Southern representatives were lobbying to strike down the legislature that outlawed slave trade by American ships, currently making it a crime punishable by death. The North wanted to fight slavery but wasn't going to allow foreign military officers to board and search American vessels with impunity. Buchanan's cabinet took a bipartisan stance, with Secretary of State Lewis Cass protesting searches of American vessels by the Royal Navy, and Navy Secretary Isaac Toucey speaking directly with Great Britain, trying to reinforce the United States's stance against slave traders.

> While on patrol with the African brigade in 1853, the USS *Constitution* took her last prize while in commission, the *HN Gambrill,* a suspected slave trader sailing under the American flag.

Secretary Toucey reinforced the African Squadron with four shallow-draft steamships and ordered the squadron commander, William Inman, to cooperate with the British. Toucey even suggested pairing American and British vessels together so that neither country's mission was compromised. The British inspections continued until 1858, when the Royal Navy relaxed its policies regarding U.S. vessels, partly due to repeated protests from the American government.

Compared to the smart action and efficiency of the East India and African squadrons, the Home Squadron was a model of indecisiveness during the 1850s. The fleet wavered between springing into action, as it did when blockading an American expedition to an island off the coast of Louisiana in 1849, to complete immovability, shown during an incident in 1854 when the American government demanded that Spain be held accountable for seizing an American merchant ship, the *Black Warrior*, in Havana harbor. In the same year, the captain of the *Cyane* shelled Greytown, Nicaragua, in retaliation for an insult to an American diplomat. In response to a riot in 1856 in which several Americans died, the Navy took over a railroad station at Colón, the Atlantic terminal of the Panama railroad, with 160 sailors. Finally, in 1857, Commodore Hiram Paulding risked his career by landing 300 men at Greytown to pull William J. Walker out of Nicaragua and return him to the United States.

OTHER ACTIVITIES DURING PEACETIME

The Navy was also active in other areas at this time, particularly in scientific research and study. Under the guidance of Matthew Fontaine Maury, head of both the Naval Observatory and the Hydrographical Office, the Navy entered another period of exploration, second only to the Charles Wilkes voyage of 1838-1842 (see Chapter 5). Navy expeditions traveled to the Amazon River, the Arctic, the Dead Sea, the Rio de la Plata in Argentina, and the Panama isthmus. Back in America, Maury was busy as well: He broke new ground in hydrology and meteorology, and he mapped the currents of the world's oceans, particularly the Gulf Stream. By calculating the fastest sea routes, his research sped up ocean travel immensely.

Another area in which advancements were being made was armaments. John A. B. Dahlgren's experiments revolutionized cannon engineering and design (see Appendix B). After 1856, all U.S. Navy warships were armed with Dahlgren guns.

> Dahlgren's experiments included measuring the pressure inside a cannon barrel for the first time and testing cannon shots against actual armor plate. His findings resulted in a completely new gun design. Dahlgren modified the powder charge for maximum velocity with minimum stress on the gun, while still increasing the new cannon's firing range and power. The soda bottle–shape barrel was cast in one piece and cooled from the outside under controlled conditions. Dahlgren calculated everything to the final degree, from the placement of the wadding and powder to how ammunition was loaded. The new smoothbore gun could shoot farther and was more powerful than any other cannon. The Navy adopted Dahlgren guns in 1850 and placed them in every ship by 1856.

As an unexpected side benefit, many Navy ships were redesigned and strengthened to support the new Dahlgren guns. For example, the *Cumberland*, a frigate laid down in 1825 and finally completed in 1842, was originally designed to carry 44 old-style cannons. A prime candidate for the remodeling process, by 1856 it carried 24 new Dahlgren guns, which technically classified the warship as an extremely dangerous sloop. Other vessels, including the venerable *Constellation*, were converted to Dahlgren guns as well. The Navy had also conceived a new frigate to carry the new weapons for maximum advantage. Displacing twice the weight of the *Constitution*, the new ship would be longer by half and would be driven by screw propellers.

Despite these advancements, the U.S. Navy trailed the rest of the world in naval technology. A stunning lesson happened at the Turkish harbor of Sinope in 1853. During a conflict between the Russians and Turks, six Russian ships of the line armed with explosive shells obliterated seven Turkish frigates and several other vessels, destroying every enemy ship in the harbor. The Turks lost 2,960 men to just 37 Russian casualties. The impervious hulls and exploding ammunition of the Russians sounded the true end for the era of the wooden ship.

In 1859, the French announced the launching of the first true ironclad vessel, the *La Gloire*. Sheathed in 4 inches of iron over a 17-inch hull of

oak and teak, the new warship was impervious to any conventional cannon, even a Dahlgren gun. The English countered in 1861 with the first
ship built completely of iron, the *Warrior.*

New advances in armament followed as well. By 1861, the French had
created a rifled cannon that could penetrate their own *La Gloire*'s armored
hull. An English inventor named Cowper P. Coles invented an armed
ironclad raft that could withstand the pounding of shore batteries, and was
on the verge of creating a prototype of the armored gun turret.

All around the world, foreign countries continued to strive for naval
advancement—except the United States, which did not come around to the
concept of iron ships for 30 more years. But first America had to undergo
the worst trial it had ever faced, a conflict that threatened to tear the
nation apart.

CHAPTER 7

THE CIVIL WAR

The causes of America's bloodiest conflict, the Civil War have been debated ever since the beginning of the war itself. Chief among the issues that led the states to wage war on each other were economic differences (an industrial North versus an agrarian South), slavery, and the differing political philosophies of an individual state's rights versus the rights of the federal government. Many Southern states felt that "the right to govern rests on the consent of the governed." When the Northern states moved to, in the eyes of the South, inhibit their sovereign rights, the South felt within its right to become free of the Union and set up another nation.

Seeds for the Civil War were sown in 1828 when influential Northern businessmen persuaded Congress to pass the "Tariff Act," which raised the price of European manufactured goods primarily sold in the South. The purpose of this law was to get the Southern states to "buy American," even more than 140 years ago. Whether they bought from Europe or from the North, Southerners had to pay more either way, which didn't sit well with them. Even though the tariff laws were changed or stricken by the time of the Civil War, antipathy about the laws remained.

Although many Southern farmers didn't even own slaves, and most Northerners had never seen one, the issue of slavery was used to drum up support for a war on both sides. Northern abolitionists denounced the idea of owning humans (even though every Northern state had owned slaves in the late eighteenth century, until increased mechanization made it unprofitable), and Southerners saw the North's efforts against slavery as an attempt to regulate their way of life (which is not far from the truth—if the South had had to pay slaves for their labor, the entire economy would have collapsed).

Slavery had been an issue since the founding of America, and several congressional measures further divided slave states and free states. The Compromise of 1850, passed after the Mexican War, addressed several concerns on both sides. The bill allowed California into the Union as a free state, outlawed slavery in the District of Columbia, and defined New Mexico and Utah as territories with no mention of slavery. The population of these last two areas would decide whether they would allow slavery when they applied for statehood. When the bill was passed in September, it was seen as the final solution to the question of slavery in new territories.

The peace lasted until 1854, when the Kansas-Nebraska Act reignited the slavery debate. The act allowed the formation of the Kansas and Nebraska territories, with the decision of slavery to be decided when they converted to states. But the act also struck down the Missouri Compromise. When the bill passed, proslavery and antislavery groups converged on Kansas, each pushing their agenda in a violent series of clashes, coining the term "Bloody Kansas." Opponents of the act founded the Republican Party, and America edged closer to civil war.

Matters came to a head in the 1860 presidential election. With the Democratic Party split between the North (and nominee Stephen Douglas) and the South (and Kentucky Sen. John Breckinridge), and the Whig party declining, the Republican Party's candidate, Abraham Lincoln, took the White House. Lincoln thought the Constitution didn't prevent the federal government from abolishing slavery where it already existed, but he was just as determined to keep it from spreading.

The Southern states, already guarding their eroding power base (millions of immigrants poured into the Northern states, providing cheap labor, while the South stagnated under its obsolete social system), saw Lincoln's election as the last straw. South Carolina representatives vowed to secede from the Union if Lincoln were elected. On December 20, 1860, South Carolina voted to secede. Mississippi left the union on January 9, 1861. Florida followed the next day, and Alabama, Georgia, Louisiana, and Texas seceded soon afterward.

For four months, the South reinforced its positions, occupying government arsenals and forts while lame-duck president James Buchanan did nothing to stop it. When Lincoln took office, he also adopted a wait-and-see stance, unwilling to make the first overt aggressive move.

When the merchant vessel the *Star of the West* was sent to reprovision Fort Sumter (with 200 federal soldiers hidden in her hold) in Charleston harbor, the Confederate ships blockading the harbor were left with no choice. After driving off the supply ship, the fort was shelled into submission on April 12–13, 1861. The Southern states had thrown down the gauntlet, and the Union had picked it up. While Lincoln called for 75,000 volunteer troops, Arkansas, Tennessee, and Virginia joined the Southern cause.

STATE OF THE NAVY ON BOTH SIDES

Although the Northern navy had 90 ships in 1860, 48 were laid-up in port, and 30 others were on duty around the world. The Navy was hurt more by the loss of more than 350 officers who resigned to join the Confederacy. But some stayed with the Union, including Samuel P. Lee, commander of the Union forces and cousin to Robert E. Lee. David G. Farragut was born and raised in Alabama, yet he joined the Union navy and became one of its greatest commanders. David Porter, son of Commodore David Porter, hero of the War of 1812, fought on the Union side, but two of his sons joined the Southern army.

Because the South imported so many of its goods, blockading its harbors would help end the war swiftly. But with only 78 working ships, almost half of them spread across the globe, an effective blockade was impossible right away. New Secretary of the Navy Gideon Welles's first task was to assemble a fleet to cut off Confederate ports on the Mississippi River, including New Orleans and Vicksburg. He did this by arming anything that would float and sending the ships out to patrol bays, harbors, and river mouths. A valuable fleet addition during these early months was the purchase of several double-ended steam ferries from New York City in 1861. Quick, shallow-draft vessels, they could carry men, supplies, or both, and proved invaluable during the 1862–1864 river campaigns.

The North's industrial base started manufacturing ships in 1861, beginning with 8 sloops, 23 gunboats, and 12 paddlewheel boats, all steam-powered. Under Secretary Welles the Navy grew with the addition of steam sloops, river gunboats, and 36 coastal monitors. Two 5,000-ton blue-water ironclads, the *New Ironsides* and the *Dunderberg*, were also begun. By 1865, 170 steam warships had been built, many completely designed and built during the war.

THE VALIANT SOUTH

The Southern navy was fighting a losing battle from the start. While bolstered by the sudden influx of trained naval officers, it had no standing vessels to put them in. Confederate Secretary of the Navy Stephen R. Mallory had to put together a fleet with no shipyards or shipbuilding capability. Knowing that the South needed ironclads, in May 1861 he sent agent James D. Bulloch to England to acquire ships, particularly ironclad rams and commerce raiders.

The converted ironclad's *Virginia*'s victory against two wooden Union ships on March 8, 1861 turned into a stalemate with the arrival of the *Monitor* the next day. Forced to wait until the British-built ironclads were finished, the Confederacy resorted to conventional methods of inflicting damage.

Commerce raiders were one popular alternative. To distract the Union, on May 6, the Confederate Congress voted to issue letters of marque and reprisal. Although the Union wanted to treat any captured privateers as pirates, at the Paris Declaration of 1856 America was one of the few nations that still supported privateering. Now the federal government was forced to watch its own policy being used against it.

Southern privateers did put a dent in Union trade and shipping (by the end of the war, more than three quarters of American merchant ships had registered in foreign ports, dealing the death blow to the American Merchant Marine), but commerce raiding was not as damaging to the industrialized North as it had been against foreign enemies in the past.

Although the blockade and various foreign laws prevented many privateering ships from making the open seas, the 19 that did captured an astounding 258 vessels, almost 5 percent of the Union merchant fleet, worth tens of millions of dollars. Southern privateers, including the *Sumter* (18 prizes), the *Tallahassee* (29), the *Shenandoah* (36), the *Florida* (37), and the scourge of the Atlantic, the *Alabama* (69 prizes), robbed from the Union to give to the Confederacy.

But by autumn of 1862, the Confederate navy had lost four of its most powerful ironclads—the *Arkansas*, the *Louisiana*, the *Mississippi*, and the *Virginia*—all but the *Louisiana* (which had been blown up) scuttled to prevent capture. That put a serious dent in the Southern fleet. Added to this were the losses at New Orleans and Memphis and the surrender of the Pensacola naval yard. The Confederate navy was retreating on all fronts.

The South also tried diplomatic means to help its cause. James Bulloch lobbied for the recognition of the Confederacy as a sovereign nation and even an alliance with Britain, which would have made the Union an enemy of the Royal Navy.

The federal government, under the auspices of President Lincoln and the ambassador to Britain, Charles Francis Adams, strongly implied that any recognition of the South would result in a declaration of war and an immediate invasion of Canada. Although he was strongly anti-Union, Prime Minister Lord Palmerton issued a proclamation recognizing the Confederacy as a belligerent, but not as a legitimate nation.

The commander of the British North American station, Sir Alexander Milne, had been watching the North's increased naval production for several months. He reported that a war with America would result in a full-scale naval battle with a fully equipped and armed fleet. Remembering the destruction during the War of 1812, Britain backed down even more, impounding the completed steam sloop the *Alexandria*, which had been about to sail for the South.

Stymied by skillful federal representatives overseas and losing on the home front to superior Northern technology, the rebels turned to alternate methods of fighting. They were the first to use maritime mines (then called "torpedoes") on a large scale, and they sank more Union vessels with them than by any other means.

The first mines were simple affairs, often watertight barrels packed with gunpowder, anchored to the bottom of the harbor or river where they were placed, and set with a contact fuse on the top. Then they sat, almost undetectable, waiting to contact with and detonate against a ship's hull. A deliverable type of mine was created by Matthew Maury for the Confederates. It was an round or cylindrical container full of explosives that was delivered to a target at the end of a long pole attached to another ship—or, in the cases of the CSS *Hunley* (see Appendix C), delivered underwater.

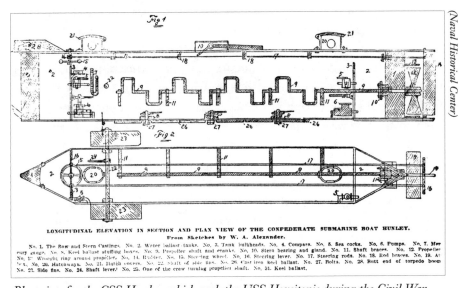

(Naval Historical Center)

LONGITUDINAL ELEVATION IN SECTION AND PLAN VIEW OF THE CONFEDERATE SUBMARINE BOAT HUNLEY.
From Sketches by W. A. Alexander.

No. 1. The Bow and Stern Castings. No. 2. Water ballast tanks. No. 3. Tank bulkheads. No. 4. Compass. No. 5. Sea cocks. No. 6. Pumps. No. 7. Mercury gauge. No. 8. Keel ballast stuffing boxes. No. 9. Propeller shaft and cranks. No. 10. Stern bearing and gland. No. 11. Shaft braces. No. 12. Propeller. No. 13. Wrought ring around propeller. No. 14. Rudder. No. 15. Steering wheel. No. 16. Steering lever. No. 17. Steering rods. No. 18. Rod braces. No. 19. Air box. No. 20. Hatchways. No. 21. Hatch covers. No. 22. Shaft of side fins. No. 26. Cast iron keel ballast. No. 27. Bolts. No. 28. Butt end of torpedo boom. No. 23. Side fins. No. 24. Shaft lever. No. 25. One of the crew turning propeller shaft. No. 31. Keel ballast.

Blueprints for the CSS Hunley, which sank the USS Housitonic during the Civil War.

The South also experimented with submarines and submersibles, but only in the waning days of the war, when it was already obvious to observers that the Confederate cause was lost. Ironically, the unconventional warfare—mines and submarines, proved to be the most effective in hampering the Union.

EARLY ACTION

On April 19, Abraham Lincoln declared a blockade of thousands of miles of open coast riddled with small bays and inlets from South Carolina to Texas. How this decision would be enforced was in doubt, especially since the Union had lost the Navy Yard at Norfolk, Virginia, on April 20 to a Southern mob.

The yard was a godsend for the Confederate forces. Although the retreating Northern forces scuttled and burned the ships under construction, the underwater hulls were still intact, so they could be raised and rebuilt. Among the vessels left behind were the huge vessel the *Pennsylvania*, the largest ship ever built by the Navy, and, more important, the *Merrimack*, the most modern warship on either side. (The *Merrimack* would be converted into the CSS *Virginia*.) Almost 2,000 cannons were stored in the yard, including at least 300 Dahlgren guns, and many buildings and raw materials were intact.

The South wasted no time in getting the yard up to full production. Lincoln then extended his blockade to Virginia, making a total of 3,500 miles of American coastline to be patrolled. It was an almost impossible task—certainly beyond the Union navy of 1861's capabilities.

THE RACE TO IRON—THE MONITOR AND THE VIRGINIA

When the Confederates took possession of the Norfolk Navy Yard and reviewed what they had captured, their first priority was to raise the *Merrimack*, convert it to an ironclad, and send her out to smash the Union blockade. Just one ship—the right one—could wreak havoc against the Union navy and reopen vital supply lines from Europe, perhaps even convincing Great Britain or France to join the South's side.

After the loss of the Norfolk Navy Yard, and knowing that the South was converting the *Virginia* into a ironclad, Wells was convinced in August 1861 to appoint an "ironclad board" to recommend the best way to proceed. The three board members, Cmdr. Charles Davis, Commodore Joseph Smith, and Commodore Hiram Paulding, recommended three ironclad models a month later. The first, an armored heavy warship called the *New Ironsides*, would carry two 50-pound cannons, and fourteen 11-inch Dahlgren guns. Although it looked great on paper, it couldn't be built in time to fight the *Virginia*, already under construction. The second, a lightly armored vessel named the *Galena*, would prove to be ineffectual when on the water. The third was by John Ericsson, who had been railroaded by Robert Stockton 17 years earlier for the *Princeton*. His revolutionary design was the most advanced American ship built thus far. Named the *Monitor*, it represented the salvation of the Navy. What followed was a frenzy of building on both sides, each trying to complete one ship.

John Ericsson achieved a major engineering miracle with the *Monitor*, launching the completed vessel 97 days after laying the keel, just 101 days after the Navy contracted for the vessel. Innovative in every aspect, the ship contained at least 40 patentable inventions, including flush toilets; a collapsible smokestack; the rotating twin-gun turret; forced-air ventilation for the crew, which worked below the waterline; and a hull that was almost entirely submerged, leaving only the turret as a viable target. Because of its design and shallow draft (just 12 feet), it was primarily a coastal defense ship. But with it rested the Union navy's hopes of stopping the Confederates.

At the Norfolk Navy Yard, crews were working seven days a week to get the *Virginia* into action. The *Virginia*'s design was similar to that of the *Monitor*, submerging the deck so that only the armored gun housing could be fired at, rendering the ship almost unseaworthy as well. With an immense draft of 22 feet, however, it could not operate in shallow water. Also, as the *Virginia*'s previous incarnation, the *Merrimac*, had been laid up awaiting new engines, the Confederates were forced to use obsolete steam engines. The ship's top speed was a plodding 8 knots.

Franklin Buchanan, who was strongly anti-Union, captained the *Virginia*. The first head of the Naval Academy at Annapolis and former commander of the Washington Navy Yard, he had submitted his resignation before his home state, Maryland, had decided whether it would secede. When it didn't, he tried to get reinstated but was rejected by Navy Secretary Welles. Embarrassed and angry, he offered himself to the Confederacy and was placed in command of its first ironclad.

Union Navy Lt. John L. Worden was known as a talented officer who had his own grievances with the South, having been imprisoned in Alabama while returning from delivering messages to the Federal fleet. He had been released in November 1861, three months before receiving what would turn out to be perhaps the most vital commission of the entire war.

The first week in March 1862 was maddening for both sides because each knew the first ship running would have the advantage. The *Monitor* tried to sail from the New York Navy Yard on February 27 but was laid up for several days while the bugs were worked out. By the time everything was fixed, it was March 5.

Fortunately for the North, the *Virginia* was also having problems. Captain Buchanan had set his ship's first voyage for the night of March 6, but the pilot refused to take the unknown vessel out of the yard into the dark, swift river filled with shoals and blocking ships sunk by Confederates. Buchanan delayed his departure until the next day, when inclement weather forced another delay. On March 8, the *Virginia* headed down the James River to engage the Union fleet at Hampton Roads, which consisted of the sloops-of-war the *Cumberland* and the frigates the *Congress*, the *Minnesota*, the *Roanoke*, and the *St. Lawrence*. Only the *Minnesota* and the *Roanoke* were steam-powered, but the *Roanoke*'s engines weren't operational.

The *Virginia* appeared on the horizon, trailing a plume of smoke, and went straight for the fleet, destroying the *Cumberland* by cannon and ram, and shelling the *Congress* until it surrendered. The Confederates set the *Congress* on fire; it exploded at approximately 2 A.M. on the morning of March 9.

With Buchanan wounded during the battle, command of the *Virginia* passed to Lt. Catesby ap Roger Jones. More that 250 sailors and officers had been killed aboard the Union ships; the Confederates had lost two men and had several wounded, some from shore fire after the battle.

Meanwhile, the *Monitor* arrived at Sewell's Point, where Lt. Cmdr. Worden reported to Capt. John Marston. While Marston had received explicit orders from Secretary Welles to have the *Monitor* set out for Washington, he disobeyed the directive and ordered the *Monitor* to Newport News to assist the *Minnesota*.

CLASH OF THE IRONCLADS

The two ironclad ships were more evenly matched than either side knew. The Union government was terrified that the *Virginia* would crush its fleet, and the destruction of the *Cumberland* and the *Congress* seemed to confirm these fears. The ship the North pinned its hopes on, the twin-gun *Monitor*, did not inspire much confidence. Smaller and not nearly as heavily armed, many thought she didn't stand a chance against the cannon-bristling Confederate ironclad.

But while the *Virginia* had won against the Union at Hampton Roads on March 8, it had cost the new ship. When the crew took stock of the damage, they found two cannons unusable and the ram torn off, causing a hull leak. The smokestack also had been shot away. Of all these, the smokestack was the biggest problem because it reduced the air draft of the steam boilers, cutting the *Virginia*'s speed to 4 knots. None of this was a real concern: The crew had seen the results of the ship in action and was confident it would be just as victorious the next day. Although Buchanan knew of the *Monitor*, he didn't inform his crew, an incredible error on his part.

On the morning of March 9, the *Virginia* returned to finish the *Minnesota* and any other Union ships there. This time, however, the crew was met with what Lieutenant Jones first thought was a floating "water tank." When it matched their movements and Jones realized this new ship was faster than the *Virginia*, he immediately moved to engage it.

The first shot fired in the battle was a pair of broadsides from the *Virginia*, which hit the turret of the *Monitor* without inflicting any damage. When the small Union ship responded with its own guns, the crew of the *Virginia* knew they had a real fight on their hands.

The battle between the two vessels began in earnest at 8:20 A.M. and continued for the next four hours. The *Virginia*'s main disadvantage was her deep draft, which meant she was in constant danger of running aground on the shoals that littered the area. At one point, she actually did hit a submerged shoal and was under fire from both the *Monitor* and the *Minnesota* until the crew could free her.

The *Monitor* was hampered by inadequate communication between Lieutenant Commander Worden, in the bow pilothouse, and executive officer S. Dana Greene, in charge of the turret and guns. Also, since the accident on the *Princeton* 18 years earlier, all U.S. Navy ships were using half-strength powder charges in their cannons. Although Greene had requested permission to use full charges the day before the battle, his request had been denied by Worden. That decision may have prevented the *Monitor* from achieving victory (this general order was rescinded immediately after the battle).

One final disadvantage the Union suffered was the lack of a critical piece of information. Captain Buchanan had been in such a hurry to put to sea that he had left the Navy Yard without finishing the armor plating at the *Virginia*'s water line. If any of the Union ships had aimed for the hull where the ship met the water instead of at its armored top, the battle would have ended much differently.

Despite the damage it had sustained and its reduced speed, the *Virginia* did manage to ram the *Monitor* during the battle. With its ram gone, the impact damaged the *Virginia* more, crushing some of its hull timbers and increasing the leak that had started the day before. The Confederates also posted sharpshooters to fire into the *Monitor*'s gun port whenever possible. This forced the *Monitor* to shoot while the turret was still moving, making the guns less accurate.

With nothing else working, Lieutenant Jones ordered his own guns to concentrate on the only other protrusion on the *Monitor*'s deck, the pilot-house. A direct hit wounded and blinded Worden, forcing Greene to take command of the ironclad and depriving the turret of its commanding officer (Worden survived the battle but lost sight in one eye and was scarred for life). But the *Virginia* still couldn't capitalize on its advantage and settled for fighting the Union ironclad to a draw, eventually retreating back to Norfolk.

The days of these two landmark ships were both numbered afterward. The *Virginia* was destroyed by her crew on May 11, 1862, when the Union army threatened to recapture the Norfolk Navy Yard. The wreck of the *Virginia* was removed between 1866 and 1876, and little survives of the gallant ironclad today. The *Monitor* stayed near Hampton Roads and participated in the Union's Peninsular campaign. In December 1862, the ironclad was ordered south. Caught in a storm off Cape Hatteras, North Carolina, it foundered on December 31, 1862, taking 16 sailors with it.

The *Monitor*'s remains were discovered in 1974, were declared a marine sanctuary the following year, and have been the focus of a long-term recovery operation ever since. The ironclad's propeller and 30-ton steam engine have been raised, and the most recent expedition recovered the famous turret in 2002.

The *Monitor* and the *Virginia* were firsts for the United States, proving once and for all ironclad vessels' superiority to wooden-hulled ships. Although each had design flaws, they were the first truly modern ships to fight each other, representing the pinnacle of American naval engineering at the time.

STATISTICS FOR THE *MONITOR* AND THE *VIRGINIA*

USS *Monitor:*

Propulsion: Screw propeller

Length: 172 feet

Beam: 34 feet

Draft: 12 feet

Displacement: About 776 tons

Top speed: 8 knots (approximately 9.6 miles per hour)

Crew: 57 officers and sailors

Casement specifications (turret): 20 feet in diameter, 9 feet high.

Armor: 8 inches on the turret, ½-inch iron plate, 26 inches of oak, and 5 inches of iron on the hull.

Armament: Two 11-inch Dahlgren guns

Date launched: January 30, 1862

CSS *Virginia* (formerly the USS *Merrimack*):

Propulsion: Twin screw propellers

Length: 263 feet

Beam: 51 feet

Draft: 22 feet

Displacement: About 3,900 tons

Top speed: 8 knots (approximately 9.6 miles per hour)

Crew: 350 officers and sailors

Casement specifications: 172 feet long, 27 feet long

Armor: 1- and 2-inch armor plate over 2 inches of oak and pine

Armament: Six 9-inch guns, two 7-inch rifles, two 6-inch rifles

Date launched: February 17, 1862

THE RIVER WARS

In the middle of the county, the Union was attempting its "Anaconda Plan," which involved strangling the South by capturing its ports on the Mississippi River, including the fortified city of Vicksburg and the port of New Orleans.

On the Atlantic Coast, the North's blockade was growing rapidly (although out of an estimated 2,700 attempts to slip through federal lines, 2,500 made it, a 92 percent success rate). Two hundred and sixty vessels were in operation by the end of 1861. The North had also seized several Southern ports and inlets, including the two forts guarding Hatteras Inlet, North Carolina, and sent a 77-ship fleet against the major harbor of Port Royal Sound in South Carolina. That became the main base of operations for the blockading fleet.

The Battle for the Mississippi

On January 9, 1862, the Navy ordered Flag Officer David G. Farragut and the West Gulf Blockading Squadron to capture New Orleans, Louisiana, the South's major port that also controlled the Mississippi River delta. With a fleet of 4 steam sloops (including his flagship the *Hartford*), 12 gunboats, and 21 schooners converted into mortar boats, Farragut launched his plan on April 18. Cmdr. David Dixon Porter, in command of the mortar boats, bombarded the defenses, allowing the rest of Farragut's fleet to charge past the Confederate and take the city on April 25. Just as surprised was the navy yard at Pensacola, Florida, which also surrendered on May 10.

Now that the mouth of the Mississippi River was secure, Farragut sailed upstream. After New Orleans, he took Baton Rouge, Louisiana and then Natchez, Mississippi. On July 1, Farragut's fleet reached Vicksburg, Mississippi, the crossroads of the Confederacy. His first attempt to take the city lasted until late July, but Farragut's fleet was exhausted and low on supplies. He was also being pestered by the *Arkansas*, an ironclad Confederate that had managed to slip past the Union ships, and escape down the Yazoo River, returning to harass the federals whenever possible.

Trouble in Tennessee—the Struggle to Memphis

Before moving on to Vicksburg, Gen. Ulysses S. Grant had cleared the Tennessee and Cumberland rivers by using four new ironclad ships, commanded by Capt. Andrew Hull Foote, to supplement his force. Confederate Brig. Gen. Lloyd Tilghman knew he didn't have the boats, men, or supplies to withstand an assault on both forts, so he evacuated Fort Henry, leaving just himself with a skeleton crew of 80 men to decoy Grant.

Foote was supposed to soften up the fort by bombardment, but he ended up capturing it instead. But before their surrender, the rebels inflicted serious damage on the ironclads. One of the ships, the *Essex*, suffered a shot to the main boiler, which released superheated steam that killed and wounded 30 officers and sailors.

> The blast of superheated steam that blasted through the *Essex* traveled so quickly that men were killed where they stood. Helmsman Marshall Ford was later found dead at his post, with one hand on a wheel spoke and the other on the signal bell rope.

Casualties among the other gunboats were fairly light, with 2 sailors dead and 40 wounded, and 4 Army sharpshooters killed and 15 wounded. Still the ships blazed away until the survivors in Fort Henry, with 10 dead or missing and 11 wounded, surrendered on February 6, 1862.

Grant and Foote next set their sights on Fort Donelson, only 11 miles away by land, but over a hundred by water. On February 11, Foote took six ships (four ironclads—the *Carondelet*, the *Louisville*, the *Pittsburgh*, and the *St. Louis*—and two wooden vessels, the *Tyler* and the *Conestoga*) out to Donelson. Grant traveled cross-country and, although he left after Foote, arrived before him. The attack began at 3:30 P.M. on Valentine's Day, February 14.

Fort Donelson had been reinforced by the garrison from Fort Henry and was commanded by Gen. Albert Sidney Johnston, who held no illusions about his chances. Regardless of the odds, the federal forces paid a dear price for the fort.

Johnston's men waited until the steamships were only 400 yards from the fort; then they opened fire. All the of the ironclads were damaged (the *St. Louis*, Foote's flagship, took 59 hits, killing its pilot and wounding him), and 59 men were killed and wounded. The *Louisville*, the *St. Louis*, and the *Pittsburgh* were all disabled in the battle, and the *Carondelet* was battered until it withdrew out of range. After the relatively easy capture of Fort Henry, this determined resistance surprised the small fleet.

Fort Donelson was taken with the help of the *St. Louis* and *Louisville*'s guns covering Grant's counterattack after the Confederates had almost broken through his line. It was here that Grant gained his nickname "Unconditional Surrender" by demanding it of Fort Donelson. After the fort was secure, Foote continued driving toward Memphis.

In mid-March 1862, a combined force of federal Army units led by Gen. John Pope met up with Foote's flotilla of 6 gunboats and 11 mortar boats on the Tennessee border. Pope had already driven the Confederates from New Madrid, Missouri, but the Southerners had dug in on Island Number 10 at a crucial bend in the Mississippi.

Foote, still suffering from the wound taken at Fort Donelson, was not willing to gamble. He began a cautious assault by staying 2,000 feet away and lobbing shells at the island, doing little damage. At dusk he retreated, unsure that his plan was having any effect on the enemy. Pope, impatient for action, suggested that his troops cross the river while Foote's gunboats shelled the island as a diversion. After conferring with his captains, Foote refused. The next plan, a 12-mile canal laboriously hacked through the Tennessee swamps, failed when the river fell, preventing the heavy gunboats from sailing. All the while, Foote continued bombarding the island with little effect.

Finally, on the evening of April 4, the *Carondelet*, loaded with protective bales, boxes, and crates, slipped past the Confederate guns under cover of a storm. On April 6, another gunboat, the *Pittsburgh*, sailed past. Pope mobilized his army, crossed the river, and captured Tiptonville, cutting off the island as planned. The 5,000-man force surrendered soon afterward, giving up more than 100 cannons, thousands of small arms, and an invaluable Confederate naval signal book, enabling Foote to intercept and translate enemy communications.

Next up was Fort Pillow, only 40 miles from Memphis, and the last defense point before the city itself. On the evening of April 12, Foote's ships anchored just inside the Arkansas border. Foote waited on Pope's men, who arrived the next day. They had planned to take Fort Pillow just like they had taken Island No. 10, with Pope advancing to the rear of the fort while Foote shelled it from the river. But new orders from Gen. Henry Hallack took Pope and his men east to Shiloh to follow up on the recent Union victory there, leaving Foote to attempt to bombard the fort into submission alone.

During the bloody battle of Shiloh on the Tennessee River, help came from an unlikely source—the U.S. Navy. During Maj. Gen. Albert Sidney Johnston's attack on General Grant's unprepared lines, the Union army's left flank received fire support from two nearby ships, the *Tyler* and the *Lexington*. This allowed the reeling troops time to gather themselves and form a defensive line, helping snatch victory from the jaws of defeat.

Foote was not able to complete the conquest of Fort Pillow; his wounded leg removed him from action, and he returned to Washington, D.C. Sent to take command of Port Royal on June 11, 1863, he became mortally ill while traveling and died on June 26.

His replacement, Capt. Charles Davis, was a highly regarded officer who had served the Navy for the past 39 years, primarily in scientific posts. He assumed command of the naval forces on the Mississippi and its tributaries knowing that he had to produce results.

Davis had no sooner arrived than he faced his first predicament. The next day, six Confederate gunboats attacked one of the mortar boats that had been shelling the fort, the first time the Southern river fleet had been seen. The speedy, lightly armed craft (eight total, the *Colonel Lovell*, the *General Beauregard*, the *General Bragg*, the *General Earl Van Dorn*, the *General Sterling Price*, the *General Sumter*, the *General M. Jeff Thompson*, and the *Little Rebel*), led by Cmdr. J. E. Montgomery, outmaneuvered the ponderous ironclads and rammed the gunboats *Cincinnati* and *Mound City*, sinking the former and damaging the latter so badly it had to withdraw. The Confederate casualties were light, with one man killed and two wounded—a small price to pay for the results.

But while the surprise attack had worked once, the Union fleet wouldn't be caught off guard again. In a straight-up fight, the Confederate ships didn't stand a chance. In the end, the rebels retreated from Fort Pillow, and the way to Memphis was wide open.

The Battle of Memphis

At Memphis, Davis's fleet received help from an unusual source: Col. Charles Ellet and his fleet of six ram boats. After the *Virginia*'s sinking of the *Congress* at Hampton Roads, Ellet received permission to build several rams and assist the Northern offensive on the rivers.

Col. Charles Ellet, a widely traveled engineer, recreated a naval weapon that had been popular thousands of years ago. The ram was just what its name implied: a ship with a reinforced prow and front hull designed to smash an enemy ship's hull. Ellet's craft was simple and strong, with three reinforced bulkheads fitted in the forward section of the ship, secured boilers and engines to prevent damage from the impact, and light armament. The entire design of the weapon depended on speed, not cannons.

Facing the combined fleet of Davis and Ellet was Commander Montgomery and his eight gunboats. Memphis had been deemed too important to abandon, so he was all that stood between the city and the federal fleet. On the morning of June 6, the Union and Confederate forces fought to decide the fate of the city.

Twenty minutes after the first shots were exchanged, Davis headed for the line of gunboats. With no real tactics decided between Ellet and Davis, the impetuous engineer attacked. Ordering his brother, Arthur Ellet, aboard the *Monarch*, to follow his lead, he aimed his flagship, the *Queen of the West*, at the enemy gunboat the *Colonel Lovell*. Arthur headed for the Confederate ship the *General Price*. The *Queen* and the *Lovell* charged straight at each other, but the rebel captain lost his nerve and turned at the last second. Ellet's ship struck the *Lovell* broadside and sank it. The *Monarch* was less successful, hitting its target but only disabling the *General Price*. But the attack sent the *General Price* near Davis's flagship, the *Benton*, which took out the gunboat's boiler with one shot. In just a few minutes, Montgomery had lost a quarter of his force.

Now the rebels fired back, concentrating their guns on the *Queen of the West*. Trying to restore order among his crew, Ellet was wounded by a sharpshooter at the same time one of his ship's paddlewheels was damaged, forcing the ram to shore. But as the crippled *General Price* hit the bank next to his ram, Ellet ordered a boarding party out and captured the ship.

The rest of the Confederate gunboats retreated down the river, with Davis's fleet pursuing. The *Monarch* caught up to the *Beauregard* and rammed it midship, causing the crew to run up white flags and head for shore. The damaged *Little Rebel* was also trying to make the Arkansas shore when the *Monarch* hit it as well, sending it deeper into the riverbank, where it was abandoned. The *Monarch* then steamed back to the *Beauregard* and towed it to a sandbar, where it sank to the boilers.

All told, the Union fleet captured or destroyed seven of the Confederate gunboats, with only the *General Van Dorn* escaping. Southern casualties were heavy, while those of the North were remarkably light: with several men wounded and none killed. Ironically, Ellet's wound later proved mortal, and he died after being taken to Cairo, Illinois, for treatment.

With no other defense, Memphis was at the Union's mercy. The infantry brigade moved in, and Memphis, at the junction of four railroads and a critical supply point for the South, fell. The campaign for the northern part of the Mississippi was over, with the hundreds of miles of river securely in Union hands.

The Siege of Vicksburg

South of Tennessee, Farragut's fleet began a slow retreat on July 25, convinced that there had to be a different way to take the city. And in the beginning of 1863, the Navy and Army came together in one of the first joint military operations in America.

Gen. Ulysses S. Grant, commander of the "Army of the Tennessee," was convinced that the 200-mile-long section of the Mississippi between Vicksburg in the North and Port Hudson, Louisiana, in the South could be taken by land with support from the Navy fleet. But the two battles weren't going to be easy: Both sites were heavily fortified, with cannons mounted on cliffs overlooking the river. Grant and the newly promoted Rear Admiral Porter would handle Vicksburg. Gen. Nathaniel P. Banks would coordinate the assault on Port Hudson with Rear Admiral Farragut.

While Grant was assaulting Vicksburg, General Banks was slow to attack Port Hudson. He was supposed to distract the Confederates so that Farragut's ships could slip by and secure the river below Vicksburg, including the critical Red River tributary used to move supplies from the West to the two cities. When two of Porter's ironclads ran the gauntlet past Vicksburg, only to be captured below the city, Farragut knew he had to move, with or without the army's support.

On March 14, he took seven ships past the Southern batteries. Farragut considered the attempt a disaster because only two of the seven made it past Port Hudson. But with those two vessels, the rear admiral blockaded the Red River, cutting off supplies to both Confederate cities.

When David Porter heard of Farragut's accomplishment, he tried to move his fleet through the tangled bayous around Vicksburg to the Yazoo River, bypassing the Confederate defenses completely. A previous attempt in February by Lt. Cmdr. Watson Smith had failed, but Porter pressed on anyway. After hacking his way through 100 miles of swamp and under fire from Confederate sharpshooters the entire way, he was forced to give up within sight of his goal.

April 1863 began badly for the Union navy when Adm. Samuel F. Du Pont's fleet of seven monitors and one ironclad frigate were pounded by the defenses at Charleston harbor for two hours while trying to gain entrance. They took over 300 shots from the rebel guns. With all of his ships battered but able to withdraw, he left without inflicting any serious damage, proving the hard way that naval power alone was insufficient to take land defenses.

Upon hearing the news, Grant and Porter devised a new plan to take Vicksburg. Grant would lead 25,000 of his men 45 miles south to New Carthage, Louisiana; then he would cross the river, march back, and attack Vicksburg. But Porter would have to send some ships past the cannon-loaded cliffs to ferry the soldiers across the river. Also, Grant couldn't attack from the South because the cliffs were in the way. His army would have to skirt the high bluffs and assault the city from the East, which would take more time and mean risking discovery all the way. He would also have no supply lines on the other side of the Mississippi, so what his men took with them would be all they would have to live on. During the night of April 16, Porter hurried his fleet (consisting of the ironclads the *Benton*, the *St. Louis*, the *Louisville*, the *Pittsburgh*, the *Mound City*, the *Carondelet*, the *General Sterling Price*, and the *Lafayette*; three army transports; and two tugboats, the *Ivy* and the *Tuscumbia*) past the Confederate guns, under fire the entire time. In the darkness, only one transport was lost. One week later, they were followed by a fleet of transports that would carry Grant's army across the river.

On May 1, the Southern forces at Grand Gulf were routed by Grant's men, giving Grant a solid base to stage the second part of his plan. He and Porter split up, with Porter continuing on to relieve Farragut at the Red River, and Grant heading north to claim his prize. He led his troops through enemy-infested territory, winning five battles along the way. By the middle of May, he was laying siege to Vicksburg. He was rejoined by Porter and his gunboats and mortar boats, which had used the now Union-held Yazoo River to bypass the river guns. The besieged city finally surrendered on July 4. The Mississippi River was under Union control from its source to the Gulf of Mexico, dealing the Confederacy a crippling blow and cutting off the western states entirely.

After the fall of Vicksburg and Port Hudson, all that was left was the occasional skirmish with Southern guerrillas and escorting merchant ships up and down the Mississippi. The only other river expedition of note was an ill-fated voyage led by Porter up the cotton-rich Red River searching for spoils of war. Trapped by the receding river, the admiral destroyed one ship and would have lost the rest, except for an inspired plan of dam building that enabled the boats to get to deeper water.

Porter returned downriver and was ordered to proceed to Fort Fisher, which protected one of the last Confederate ports of Wilmington, North Carolina, at the mouth of Cape Fear River. There he would shell the fort in preparation of an army assault. But first, the last Southern port in the Gulf of Mexico had to fall.

THE BATTLE OF MOBILE BAY

After Vicksburg fell, Admiral Farragut headed south in January 1864 to take Mobile Bay, Alabama, the last pocket of resistance in the Gulf. Protected by shore batteries in Forts Morgan and Gaines on either side of the entrance to the 30-mile harbor, the port was also protected by the ironclad ram the *Tennessee* and several gunboats, forcing Farragut to request his own ironclads to face this new menace.

Fortunately, by this time General Grant had been placed in command of the entire Union army. He made taking Mobile Bay a priority, with the understanding that it would be a joint navy/army operation.

Farragut's plan was to run a two-line convoy of his ships into the harbor past Fort Morgan, with his four ironclads (the *Chickasaw*, the *Manhattan*, the *Tecumseh*, and the *Winnebago*) acting as a shield for the seven wooden sloops (the *Brooklyn*, the *Hartford*, the *Lackawanna*, the *Monongahela*, the *Oneida*, the *Ossipee*, and the *Richmond*), each with a gunboat lashed to it for maximum speed. Farragut had originally wanted his flagship, the *Hartford*, to lead, but his captains feared the first ship would suffer the brunt of the Confederate guns, so they moved him to second in line, after the *Brooklyn*.

The army, led by Gen. Gordon Granger, arrived on August 1. They landed on Dauphin Island and marched on Fort Gaines on August 4. At 7:00 A.M. the next morning, Farragut gave the order to begin firing on Fort Morgan as the Army's guns commenced battering Fort Gaines.

As Farragut's fleet began taking and returning fire, the air around the convoy filled with so much smoke that the admiral couldn't see. He climbed higher and higher into the *Hartford*'s rigging to get a better view of the action. He went so far up that the *Hartford's* commanding officer, Captain Drayton, sent a man aloft to tie the 63-year-old Farragut to the mainmast so he wouldn't fall. Farragut tried to countermand the order, but the quartermaster refused and lashed the admiral to the mast as his fleet entered Mobile Bay.

The ironclads started out ahead of the wooden fleet, but they slowed as they looked for mines. This was not in Farragut's plan. He needed the ironclads to take out the *Tennessee* before it could form a line with the gunboats and demolish his wooden ships with raking fire.

Suddenly a massive explosion echoed through the harbor. The lead ironclad, *Tecumseh*, had hit a mine and had sunk in less than 30 seconds, with most of its 93-man crew going with it. Rescue boats were sent out and eventually retrieved 10 survivors; more were bobbing in the water. Meanwhile, the lead wooden ship the *Brooklyn* had stopped and was blocking the harbor entrance. In the strait with nowhere to go, the fleet began to cluster together, making the ships easier targets for Fort Morgan's batteries.

Farragut pulled alongside the *Brooklyn* and took charge. When he asked what the delay was and the answer came back "Torpedoes," he gave the immortal order, "Damn the torpedoes. Four bells, Captain Drayton," telling his captain to proceed at full steam. Farragut was gambling that the old mines wouldn't detonate under his passage.

His gamble paid off. The *Hartford* began chasing the three rebel gunboats escorting the *Tennessee*. When the Southern ironclad, commanded by Franklin Buchanan, the former captain of the *Virginia*, turned to pursue, it was pummeled by half of Farragut's wooden fleet. Three ships—the *Monongahela*, the *Lackawanna*, and even Farragut's *Hartford*—attempted to ram him with minimal results; they merely damaged their own vessels. But when the other three ironclads entered the fray, the tide of battle turned rapidly. The *Chickasaw* pulverized the *Tennessee*'s hull and took out four of her six guns. Admiral Buchanan's leg was broken during the battle. With no choice left, the *Tennessee* surrendered—and with it went Mobile Bay.

With the fall of the last large port, it remained for David Porter to take Fort Fisher. On Christmas Eve 1864, after an initial barrage, he began the shelling the fort in earnest with 5 ironclads and more than 40 various ships. When the army units that were supposed to take the fort didn't appear, he suspended the bombardment until they showed up on December 25 and then resumed lobbing two shells per second at the defenses.

After an attempt to send a barge laden with 185 tons of gunpowder near the fort as a floating bomb failed, the ground assault began. The soldiers approached to within 100 hundred yards of the enemy and then turned back, their commanding officers deeming the fort not damaged enough to successfully attack. Porter continued his bombardment. When another army of 8,000 men arrived, he supplemented it with 2,100 of his own sailors and Marines. Landing in the wrong place, the Navy men and the Marines headed for the fort with no fire support. The Confederate defenders thought they were the primary Union force opened fire. Although the unit was repulsed with more than 300 men killed or wounded, they had diverted the fort's attention from the real main assault group. The fort fell on the evening of January 15, 1865, completing the Anaconda Plan's hold around the South.

In February, Charleston, long blockaded by Union ships, fell as the southern defenders abandoned their posts after a siege that had lasted for years. With the Confederacy cut off from any assistance and having been cut to pieces by Sherman's march to the sea and the capture of Richmond, all that was left was to make the Northern victory official at Appomattox.

THE END OF THE WAR

News of the South's surrender took a while to travel. The commerce raider the *Shenandoah* kept taking American whaling vessels in the Pacific for seven months after the war's end.

The U.S. government brought a lawsuit against Great Britain, charging it with aiding the raiders by selling them ships. In 1872, an international arbitration panel awarded the United States $14.5 million in damages.

As so often happens during war, military technology advanced out of sheer necessity. With the advent of Dahlgren guns, metal-hulled and armored ships had to be built to withstand them. The major change on the seas was the overwhelming superiority of steam power versus sail. After the successes of the steam-powered ships, it would have seemed logical that the U.S. Navy would embrace steam as the method of propulsion for all future vessels. However, this would not be the case.

While many of the men who led the Army went on to influential posts in the government or elsewhere, the men of the Navy did not receive the respect they deserved for their role during the war. But one man acknowledged the debt America owed the Navy in 1863, just after the fall of Vicksburg. "At all the watery margins they have been present. Not only on the deep sea, the broad bay, the rapid river, but also up the narrow muddy bayou, and wherever the ground was a little damp they have made their tracks," said President Abraham Lincoln.

CHAPTER 8

RECONSTRUCTION AND IMPERIALISM

At the beginning of the Industrial Age, America could have taken an interest in what was happening in the rest of the world. But rather than keep up with progressive Europe, the United States developed an isolationist policy after the Civil War. With an immense country to explore and settle (after purchasing Alaska in 1867, America was at its current size with only one tenth of today's population), and the wounds of the recent war still fresh, no one wanted to provoke a conflict with another power. So the nation turned inward, healing and strengthening itself, at the cost of becoming a geo-political force for several decades.

THE DARK YEARS—THE NAVY IN DECLINE

With the War Between the States over, a weary country began rebuilding, particularly the battle-torn South. As Reconstruction began, there was no question as to what would happen to the American fleet, which had swelled to 671 ships, 5,000 officers, and 51,500 enlisted men by the end of the Civil War. Once again, hundreds of ships were sold off as the Navy was reduced to essential vessels only. The rest of the active ships were shuffled into several squadrons and dispatched to protect the interests of American citizens and merchants traveling around the globe. By the time the bloodletting was over, the Navy had been reduced to 237 ships, 2,000 officers, and 11,000 men.

The first attempt at a new global policy was carried out by the *Hartford*, which was assigned to re-establish the East India Squadron and the American presence in the South Pacific Ocean. But when the steam vessel arrived at Macao in early 1866, it found no U.S. commercial ships to protect. More than a million tons of merchant vessels had registered with foreign nations to protect themselves from Confederate raiders, and the U.S. government didn't allow re-registering after the war. While foreign trade burgeoned following the Civil War, American merchant ships weren't a part of it. With this decline went another reason for the Navy's existence.

In 1869, Ulysses S. Grant was elected president, and the Navy continued to waste away, attacked by Congress from outside and rotting within. Weak-willed or placid men like Adolph E. Borie, advised by Vice Adm. David D. Porter (who, in effect, ran the Navy during Borie's three-month term) and his successor, George M. Robeson, froze the Navy at a postwar level of inactivity for eight years. Robeson's replacement, Richard W. Thompson, was even worse: He knew next to nothing about ships or the Navy in general, even remarking in surprise upon finding Navy ships to be hollow!

> Even after the effectiveness of steam power was proven beyond any doubt in the Civil War, Rear Adm. David D. Porter, who had used steamships in the successful assault of Fort Fisher and during his Mississippi River campaign, ordered the Navy to return to sail power. To enforce his decision, he decreed that any captain using coal for sailing or maneuvers would be charged for the coal burned. Unfortunately, Admiral Porter wasn't alone in his dismissive attitude toward steam power, and the U.S. Navy's technology continued to lag behind the rest of the world's fleets.

The rivalry between traditional line officers and the rising engineer officers didn't help matters. Practically all senior positions in the Navy were held by line officers who detested the "stink pots," their jeering name for steam vessels. Their scorn of the men who made these newfangled ships run didn't help the engineers one bit. Despite being at the forefront of naval technology, in the U.S. Navy they were second-class citizens and were constantly battling for equal pay and treatment.

Even an early possible threat of war with Great Britain in 1867 couldn't raise the Navy from its doldrums. Many Congressional representatives were still angry at England for its involvement in the building of Confederate raiding ships. By 1871, however, the two countries had set aside their differences and signed the Treaty of Washington. Great Britain also expressed its regret that the ships it had built for the South had operated outside its governance.

Faced with a shortage of funds, antiquated thinking by the top Navy bureaucracy, and a fleet that grew shabbier and more dilapidated each year, enlisted men's morale plummeted. It didn't help that American sailors saw new, advanced-technology iron steamships from Great Britain, Germany, and Japan docked next to them in foreign ports.

This continued for more than 15 years. In 1876, when America celebrated its first centennial, a study of world naval powers was published. Fifteen countries were listed, and America wasn't one of them. Nations such as Austria, Brazil, Peru, and Turkey were considered ahead of the United States in naval power. In 1881 another survey, "Warships and Navies of the World," came out, and again the United States wasn't even close. China, Egypt, Greece, Japan, and Portugal saw their fleets added, but the U.S. Navy was nowhere to be seen. The mighty fleet was now a laughing-stock to the rest of the world, the once impressive Navy now a ramshackle collection of motley ships manned by indifferent crews.

But as always, the Navy made do. In 1867, a coaling station was established at Midway Atoll. A treaty for a naval station at Pago Pago was ratified in 1872 with Seoul. Not all of the foreign negotiations went as smoothly, however. In 1871, a small fleet of five steamships, the flagship *Colorado*, the *Alaska*, the *Benicia*, the *Monocacy*, and the *Palos*, all led by Rear Adm. John Rodgers, sailed to Korea to open diplomatic talks after a series of attacks on merchant ships. After making contact with the Koreans, the American contingent waited for a reply for several days and then began mapping and sounding the shoreline. In the Salee River, the ships were fired upon by island forts.

Rear Admiral Rodgers immediately put a landing party ashore to capture the fortifications. A group of sailors and Marines eventually captured 5 forts and 481 cannons. When the mini-campaign was over, 243 Koreans had been killed. American casualties were amazingly slight, with 3 dead and 10 wounded. Back home, the operation was lambasted in the media, saying that the Navy had sent too large a force to deliver a message of peace, but too small a force to conduct a war.

The only bright spot during this time was the founding of the U.S. Naval Institute in October 1873. A private think-tank dedicated to advancing naval knowledge, its members were a who's who of current Navy officers, including future Cmdr. George Dewey, leader of the American naval forces in Cuba; Capt. Stephen B. Luce; and Cmdr. Alfred Thayer Mahan. Because the organization was not a military one, lieutenants could debate technology and tactics with their superiors without fear of reprisal.

Along with the U.S. Naval Institute, change was coming to the Navy at last. Two incidents caused the Secretary of the Navy and Congress to re-examine their current maritime policy. In 1873 the *Virginius*, a gunrunner sailing under the American flag, was captured by Spain and impounded in Cuba while trying to supply Cuban rebels. After a quick trial, 53 passengers and crew were condemned to death and executed by firing squad. Secretary Robeson ordered the fleet down to Key West in case a war broke out.

The scare abated when it was learned that the ship had been illegally flying the American flag. Robeson instead had the assembled fleet exercise at the islands. The results were pathetic. Not one ship could muster a speed of greater than 4.5 knots, and all of them were in terrible condition, with outmoded boilers, engines, and armament.

Even when confronted with this appalling lack of naval ability, no changes were made during Robeson's tenure. Not until 1879, when the Chilean government went to war against Peru and Bolivia, did the United States suffer a diplomatic slap in the face that got results. Chile's navy was the most advanced in the world at the time, with two armored iron ships purchased from Britain armed with breech-loading cannons. When the United States sent a group of antiquated wooden ships to intervene (and protect the nation's economic interests in Peru, which was losing the war), the leaders of the Chilean navy told the Navy commander to stay out of the conflict or his ships would sink the fleet. The American captain couldn't believe his ears, but it was a good thing that Chile never made good on its threat: It would have been a slaughter.

UP ON CAPITOL HILL—THE BATTLE TO REBUILD THE AMERICAN NAVY

Finally realizing that most other foreign navies outmatched the U.S. fleet, changes were called for at last. In 1881, the new Secretary of the Navy, William H. Hunt, requested a state of the fleet report from Rear Adm. John Rodgers, including what the Navy would need in the future. Four months later, he reported back with very bad news: The current naval fleet was completely insufficient for any type of sea duty. Although U.S. ship-yards had little experience with the new steel vessels that were being built in Europe, the review board strongly suggested using steel for new ships. The board also emphasized installing new, breech-loading, rifled guns, citing both as vital for the nation's defense.

The Navy requested $29 million to build a new fleet from the keel up. These new ships would consist of 18 unarmored steel cruisers, 20 wooden cruisers (apparently some habits still died hard), 5 steel rams, 5 torpedo gunboats, and 20 torpedo boats. Over the next 8 years, they endorsed adding 21 more iron warships and 70 unarmored cruisers.

Although these suggested changes would have been a tremendous boon to the Navy and America, Congress could not assimilate the vast scope of the operation. In fact, the House Naval Affairs Committee couldn't agree with any portion of the report, citing the typical reasons against it: the massive cost of retooling the fleet and the lack of a demonstrable enemy. The American government had reverted to Thomas Jefferson's coastal defense idea of almost 75 years earlier, pushing for mines, torpedo boats, gunboats, and monitors. A blue-water fleet was seen as impractical and unnecessary.

According to Congress, relations with the rest of the world were good. In 1882, 11 years after John Rodgers's violent expedition to Korea, Capt. Robert W. Shufeldt negotiated a trade agreement with the same nation. With no country threatening the shores, Congress saw no need to over-haul the Navy.

During this time, the fleets of Europe advanced naval technology even further. Great Britain's huge battleship the HMS *Dreadnought* was sheathed in 24 inches of iron armor. The French navy of 1881 boasted several ships with 20 inches of steel armor. The proposed lightly armored cruisers of the naval board, with protection around the engines and boilers only, would be gnats next to an elephant by comparison.

With the appointment of Rear Adm. Robert Shufeldt as the chairman of the Naval Advisory Board, the time had come at last to begin renovating the Navy. After sailing around the world looking for global markets and opening Korea to American trade, Shufeldt knew how to get what the Navy wanted from Congress. Citing a need for ships to protect Americans and their commerce abroad, he asked for five vessels. This was much more agreeable to the House Naval Affairs Committee than the previous year's request. On March 3, 1883, Congress passed a bill to build four steel warships, taking the first steps to refit the Navy.

Shufeldt and his board designed three main ships and a smaller "dispatch" vessel. The cruisers, the *Atlanta*, the *Boston*, and the *Chicago*, followed the proposal for a lightly armored steamship (they also had sails, as a secondary means of propulsion) with modern breech-loading rifled-barrel cannons. Not suitable for going up against a modern battleship, these agile ships were designed to protect American merchant vessels in foreign ports, able to fend off poorly armed pirates or angry native populations with relative ease. Almost more important than their purported role in the Navy was the fact that they were built at all. But once Congress took this small step of modernizing the fleet, more initiative, approval, and money were soon to follow.

Founded in 1884 by Commodore Stephen B. Luce, the United States Naval War College, in Newport, Rhode Island, is the foremost school for the study of naval tactics, theory, and technology in the world. Its goals of training officers in the arts of logistics, tactics, strategy, and battle apply to all branches of the armed forces.

Luce chose Capt. Alfred Thayer Mahan as one of his four faculty members. The publication of Thayer's *The Influence of Seapower Upon History, 1660–1783*, was an acclaimed success, and the young university gained international recognition.

In spite of this, the college faced opposition by Navy personnel who believed sailing and tactics could be learned only on a ship. In response, the college developed naval science. A system of tactical analysis was created and refined, covering everything from appraising a situation to drafting correct orders, to evaluating the outcome. The college implemented war-gaming scenarios for strategic experiments, and almost every

American war plan during the next 30 years was conceived by Naval War College officers, either alone or in conjunction with the Office of Naval Intelligence.

After World War I, the collegiate program was expanded to include four basic areas of study: command, strategy, tactics, and policy. By World War II, the war in the Pacific had been played out so many times that the Americans had anticipated everything except the kamikaze attacks. The post–World War II years also saw the precursor of the current publication *Naval College War Review* and the first session of what would become the Current Strategy Forum. The 1950s and 1960s saw the founding of the Naval Command College. The invention of computers revolutionized how the war games were run as well.

The college celebrated its centennial in 1984 and then celebrated the hundredth anniversary of war-gaming in 1987. The Naval War College continues its tradition of excellence as the U.S. Navy moves into the twenty-first century, training the best and brightest men to become the best officers in the Navy.

A LIGHT IN THE DARKNESS—RE-ENGINEERING THE FLEET

With President Grover Cleveland came William C. Whitney as Secretary of the Navy in 1885, and maritime advancements continued. American shipbuilders mastered the techniques of steel construction, and new ships came out of the yards. Whitney's tenure saw the addition of the cruiser the *Baltimore*, built on the same lines as the *Chicago*, but much faster; the battleships the *Maine* and the *Texas*; and the large armored cruiser the *New York* and the smaller cruiser the *Olympia*, which would play an important role in the Spanish-American War.

This increased production came at an opportune time, for America was being pulled into global politics almost against its wishes. A successful coup in Panama in 1885 almost cut off U.S. trade across the isthmus. In March 1889, a hurricane sank the only three antiquated Navy vessels in the Pacific, stationed at Pago Pago on the island of Tutuila, Samoa. The Samoan Islands in general had already been contested by Great Britain and Germany over using the harbor as a refueling station. By June of the same year, the three nations had worked out an arrangement to let England and Germany use Pago Pago without encroaching on the American station.

More important, the incident gave new Secretary of the Navy Benjamin F. Tracy ammunition for upgrading the fleet. Capt. Alfred Thayer Mahan's groundbreaking book *The Influence of Sea Power Upon History, 1660–1783*, also did more to influence naval power around the world that its author could have possibly realized.

Published in 1890, Alfred Thayer Mahan's book *The Influence of Sea Power Upon History 1660–1783* stated that the most powerful nations were ones with a strong sea power, including a navy to defend trade routes and merchant ships, and naval bases and colonies around the world. The book does not take into account the rising technology of steam power, but instead it uses a set of general principles that navies of all kinds the world over should adhere to in order to be successful:

- Concentrate the naval force, or don't split up the fleet.
- Identify and concentrate on the main objective, usually the defeat of the enemy navy.
- Adopt a single-minded determination to achieve this goal, attacking the enemy's fleet and not merchant ships or land targets.

Although the book received a wary reception from officers and critics in the U.S. (except for future President Theodore Roosevelt, who loved it), it revolutionized naval thinking around the world, particularly in Great Britain, France, and Germany. Mahan's concepts and theories were studied and adopted by several foreign navies, Germany in particular, where the book was required reading for every officer.

Secretary Tracy's 1890 evaluation revealed that the fleet still lagged behind smaller nations with a fraction of the resources. Tracy estimated that the U.S. ranked twelfth among world naval powers, below Austria-Hungry, Turkey, and China. In his annual report, he recommended building 20 coast-defense vessels, 60 cruisers, and 20 battleships over the next 12 to 15 years. His report attracted allies like War College founder Stephen Luce, who wrote bluntly, "The battleship is the foundation of our Navy, the United States has no battleships, therefore she has no Navy."

UNREST IN AMERICA'S BACKYARD AND AROUND THE WORLD

Meanwhile, American involvement in foreign affairs continued. In 1891, after the successful Chilean revolution, a mob clashed with a group of American sailors from the USS *Baltimore*, killing 2 of them and injuring 18. The *Baltimore* was recalled home, and only the gunboat the *Yorktown* was left in the harbor while the local court sorted things out. Nevertheless, the ship's gun crews slept by loaded weapons during their stay. President Benjamin Harrison was pushed to the brink of declaring war on Chile, even though several European nations took Chile's side in the dispute. The Chilean government quickly made a demanded apology, and the body of one of the slain sailors was returned home to a posthumous hero's welcome.

Hawaii felt the fires of unrest the next year, and the ruling government actually asked the United States to annex the entire island group. The government refused, but high-ranking Navy officers were already marking the small cluster of Pacific islands as the most important strategic point for America; as such, they could not fall into another nation's hands. The decision not to annex had violent repercussions later.

The Senate and the House of Representatives were in agreement, thanks to Stephen Luce's political acumen. Democrats and Republicans united across party lines on naval expansion, seeing it as for the good of America. Although some still clung to the idea of coastal defense, the majority of Congress overrode their protests. The naval act of June 1890 called for three battleships, one protected cruiser, one torpedo cruiser, and one light torpedo boat. (In a clever conceit to the coastal defense proponents, House Naval Affairs Committee Chairman Charles Boutelle wrote the request for "three seagoing coastline battleships," a term that no one would ever think to use upon seeing the finished ships.) All of the other vessels were really just window dressing to get the battleships, the beginnings of this modern Navy.

While building the new fleet, America kept a watchful eye on its neighbors. Count Ferdinand de Lesseps failed to dig a canal across the Panama isthmus from 1881 to 1887, but his project attracted interest from U.S. naval leaders and Congress. They realized that, sooner or later, a canal would be completed and the oceans would be joined in Central America, opening a new route from east to west. To guard the nation's West Coast, plans were made to gain possession of Hawaii, still ruled by a monarchy. President Benjamin Harrison's Secretary of State, James G. Blaine, was all for the annexation of Hawaii, and his minister to the nation, John L. Stevens, created a revolution that deposed Queen Liliuokalani in January 1893.

The cruiser the *Boston*, then in Honolulu harbor, landed a force of 164 men and took the royal palace. Stevens established a provisional government, and Washington moved to annex the islands in the last hours of Harrison's term. The attempt failed, and Hawaii had to wait until after the Spanish-American War to be brought into the American fold.

In 1894, revolutionary fever swept through Brazil, causing a squadron of five modern cruisers and an old gunboat to be dispatched to protect American merchants in the area. The next year, tensions were renewed between America and an old enemy, Great Britain. Venezuela was pressing its claim on part of its neighbor, British Guiana. When Britain refuted the claim, the United States, with only one first-class battleship (two second-class battleships were still under construction) and one armored cruiser in the fleet, demanded that the dispute go to arbitration. When the War College began running battle simulations against the Royal Navy's 16 cruisers and more than 36 modern battleships, it was discovered that President Grover Cleve-land (who had suspending the naval building program during the worst economic recession of the century) might have gone too far. Nevertheless, a war plan was drawn up that relied on the tiny fleet and a lot of luck, even involving an invasion of Canada, if necessary. Fortunately, the British seemed more amused than insulted by the U.S. demand and agreed to the mediation. When the judgment came down for Britain, the under-equipped Navy breathed a sigh of relief that it wouldn't have to back up the American government's posturing.

During all of this, the Secretary of the Navy, Hilary A. Herbert, was doing everything possible to improve the fleet. With Mahan's theories completely accepted in America by 1894, Herbert regrouped the active ships of the fleet into two main battle groups instead of the current five squadrons around the world. He also carried out a strategic strengthening of the Pacific Squadron in response to Japan's maritime buildup, which by 1895 was second only to Great Britain's in naval power.

In 1895, the prelude to the Spanish-American war was intensifying in Cuba, with the bloody revolution getting major coverage in U.S. newspapers. The assistant Navy secretary, William G. McAdoo, used the possible flashpoint to suggest forming a naval war board, staffed by officers who would advise the Navy on primarily military matters. The General Board of the Navy would be created five years later, but the seeds were sown now. Cuba was also important to Secretary Herbert, who pushed through a request to build 3 more battleships and 10 torpedo boats.

When John D. Long assumed the secretarial post in 1897 (along with the most famous assistant secretary ever, Theodore Roosevelt), the Navy was becoming a true military power. In January, the battleships the *Indiana*, the *Massachusetts*, and the *Oregon* all began active duty. The second-class battleships the *Maine* and the *Texas* had been sailing for two years, and five more battleships (the *Alabama*, the *Illinois*, the *Kearsage*, the *Kentucky*, and the *Wisconsin*) were in various stages of construction, with all of them completed in 1899. Supporting this new Navy were seven cruisers, four monitors, an armored ram, an experimental submarine, and six 1,000-ton gunboats.

After suffering through some of the worst years in its history, the United States Navy was regaining its pride and poise. With the long-delayed embrace of steam technology and steel shipbuilding, America did what it had often done during the past century—come from behind and take an unassailable position ahead of other fleets. From here it was a short step into the ranks of those nations known as world powers.

CHAPTER 9

THE SPANISH-AMERICAN WAR

At the beginning of 1898, Spain owned the colonies of Cuba, the Philippines, Puerto Rico, and Guam. None fared well under Spanish rule, and each eventually tried to rebel and govern itself. In 1868, native Cubans rallied against Spain in what became known as the 10 Years Revolt. They didn't win their freedom, but their actions garnered sympathy in America. Freedom fighters came to the United States to gain weapons and support for their uprising. Hundreds of Americans traveled to Cuba to fight for the country's freedom. Others supported the rebellion because they owned land or had investments in the sugar- and tobacco-rich island.

In October 1896, Spain sent Gen. Valeriano Weyler to Cuba to deal with the insurgents. Weyler forced peasants into concentration camps, burned farms, destroyed crops and livestock, and ordered any resistors to be killed. Many prisoners in the camps were women and children. It has been estimated that at least 200,000 people died of starvation and disease in the camps.

Just before General Weyler's arrival, President Grover Cleveland tried negotiating peace between Cuba and Spain. Afterward, the next president, William McKinley, attempted to purchase

Cuba outright in 1897, the third time an offer had been tendered since John Adams's first proposal in 1823. The Spanish refused again and said it would rather fight than give up the colony. At this point, the Monroe Doctrine was brought up to justify going to war.

The press was also trying to justify a war. New York boasted two newspapers, the *Journal*, owned by William Randolph Hearst, and the *World*, owned by Joseph Pulitzer. These two editorial giants used sensationalism and half-truths to sell papers and incite public opinion in a practice called yellow journalism. This would be well demonstrated in the sinking of the *Maine*, which had been sent to Cuba as a message to the Spanish that they were being watched.

On the evening of February 15, 1898, the USS *Maine* was anchored in Havana harbor under the command of Capt. Charles D. Sigsbee. At 9:40 P.M., a massive explosion rocked the ship, followed by a second smaller blast. The *Maine* sank quickly, taking 266 crewmen out of the 354 aboard down with it. Captain Sigsbee first thought he was under attack, but he didn't see any Spanish ship or rebels nearby except for the *Alfonso XII*, which was rushing over to help the wounded.

There were three theories about what had happened. A Spanish mine could have been planted near the hull, the rebels may have blown her up to force America to get involved in the conflict, or bituminous coal may have ignited in a poorly ventilated ordnance bunker, setting off the powder. The first theory was unsupported because there were no known Spanish ships in the area. The rebels also had no reason to destroy the *Maine* because her presence was proof of America's involvement. On March 28, 1898, a Naval Court of Inquiry declared that the Maine had been most likely sunk by a mine. After several more reviews, including one in 1976, it is thought that a coal explosion caused the accident.

The *Maine* sat on the harbor floor until 1911, when the hull was repaired enough to tow it out to sea and sink it. Many parts of the ship were salvaged, including her mainmast, now in Arlington National Cemetery; her foremast, located at the Naval Academy in Annapolis, Maryland; and one of her bow anchors, now in Reading, Pennsylvania's City Park.

The sinking of the *Maine* galvanized American interest in the conflict. Fueled by even more rampant yellow journalism, it popularized anti-Spanish sentiment, characterized by the infamous slogan, "Remember the *Maine* and to hell with Spain!" It also gave hawks in Congress another reason to press for U.S. military intervention, which, despite President William

McKinley's efforts to avoid sending Americans to fight, now seemed a foregone conclusion.

Hearst and Pulitzer took their journalistic war to new heights during the Spanish-American War, each trying to outdo the other in vilifying Spain. Huge daily headlines screamed that U.S. naval officers were sure a Spanish mine had destroyed the warship. The *Journal* offered a $50,000 reward for the perpetrators. By the time they were through, America was crying out for war, as were many politicians and the Assistant Secretary of the Navy, Theodore Roosevelt.

A passionate imperialist, Roosevelt believed that *The Influence of Sea Power Upon History, 1600–1783* was the blueprint for the future of the Navy. Rear Admiral Mahan advocated controlling the Caribbean Islands, Hawaii, and the Philippines due to their strategic placement. He also recommended creating a canal through South America and building a fleet of steel steamships (this part Congress and the Navy had already done). Already a cunning politician and strategist, Roosevelt made sure he had others who agreed with his ideas in key places when he needed them. One of these allies was Rear Adm. George Dewey.

Stationed in Hong Kong, Dewey awaited further orders while Congress made preparations for battle. The government allocated a war budget and issued an ultimatum to the Spanish government to leave Cuba. When Spain's negative response was received, President McKinley called for authorization to intervene in Cuba. This vote included the Teller Amendment, which stated that the U.S. would not try to govern Cuba after the war was over. On April 21, Spain announced that it considered the joint resolution to be an act of war. McKinley responded by calling for a blockade of Cuba and declaring war with Spain on April 25, 1898.

OLD FISH IN A LARGE BARREL—THE BATTLE OF MANILA BAY

Commodore Dewey moved his fleet to Manila Bay in the Philippines as Spanish Adm. Pascual Cervera y Topete raced to Cuba. The improved state of the U.S. Navy was the result of a deliberate buildup of the new steel industry after 1883. The first four ships built were the *Atlanta*, the *Boston*, the *Chicago*, and the *Dolphin*. The fleet now consisted of 5 battleships,

6 monitors, 2 armored cruisers, 8 protected cruisers, 9 small cruisers, 1 ram, 1 dynamite gunboat, 6 torpedo craft, and 10 gunboats. All but nine of these ships were constructed after 1890. The Spanish fleet consisted of 32 ships built before 1890, and most were in a state of disrepair, with barnacled hulls, decrepit or broken boilers, and inadequate, obsolete firepower.

When he sailed into Manila Bay, Dewey commanded the cruisers the *Olympia* (his flagship), the *Raleigh*, the *Boston*, and the *Baltimore;* two gunboats, the *Concord* and the *Petrel;* the cutter the *McCulloch;* and two colliers.

Dewey faced Adm. Patricio Montojo y Pasaron and his fleet, comprised of the cruisers the *Reina Cristina* and the *Castilla* and the gunboats the *Don Antonio de Ulloa*, the *Don Juan de Austria*, the *Isla de Cuba*, the *Mauques del Duero*, the *General Lezo*, and the *Argos*. The Spanish ships were in such poor condition (the *Castilla's* propeller shaft leaked so badly that it was plugged with cement, preventing the ship from moving) that Admiral Montojo sat anchored in the harbor, praying the shore batteries would weaken the American fleet as they came in so he could finish them off.

Dewey scouted nearby Subic Bay first, thinking the Spanish might have left a force there. (The last thing Montoyo could afford to do was split up his meager fleet.) When no attack came, the U.S. fleet proceeded into Manila Bay.

Met with one cannon shot upon entering the harbor in the early morning of May 1, the fleet advanced until it spotted the enemy in the rising dawn. At 5:15 A.M., Admiral Montojo gave the order to open fire. Not until 25 minutes later did the commodore feel his ships had reached the optimum range. When Dewey uttered his famous order at 5:40 on the morning of May 1, 1898, "You may fire when you are ready, Captain Gridley," he unleashed a barrage that lasted nearly seven hours. Although the battle was impressive, the American sailors' gunnery skills weren't. Out of almost 6,000 shells fired, only 142 actually hit their targets, primarily because the sailors were still using the antiquated method of matching the roll of their ship and firing when their target rose into the gun sights.

When the smoke cleared, Admiral Montojo had lost every ship in his fleet. In a brave but foolish effort, he had sailed the *Reina Cristina* straight for the American line, trying to take out at least one ship and salvage a bit of Spanish pride. Unfortunately, his lone cruiser was severely damaged by the U.S. warships. He also lost a total of 400 men, many from the *Reina Cristina*, with hundreds more wounded. Dewey had not lost a single man in battle (an engineer on the *McCulloch* died of heatstroke during the battle) and counted eight injuries, none serious.

The Philippines were now firmly under American protection, and although Dewey lacked an occupying force, he didn't back down from any attempt to intimidate him. When German Vice Adm. Otto von Diederichs protested the American fleet's investigation of one of his ships working among the islands, Dewey, already suspicious of his intentions, told him through his interpreter, "Tell your admiral if he wants war, I am ready." The two sides maintained an uneasy peace. When a relief convoy of monitors, cruisers, and much-needed ammunition arrived, Dewey's concern over the German squadron was alleviated.

Back in Washington, McKinley, aware of Hawaii's importance in the Pacific, called for it to be annexed and become a U.S. territory. Secretary of the Navy John D. Long ordered Capt. Henry Glass of the *Charleston* to take Guam on his way, to support Dewey in the next phase of clearing the Philippines of Spanish rule. Glass had no trouble taking the island. Until his arrival, the Spanish garrison had not heard of the war (when Glass fired a few ranging shots at the fort as he approached, the officers inside thought he was saluting them) and were not prepared to defend themselves. Even the men who had sailed to take the island had no idea of its importance—but a little more than 40 years later, possession of Guam would be much more fiercely contested.

While many Americans supported their government's imperialist efforts, these actions were not supported by a large segment of the nation. The American Anti-Imperialist League was forming and included such famous people as Andrew Carnegie and Mark Twain. The former Secretary of the Treasury and Massachusetts Sen. George S. Boutwell served as president of the league. Despite those protests, Hawaii was annexed on July 6, 1898.

HIDE AND SEEK OFF CUBA: THE BATTLE OF SANTIAGO

Less than a week after war was declared, the leader of the Spanish navy, Admiral Cervera, was sent to defend Cuba and Puerto Rico. Cervera had no illusions about the outcome. With inadequate supplies and no funds, he knew his mission was doomed—and had told his superiors so before leaving. His ships did not have enough coal to make the journey, forcing him to refuel at several Caribbean Islands. His lateness sowed confusion among the American patrol boats, which had expected Cervera to arrive in Havana in early to mid-May. The biggest advantage the Spaniards had was that the Americans didn't know where the enemy fleet was. Cervera arrived instead at the port of Santiago on May 19. It was such a strange place to land that when the U.S. spy reported it, many in the Navy didn't believe him.

Until the Spanish fleet was neutralized, the Army could not land in Cuba. Rear Adm. William T. Sampson, commander of the North Atlantic Fleet, sent a group of ships known as the Flying Squadron, under Commodore Winfield Scott Schley, to search for Cervera west of Cuba. The squadron included the battleships the *Texas* and the *Brooklyn* and the protected cruisers the *Columbia* and the *Minneapolis*, all out of Hampton Roads, Virginia. Meanwhile, the *Oregon* was making full steam from San Francisco, rounding South America and arriving at Cuba in 67 days.

By May 26, word came that Cervera had arrived, and the American force set out to meet him. Finding him at Santiago, the Navy blockaded the harbor. While Cervera's fleet couldn't get out, the Americans couldn't come in to get him as they had at Manila. The small harbor entrance only allowed for one ship to enter or leave at a time.

The next month passed slowly, with Cervera showing no inclination to come out and fight. The U.S. was limited to assembling the fleet in a semicircle to wait the Spanish out. An attempt to sink one of the obstinate colliers, the *Merrimac*, as a barrier in the harbor failed. The ship sank in line with the channel, not across it, as planned.

By July 1, the Spanish forces realized they were as good as defeated. Cervera knew he couldn't outwait the Americans forever, but he also knew he wouldn't win a fight with them. Although his ships were newer than the ones at Manila Bay, several did not have their full complement of guns, and some were carrying the wrong type of ammunition. But Cervera's personal and national honor demanded that he fight his way out rather than surrender.

On July 3 the battleship the *Massachusetts* was refueling at Guantanamo Bay, and Admiral Sampson had chosen to rendezvous with Army Gen. William Shafter, sailing on the fleet's flagship the *New York*. Seizing the best opportunity to escape, Cervera sailed his ships out single file to try and outmaneuver the American blockade, which consisted of the battleships the *Oregon*, the *Indiana*, the *Iowa*, and the *Texas*; the cruiser the *Brooklyn*; and the smaller yacht the *Gloucester*.

The American force was taken by surprise, to the point that the *Brooklyn*, commanded by Schley, swung across the bow of the *Texas*, forcing the battleship to reverse its engines to avoid a collision. Then the *Oregon*, picking up speed, narrowly missed the *Iowa* and the *Texas*. They recovered quickly and began moving to parallel the enemy fleet, which was sailing west along the Cuban coastline. The Spanish might have gotten away: Their ships had a full head of steam in their boilers, while most of the American ships were running at half power to conserve fuel. However, the first-class battleship the *Oregon* was running at full steam, and its captain, Charles E. Clark, and crew were spoiling for a fight. Stoking the ship's boilers until she reached the incredible speed of 18 knots (21.6 miles per hour), he overtook the Spanish ships and shelled them until the entire battered squadron turned toward land. All the cruisers went aground off Cuba, where the rest of the U.S. force overtook them.

Commodore Schley and his squadron destroyed every enemy ship, with 350 Spanish dead and 160 wounded. The Americans had lost only one man, with two wounded. The jungle coast of Cuba was a terrible sight afterward, with the wrecks of the destroyer the *Furor*; the armored cruisers the *Infanta Maria Teresa*, the *Almirante Oquendo*, the *Vizcaya*, and the *Cristobal Colon*; and the torpedo boat the *Pluton* scattered across the water.

Admiral Sampson had missed the entire battle and was livid over it. When Schley gallantly sent a cable to the Secretary of the Navy informing him that the battle had been won under Sampson's auspices, the admiral sent along a coded message criticizing Schley's handling of the blockage over the past month, which was unmerited. Reviewing his medical history later revealed that Sampson was suffering from an Alzheimer's-type disease, which clouded his judgment even then.

Meeting the Spanish survivors who swam away from the wreckage was none other than William Randolph Hearst himself, who had accompanied the squadron to see the war in Cuba and create more news first-hand. Armed with a revolver and his own unit of journalists and sketch artists, he rounded up the dazed sailors and took them into "custody" aboard his newspaper ships.

THE END OF THE WAR

After this second devastating blow, Cuba surrendered to U.S. troops on July 17. The next day, the Spanish government sent French Ambassador Jules Cambon to request that President McKinley negotiate for peace. After the success at Cuba, the army assigned to the Philippines occupied the islands while governments sat down to figure out how to divide it all up.

After months of negotiation, the Treaty of Paris was signed on December 10, 1898. In a very controversial decision, McKinley saw Spain renounce all rights to Cuba and cede Puerto Rico, Guam, and the West Indies. Strangest of all, America purchased the Philippines outright for $20 million. Suddenly the Monroe Doctrine was thrown out the window as soon as it conflicted with U.S. self-interest. The fact that the Philippines weren't in the Western Hemisphere and, therefore, were outside the area covered by Monroe's speech, was no doubt used as an excuse to purchase the island group outright.

To avoid losing face, a secret agreement was struck between Spain and the United States. Spain would pretend to defend the Philippines, but when the U.S. forces arrived, would hoist a white flag and allow America to take the islands without alerting the Filipino insurgents to their new rulers.

Mahan's plan for a new navy with strategic and modern advances was slowly becoming reality. With the proper guidance, the U.S. Navy was poised at the beginning of the coming decade to exhibit a readiness and control around the world that had never existed for any nation.

CHAPTER 10

ENTERING THE TWENTIETH CENTURY

While the nation's victory in the Spanish-American War (where the U.S. faced an obsolete enemy fleet) seemed to come with ease, naval insiders knew they had to integrate the new technology with the men who operated it more efficiently. To the world, the United States was riding high and appeared to have the ability to back it up. In just 124 years, the nation had progressed from a fractious group of colonies that had almost split over slavery and states' rights to a unified and committed nation, ready to defend what it saw as its interests around the world. Now the U.S. Navy had an opportunity to create a fleet that could realistically do just that.

The overseas intervention began with the Philippines. According to the imperialists, the Philippines were needed to keep an eye on the burgeoning Japanese fleet as well as crumbling China, who was under threat from several European powers. When the government said the Philippines must contain a U.S. military base, more than two years of bitter fighting followed, with American soldiers clashing with Filipino rebels. By the time it was over, 4,200 Americans and 20,000 Filipinos had been killed.

Navy ships were crucial during the battles, transporting troops from site to site and conducting offshore shelling in preparation for military landings. With most destroyers patrolling the Atlantic, smaller vessels such as gunboats, monitors, and cruisers handled the operations. In March 1901, the Army captured the Filipino leader, Gen. Emilio Aquinaldo, and secured the islands by July 4.

At the same time, another hot spot was developing in China. The Righteous Society of Heavenly Fists, or "Boxers," as they came to be known, a radical nationalist group, rebelled against the increasing foreign influence in their homeland. As a large group marched on Peking, the Navy was called in on May 31, 1900, to help guard the various diplomats in the city. The international group of 337 men came from several countries, including Britain, France, Germany, Italy, Japan, Russia, and the United States, which contributed 48 Marines and 5 sailors. They soon found themselves overwhelmed by thousands of furious Chinese protesters and called for reinforcements. Four hundred eighty-two Marines and 2,000 soldiers were sent to the International Relief Expedition, which eventually grew to 18,600 men and several international fleets of ships, including 46 from the United States. Eventually, the Navy removed the Marines there, leaving the fighting to the Army.

The passing century marked the end of an era. On January 1, 1900, the last Spanish governor of Cuba left the island, ending four centuries of European control in the Caribbean Ocean. In September 1901, President William McKinley was assassinated and Vice President Theodore Roosevelt was sworn into office.

Having already served as assistant Secretary of the Navy during the Spanish-American War, Roosevelt was a staunch ally of the Navy. He also agreed with Secretary of the Navy John D. Long that there was a need to create overseas bases, particularly in the Pacific Ocean.

Long and Roosevelt laid the foundation of the fleet and policy of today. Long created the General Board, a panel of senior officers who guided and advised the Navy in strategy, operational planning, and fleet design. The first president was Adm. George Dewey, which cleverly limited him to the bureaucratic side of the service. Long also made the line officers part of the engineer corps so that every future officer would learn about steam power and engineering, ensuring no more division of classes.

By 1901, 60 vessels were under construction, including cruisers, the first destroyers, gunboats, monitors, and a new class of submarine, the *Holland* class (see Appendix C). When Secretary Long retired in 1902, the U.S. fleet was ranked fourth in the world, after Britain, France, and Russia.

FLEET DIPLOMACY IN AN UNCERTAIN AGE

Unlike his predecessors, President Roosevelt tried to uphold the Monroe Doctrine when possible. Having inherited the Philippine insurrection, he tried to prevent the same situation from happening again. However, when an opportunity arose that could benefit the United States in Central America, he quickly took advantage of it using the U.S. military.

Various Caribbean nations also took refuge behind the Monroe Doctrine, trusting their American protector to ward off foreign reprisals. Venezuela was one of the worst offenders, having borrowed $12.5 million in bonds from various countries, including Great Britain, Germany, and Italy, and then refused to repay the debt. The three naval powers all sent ships down to blockade Venezuelan ports.

Coincidentally, the U.S. fleet, commanded by Admiral Dewey, was practicing maneuvers off Costa Rica at the time. Dewey's relationship with the German Navy had never been great, and now, even though the Venezuelans were in the wrong, Dewey thought the foreign blockade should be watched. With Roosevelt's approval, he sailed over to keep an eye on the situation. The blockade continued until Venezuelan president Cipriano Castro accepted an offer of arbitration from The Hague, which eventually satisfied all of the involved parties.

In 1902, Great Britain rocked the world by announcing that after nine months of secret negotiations, it had entered into an alliance with Japan. Among other provisions, the main thrust of the agreement seemed to be keeping Great Britain neutral in the event of Japanese aggression. Under the terms of the treaty, if Japan attacked another nation, Great Britain would not interfere. If Japan went to war with two nations, Great Britain would be obliged to join the fight on the side of Japan!

The U.S. government suspected that Japan had made the deal with an eye toward foreign expansion. In response, all of the four great naval powers increased production, with Germany planning 38 first-class battleships by

1920. President Roosevelt also became more wary of German intentions, particularly when news of the Büchsel plan came out, which advocated German expansion into South America and eventually making the United States discard the Monroe Doctrine .

By this time other countries were complaining about the doctrine as well because it seemed to imply, "Do as I say, not as I do." America forbade other countries from interfering in the Western Hemisphere, but it magnanimously allowed its own government to do as it pleased, as Roosevelt proved during the Panama rebellion of 1903.

A colony of Colombia, Panama, was vital to U.S. Navy concerns because a canal there would cut the transoceanic passage time from 14,000 miles to 5,200 miles. In January, Secretary of State John Hay worked out a treaty allowing the United States to lease a 10-mile-wide strip of land on the isthmus from Colombia for 100 years at a total cost of $10 million. But when it came time to sign, Colombia balked, not liking the specific terms of the agreement that stipulated that Colombia would have sovereignty over the land in name only, with the United States in real control.

With unrest fermenting among the populace, aided by French merchants who wanted to negotiate with the United States regarding their own treaty, revolt seemed imminent. Seizing the opportunity, Navy ships were dispatched in October with orders to take the railway in the event of a revolution and prevent Colombian soldiers from entering the country. On November 3, the insurrection began, the railway was seized, and Colombia was shut out. On November 4, an interim government was created, and two days later, the United States officially recognized the new Panamanian nation. Less than two weeks after the revolution, the United States and Panama signed the Hay-Bunau-Varilla Treaty, an accord identical to the one Colombia had rejected earlier. Although many Americans denounced the blatant illegality of the action, no real action was taken by anyone. The rapidly changing modern world would prove the necessity of protecting America first and dealing with any repercussions later.

FACING OFF WITH THE EMPIRE OF THE RISING SUN

Meanwhile, Japanese expansion continued, culminating in the Russo-Japanese war of 1904–1905. The Japanese showed their naval prowess during the brief conflict, from their sneak attack on the Russian navy at

Port Arthur, Manchuria, to victories in the Yellow Sea and the Strait of Tsushima. Taking Mahan's lessons to heart, the Japanese had targeted only the Russian navy, they had kept their own fleet together, and they had not engaged in any commerce raiding. The only mistake the emperor's government made was deciding not to continue the war. Faced with the massive resources of Russia, which would eventually overwhelm the Japanese, Tokyo asked Roosevelt to negotiate a peace accord, which gave the island nation territorial recognition in Manchuria and Korea. However, no money was paid to Japan, which displeased its population. Four months after the war ended, its own citizens overthrew their government.

Although Roosevelt was awarded the 1906 Nobel Peace Prize for his actions, there was still concern about Japan's aggressive policies. Roosevelt continued to strengthen the Navy, though he underestimated what would be needed in the future. Still, during his first term, naval allocation increased by 25 percent (from $85 million to $118 million), and another 250,000 tons were either under construction or approved, including 10 first-class battleships. In December 1905, Roosevelt was confident that one new battleship a year would be plenty for the Navy, but he would later regret those words in the face of increased foreign naval buildup.

In 1906, diplomatic matters almost came to a head with Japan when the San Francisco school board passed a resolution to segregate Japanese students. Riots soon followed, and radical Japanese newspapers advocated sending warships to the West Coast. Faced with possible foreign invasion, California and other Pacific states eagerly clamored for a stronger navy. Although Roosevelt knew California was too far away for a successful assault, he used the West Coast's fear to his advantage. And when the HMS *Dreadnought* was launched by Great Britain, it sealed the deal.

With one ship, Britain rendered every ship in navies around the world obsolete. Laid down in October 1905, the 18,100-ton vessel was completed just four months later. It was launched in February 1906, and outfitted by December. Powered by the brand-new steam turbine, its top speed was 21.5 knots (25.8 miles per hour), with a range of 6,000 miles. The ship's main battery consisted of ten 12-inch guns, paired and mounted on the centerline of the ship, and twenty-eight 3-inch guns. The HMS *Dreadnought* ushered in a new class of maritime vessel, and capital ships from then on were known as "dreadnoughts."

Faced with the obsolescence of their own fleets, other nations scrambled to catch up. The Italians had created the idea of a dreadnought-class ship first, but the Japanese had been first to begin building one, the 20,000 ton *Aki*. It would have been finished before the *Dreadnought* if Japan hadn't gone to war with Russia. Germany approved the building of the *Nassau* right after the *Dreadnaught's* launch but reconfigured the plans after realizing the power of the British ship's all big-gun battery. When the German warship was completed, it was an ineffective hodgepodge of old and new designs.

America didn't waste any time, either, having submitted plans for its own large battleships, the 16,000-ton vessels the *Michigan* and the *South Carolina*. Although smaller and slower (18.5 knots) than the British ship, they would also take advantage of the big gun concept, carrying eight 12-inch guns apiece. But an entrenched House and Senate and an ineffective Secretary of the Navy, Josephus Daniels, made progress slow. Congress authorized only one new battleship in 1907, the *Delaware*, and threw Roosevelt's "one battleship per year is enough" comment back at him.

Aware that he needed public support for the Navy as well as a show of force to the world, Roosevelt ordered the fleet to embark on a world tour. "The Great White Fleet" steamed 46,000 miles in 14 months, reaching almost every major world port. It was a huge success, greeted by cheering crowds of foreign admirers. The fleet even stopped in Japan, where it was welcomed by the ruling government. The voyage calmed American fears and helped secure an agreement between Japan and the United States to keep the status quo on the Pacific. Roosevelt stayed in office long enough to see the fleet return to America in 1909, just two weeks before relinquishing his office to William Howard Taft.

President Roosevelt left a greatly improved Navy after his eight years in office. The number of officers had increased from 883 to 1,096, and the enlisted ranks had grown from 25,050 to 44,500. Twenty-seven submarines had been approved, and the main units had been brought together instead of being scattered around the globe. The U.S. Navy was now second only to Great Britain in strength and capability.

But as successful as the "Great White Fleet" tour had been, Congress still opposed building dreadnought-class ships. With Roosevelt's 1904 announcement that he would not run for a third term, his influence over the legislature waned. Opponents cited the same arguments that had been brought up since the Revolutionary War: New ships were too expensive—they would cause an arms race and a greater chance of going to war. But while opponents' reasons were the same, the world had moved on. A strong Navy would be vital for America's protection—and soon the world's.

STORM CLOUDS OVER EUROPE

Fortunately, Taft was still wary about the threat of European and Asian expansion, and he agreed with Roosevelt's naval policies. The battleship program continued, and new ships were started, including the first two American dreadnoughts, the *Michigan* and the *South Carolina*. In 1911, the first oil-powered battleships, the *Nevada* and the *Oklahoma*, were approved as well. The transition from coal to oil meant a 40 percent longer cruising range than previous vessels.

Also in 1911, Congress voted to provide $5 million of fortifications to the almost-completed Panama Canal, guaranteeing the fleet unhindered access to the waterway. Construction was also proceeding on the major naval base at Pearl Harbor, Hawaii, with the dredging of the main channel into the harbor completed before the end of the year.

The years before World War I found national attention divided between two fronts. Although tensions were rising in Europe, many American politicians and naval officers were also focused on China and Japan. The Asiatic fleet, weakened over the past decade, now consisted of three cruisers and six gunboats that primarily patrolled the Yangtze River. While the United States was expanding trade with China, the American minister there was concerned about Japan taking advantage of the cash-rich but militarily weak nation. There was also a strong possibility that Japan was laying groundwork to secure a harbor at Magdalena Bay, Mexico, which the American government would not tolerate.

Taft, however, always kept one eye on Germany and constantly measured the Kaiser's fleet strength against the United States'. His Secretary of the Navy, George von Lengerke Meyer, advocated adding dozens of ships, including 7 battleships, 8 large cruisers, 33 protected cruisers, 132 destroyers, and 38 submarines, along with the necessary support craft. But with the chair of the House Naval Affairs Committee being held by a Democrat, such a large request was impossible. Congress did allow $60 million more for the Navy than had been given during Roosevelt's last four years. But the idea that Germany, already racing the British for naval superiority, would divide its fleet to move against America and weaken its home defenses, was seen as absurd. Nevertheless, the arms race continued.

South of the border, U.S. Secretary of State Philander C. Knox mobilized a Navy gunboat, the *Dubuque*, and Marine units to establish a neutral zone in Nicaragua that would assist the rebellion happening there. After the new leader, Adolfo Diaz, gained power, the Marines stayed on to fight the remains of the old guard, who were now the rebels. American forces were withdrawn from the country in November 1912 as Taft was losing his bid for re-election to Woodrow Wilson.

Wilson was chiefly interested in America's internal affairs and had no interest in getting involved in the growing storm about to break in Europe. While Secretary of the Navy Daniels agreed with the commander-in-chief, his assistant, Franklin Delano Roosevelt, had no such qualms. Like his cousin Theodore before him, FDR was willing to act without official permission to protect the country. When Japan protested in 1913 over another California bill prohibiting Asians ineligible for citizenship to own land, Roosevelt sent secret communiqués to Navy commanders outlining plans in case of war. Despite the U.S. Navy's limited presence in the Far East, Roosevelt wanted to take preliminary action, just like Teddy had prepared for against Spain. Cooler heads prevailed, however, and governmental, not gunboat, diplomacy cooled the Japanese ire.

Like Roosevelt before him, Wilson used the Navy as his "big stick," particularly when he could enforce the Monroe Doctrine. In April 1914, Mexico was undergoing another rebellion, this time against the military dictator Gen. Victoriano Huerta. Wilson actively supported the rebels, supplying them with arms and even sending warships to Veracruz and Tampico. Matters almost came to a head when government troops arrested eight U.S. sailors unloading a whaleboat at Tampico. Although they were quickly released and an apology was tendered by the local commander, he declined to fire a 21-gun salute in deference to the Americans. This was the excuse Wilson had been waiting for. When a German arms ship arrived at Veracruz for the dictator, he ordered troops ashore. Four thousand Marines and sailors landed at the city and engaged Huerta's men.

Seventeen Americans and 126 Mexicans died before the city was secured. However, the battle united the Mexican population behind General Huerta, and the naval forces were withdrawn in November.

By this time, the regional wars in Europe had turned into a full-continent brawl, drawing in the major countries. The U.S. military watched and waited to see how its government would respond.

Since the middle of the nineteenth century, U.S. Navy divers have performed a variety of jobs, including underwater reconnaissance, ordinance disposal, construction, search and rescue, and salvage operations. During the Civil War, Adm. David Farragut used divers to clear mines in Mobile Bay before the battle. In 1898, Navy divers examined the wreck of the USS *Maine* at Havana to provide information to the court of inquiry.

In the early twentieth century, military diving teams experimented with different equipment to improve the safety and length of time underwater. In 1915, the divers applied their knowledge in salvaging the submarine F-4, which sank off Honolulu, Hawaii, in 304 feet of water. The divers recovered the submarine and the bodies of the crew, even though they were unknowingly affected by nitrogen narcosis at the time. The operation led to the establishment of the Navy Diving School in Newport, Rhode Island, and the publication of the first *U.S. Navy Diving Manual.*

After World War I, experiments with a helium-nitrogen mixture led to a greater understanding of decompression, as well as advances in deep diving technology.

The attack on Pearl Harbor brought a major effort from Navy divers who participated in underwater search and rescue, salvage, and repair operations. The divers spent 16,000 hours below the harbor's surface on 4,000 dives. Divers also worked in the Pacific theater, recovering intelligence and other valuable information on the Japanese. In 1943, the Underwater Demolition Teams (UDT) were created to remove beach obstacles both in Europe and the Pacific islands.

Since then, Navy divers have participated in salvage, repair, underwater construction, and location and recovery of sunken aircraft. They have experimented with saturation diving, or spending extended time underwater, as an efficient means of executing salvage operations. Along the way, they have set and reset the open-sea diving record, although it is currently held by the French, at 1,643 feet below sea level.

CHAPTER 11

WORLD WAR I

It seemed to begin with the assassination of the heir to the throne of a second-rate empire. But the murder of Archduke Franz Ferdinand set in motion plans that had been laid years before, igniting racial hatreds and enveloping most of European continent in war. The conflict eventually drew in countries that had no initial stake in the war, such as Japan, which was pursuing its own agenda, and finally the United States of America.

SMALL COUNTRIES, BIG BATTLES: THE BALKAN WARS

A series of regional conflicts swept through the Balkan States in 1912 and 1913. Austria-Hungary, Bulgaria, Greece, Montenegro, and Serbia clashed over territory once belonging to the Ottoman Empire, a four-century flowering of culture and science in the Middle East that declined after a series of wars.

Other countries, including Russia, Germany, and France, observed the battles with great interest. Russia had already carved out its portion of the empire but had supported Serbian and Bulgarian advances when necessary. Germany, on the other hand, backed Austria-Hungary's aggression against Serbia. France was concerned that if Austria-Hungary went too far, it would end up fighting Russia, which would bring in Germany and start a continental war.

Serbia and Bulgaria tried to defend themselves against Austria-Hungary by forming the Balkan League in March 1912. Together they planned to take over Macedonia, which had recently revolted against the Ottomans. Greece also joined Serbia and Bulgaria in secret. In October, the Balkan League went to war with the Ottomans and defeated them. The league's push to the Adriatic Sea and almost to Constantinople caused France, Russia, and Austria to mobilize their troops in case the fighting spread further. Germany's Kaiser Wilhelm wanted to declare war against France and Russia immediately but was delayed by Adm. Alfred von Tirpitz, who said his navy wasn't ready.

A council of nations arbitrated the conflict and got Serbia to withdraw from the Adriatic Coast. Austria agreed to abandon its claim to Novibazar, which it had occupied with military troops until 1909. Serbia and Bulgaria were allowed to keep and divide Macedonia.

But the Bulgarians decided they hadn't gotten enough, so they attacked former ally Serbia, causing Greece, the Ottomans, and Romania to ally with the Serbs against them. After Greek troops pushed the Bulgarian forces back from Constantinople, the Serbs reneged on the agreement and refused to leave the Adriatic. This enraged the Austrians, who threatened war if Serbia didn't leave immediately. Wilhelm sided with Austria, trying to drag Russia into a war on the Serbian side, wherein he could enter the fight against them. French and Russian negotiations convinced the Serb forces to withdraw in late 1913. The Balkan War hadn't achieved anything, and the area returned to an uneasy peace.

Kaiser Wilhelm wasn't finished, however. In December 1913, a German military contingent arrived in Constantinople to "advise" the Turkish army. Along with this help, the Germans took command of the local forces guarding the Dardanelle Straits, used by Russia as a conduit from the Black Sea to the Mediterranean. With everyone poised for war, all that was needed was the right incident to set it off.

A SPARK IN THE POWDER KEG

Nothing had happened since the Serbs had left the Adriatic in 1913, and European countries thought everything might be returning to normal.

Even the recent naval buildup between Great Britain and Germany had lessened in recent months.

But others had different plans. Serbian students planned to protest Austria's recent annexation of the province Bosnia-Herzegovina. Their target: Archduke Franz Ferdinand, who was touring the new addition to the Austrian empire, despite so much civil unrest that the Serbian government warned him not to come. Ferdinand persisted and was assassinated in Sarajevo on June 28, 1914.

Austria-Hungary was properly outraged at the crime and demanded impossible concessions from Serbia, among them the suppression of all anti-Austrian misinformation, the dissolution of all nationalist and terrorist groups, and the right to investigate the murder of the archduke with its own representatives. To prevent Russia from joining Serbia's side (even though that was exactly what the Kaiser wanted), Germany pledged full support of Austria.

When the Serbian government said it would agree to all the demands except Austria's participation in the investigation, it was the excuse the empire had been waiting for. Austria broke off diplomatic relations and began preparing for war, backed by Germany.

Russia responded by partially mobilizing its troops to defend Serbia, if necessary. Any hope for a last-minute peace was foiled by German Chancellor Theobald von Bethmann-Hollweg, who sabotaged Britain's efforts to bring the major nations to the negotiating table to discuss limiting the war to Serbia and Austria. Bethmann-Hollweg delayed the British message to Austria, ensuring their course of action.

On June 28, 1914, Austria declared war on Serbia. A little over a month later, Germany declared war on Russia, forcing the involvement of France and Great Britain. The European continent prepared for war.

THE NEUTRAL GIANT: AMERICA AT THE BEGINNING OF WORLD WAR I

At the beginning of World War I, the United States was neutral and comfortable. The nation was stable and growing, and there was no enemy that could possibly move against it. The Japanese-British alliance treaty had been reworded to exclude America from the list of possible targets, so the Pacific was truly peaceful. Britain and Germany, the only real naval threats, were too busy trying to outbuild each other to concern themselves with the United States.

The Navy was very warship-heavy at this time. Of the 173 commissioned vessels in 1911, there were 33 battleships, 50 destroyers, 12 armored cruisers, and 17 protected cruisers, with 1 destroyer tender and 3 scout cruisers. The fleet had no battle cruisers, no ammunition ships, and only one hospital ship and one repair ship. There were 38 submarines but only 2 submarine tenders.

> The backbone of any modern navy until World War II, the battleship was designed to find and destroy other enemy warships, whether alone or in a fleet. Classes of battleships included the following:
>
> **Monitor:** This slow, turreted vessel was primarily designed for coastal defense. Monitors were different from coastal battleships in that they did not engage an enemy at sea; instead, they stayed close to shore and waited for a target to come to them.
>
> **Coast defense battleship:** A step up from the monitor, this warship was also slow but was more heavily armored and armed. It could operate at sea for limited periods.
>
> **Pre-dreadnought:** The class of ship built before the dreadnought-class warship in 1906 (see Chapter 10). Slower than their replacements, these ships still carried a broad mix of armament, small to large, for use against other battleships.
>
> **Dreadnought:** Epitomized by the British ship *Dreadnought* built in 1906, the dreadnought-class was the first to use all big guns in its main batteries. It was solely designed to engage enemy battleships.
>
> **Super dreadnought:** This ship carried guns larger than 11–12 inches. It was rarely used in actual battle.
>
> **Light battleship:** The standard definition of a battleship was any vessel that could survive a hit from one of its own guns. The light battleship wasn't as heavily armed or armored as the bigger warships, but it was still classified as a battleship.

In December 1913, Secretary Daniels asked Congress for two battleships, eight destroyers, three submarines, and the reopening of several closed Navy yards and the expansion of all naval building facilities. The most controversial ruling was the banning of alcohol on all ships as of July 1, 1914. President Wilson signed the bill with little fanfare, probably not even realizing how important those reactivated yards would be in the future. He was unmindful of the European political situation, paying no attention to concerns from his own administration. He even advocated an international arms-reduction summit, which was ignored by just about everybody. But before anything could be done, war broke out.

Wilson moved swiftly afterward, issuing the first of several neutrality announcements on August 4. However, this time other factors to remaining neutral worked against America. In the hundred years since the last major conflict with a European power (the Spanish-American War was too short and one-sided to count), America was now exporting mass quantities of agricultural and manufactured goods, including weapons, around the world. Wilson wanted to follow established policy, remaining uninvolved yet selling goods to every warring country.

However, as it had done before, Great Britain moved to block the import of goods vital to the war effort, including copper, iron ore, rubber, and petroleum. It even planned to use the Royal Navy to intercept American merchant ships. Wilson's administration protested, and the historical cycle continued.

In November, Secretary Daniels went head-to-head with the Navy Board, which advocated building 36 new vessels, including 4 battleships and 16 destroyers, and enlisting 20,000 men. Daniels didn't agree that the Navy was under strength and had the manpower recommendation stricken from the report. He also reduced the request to 18 ships, including 2 battleships, 6 destroyers, and 7 submarines.

Originally a class designed to destroy enemy torpedo boats, the destroyer class's role became more varied as the twentieth century progressed, encompassing antisubmarine and antiaircraft duties. The vessels operate in groups and primarily serve a defensive role in combat.

Destroyer (DD/DDG): The basic destroyer model is a small, fast, heavily armed vessel designed to escort and protect a battle fleet from enemy ships, submarines, or planes. Today DD-class destroyers are antisubmarine ships, and DDG-class destroyers are primarily antiaircraft ships, but each can fulfill a variety of missions.

Frigate (DL/DLG): Designed in the mid-1960s, the frigate ranked between a cruiser and destroyer in size and carried a cruiser's armament on a destroyer's hull.

Destroyer escort (DE): Created in World War II for antisubmarine convoy defense, these mass-produced ships were built quickly and cheaply during the war. Older destroyers were often converted into this class. They were later classified as an ocean escort (DE), then a frigate (FF), and then an escort destroyer (DDE). Usually this was a single-purpose ship, either antisubmarine (ASW), or antiaircraft (AAW). These vessels have served as general-purpose warships in modern times.

THE BATTLE AGAINST THE U-BOATS

Germany and Great Britain were already taking steps to prevent needed supplies from getting to each other. Port blockades were enacted, with London announcing that any ship suspected of trading with the enemy would have its cargo confiscated. Although these steps were useful, they severely hurt American trade, particularly in the South, which sent thousands of tons of cotton to European textile mills.

A major part of Germany's naval strategy was to use its deadly *untersee-booten*, or U-boats, to harass merchant shipping. Soon the assault took a more deadly turn. In February 1915, Germany declared the waters around Great Britain a war zone and stated that suspicious vessels from any nation would be fired upon, since England had been using flags of neutral nations to move ships through the area. Over the course of the war, 274 U-boats would sink 6,596 merchant vessels from around the world.

The announcement threatened American neutrality, since ships flying the Stars and Stripes had been exempt from U-boat attacks. Three months later, the Germans made good on their threat on May 1, when a U-boat torpedoed the U.S. oil tanker the *Gulflight*, killing three Americans. One week later, the British ocean liner *Lusitania*, which was carrying an illegal cargo of rifle ammunition and artillery fuzes in addition to its 1,959 passengers, was sunk by the *U-20*, killing 1,198 people, including 128 Americans.

The United States was outraged. Wilson demanded reparation and guaranteed such an event wouldn't happen again. He also called for increased Navy appropriation bills to be prepared for Congress in November. Assistant Secretary of the Navy Franklin Roosevelt was happy to comply. The bill asked for $285 million for, among other things, 4 battleships and 4 battle cruisers, enlarging the current fleet by 186 vessels by 1921. Despite the firestorm raging in Europe, the bill was divided in Congress, supported by states on both coasts and opposed by Midwest and Southern states. Wilson got no support from Secretary of the Navy Daniels, who couldn't even contemplate preparing for war.

The cruiser fell between a battleship and a destroyer, and it often combined elements of both. The Royal Navy defined a heavy cruiser-class vessel as any ship carrying 6.1- to 8-inch guns. The vessels often were used in fire support roles and escort duty.

Armored cruiser, or first-class cruiser (also known as a heavy cruiser) (ACR): The largest cruiser class, these ships serve both offensive and defensive purposes, from hunting enemy commerce to acting as screens for other fleet units against enemy ships.

Battle cruiser (BC): The battle cruiser was a high-speed battleship, sacrificing armor and guns for speed.

Large cruiser (CB): This subclass of cruiser was created in the late 1930s and early 1940s. It was generally a larger version of the heavy cruiser, with 11- to 12-inch guns and armor to protect them against a standard cruiser's shells.

Semiarmored cruiser: This class tried to strike a balance between the armored cruiser and the protected cruiser, but it accomplished neither. This class saw only limited action and was phased out quickly.

Protected cruiser, second-class cruiser, light cruiser (CL): A smaller version of the heavy cruiser (defined by the Royal Navy as any ship with 6-inch guns and smaller), these ships did escort duty and served as commerce raiders, scouts, and defensive screens for larger cruiser fleets.

Guided missile cruiser (CG): Developed during the Cold War, the two types of missile cruisers are either offensive antiship and antisubmarine cruisers or defensive antiaircraft vessels. A few cruisers have been built with both types of armament, but these are the exception rather than the rule.

Third-class cruiser, sheathed cruiser (PG): This smaller ship was designed for secondary coastal defense in areas where a naval presence was required but there was no immediate threat. These cruisers were slower and more lightly armed and armored than a normal cruiser.

Scout cruiser (SC): These small, very fast cruisers served as scout ships for a battle fleet. This class was combined with the light cruiser class by the 1930s.

Antiaircraft cruiser (CLAA): Essentially a large destroyer, this cruiser often led destroyer-class ships in battle. The class often refers to modern cruisers that have been commissioned for the antiaircraft role.

Wilson toured the Midwest in January and February 1916 to gain support for his plan, and he coined the demand for "the greatest Navy in the world." After a bit of compromising, with a couple of battleships replaced by battle cruisers, the proposal moved forward.

On the day the first version of the bill passed Congress, British and German fleets met in the Battle of Jutland, with heavy damage inflicted on the type of battle cruisers Congress had been advocated building. With this distressing news came a new bill, passed on July 21, 1916, that added 10 battleships, 6 battle cruisers, 10 scout cruisers, 50 destroyers, 9 fleet submarines, and 58 coast submarines to the fleet. The bill also compressed the five-year building plan into three years.

Since 1916 was an election year, Wilson ran using the slogan "He kept us out of war." He won by 3.3 percent and assisted with a peace offering to Britain from Germany. The British terms were too strict; the German terms were too lenient. Peace would not be achieved that year, although Wilson used the brief negotiations to announce his idea for an international league of nations. Then British cryptoanalysts intercepted a coded message from Germany's foreign secretary, Arthur Zimmerman, to its Washington ambassador, Count Johann von Bernstorff. It was the infamous Zimmerman telegram, and that more than anything brought America into the war.

> The missive from Germany, known as the Zimmerman telegram, stated that if the peace talks weren't successful, total U-boat warfare would start and continue until Germany was victorious. The other item in the telegram that swayed America consisted of orders for Germany's ambassador to Mexico, Heinrich von Eckhardt to convince Mexico to join the war on Germany's side; if they won, Mexico would get back the lands it had lost in the Mexican War.

On April 6, 1917, the United States declared war on Germany. Adm. William Sims headed to Europe to oversee the American naval force. Upon learning that U-boats had sunk almost one million tons of British shipping since February, Sims requested as many destroyers as could be spared be sent to Britain immediately.

Back in Washington, the general board and Chief of Naval Operations were surprised by the appeal. Concerned that this would not be America's last war, they didn't want to squander the fleet in a battle to help Great

Britain. If the island nation fell, they feared Germany, Austria, and Japan would begin a campaign of world domination, with only the United States to oppose them.

A better way had to be found to combat the U-boat menace. The convoy, a group of merchant ships escorted by destroyers and other escort ships, was tried and was instantly successful. From a high of 835,000 tons of merchant shipping lost in April 1917, the figure had dropped to 250,000 tons by November.

In July, Secretary Daniels approved a building program that swelled the fleet's destroyers to 273. To further combat the U-boats, the U.S. Navy created the submarine chaser, a swift 120-foot boat designed to chase and destroy submarines. Eventually, more than 400 submarine chasers were built, with many sailing across the Atlantic to hunt the Germans.

The first official sinking of an enemy submarine by a U.S. warship occurred on November 17, 1917, when the destroyer the *Fanning* encountered the *U-58* while on escort duty with her sister ship, the *Nicholson*. Spotting the periscope of the German submarine, the destroyer dropped depth charges over the enemy's last sighted position. Nicholson joined in the bombing when the hull of the submarine broke the surface, with sailors pouring out of the hold in surrender. The American ships managed to offload 40 prisoners before the submarine sank, apparently ordered by the commanding officer. The sinking of the U-58 was also the only combat between a U.S. ship and a U-boat in World War I.

Meanwhile, the destroyers stationed in Britain grew from 6 to 34. The warships ferried American soldiers across the ocean and also escorted cargo and troop ships. They helped execute Roosevelt's plan to salt the North Sea with thousands of mines, formerly deemed impossible by the Royal Navy, who claimed that 400,000 mines would be needed. But the Navy Bureau of Ordnance had just created the antenna mine, which had a much greater range than contact mines, the only kind available in Britain.

Britain agreed to the idea in November 1917. By March 1918, mines were being completed at Inverness and Ingordon at the rate of 2,000 per day. When they were finished, 70,000 American and British mines littered the North Sea in a 35-mile swath, with each square mile containing about a dozen mines on average. The North Sea minefield was known to have sunk at least six U-boats, and the psychological edge it gave the Allies was profound. The mining of the North Sea remains one of the great naval engineering feats of the twentieth century.

> Before the antenna mine, underwater mines had to make contact with a ship's hull to detonate. But Adm. Ralph Earle's antenna mine contained a float with a 70-foot wire attached to the body of the mine itself. When a ship hit any part of the wire, it completed an electric circuit and detonated the mine's 300 pounds of TNT. This new mine had a greater range and allowed fewer mines to cover a larger area.

EARLY NAVAL AVIATION

The other innovation that had profound effects on warfare was the development of naval aviation, including the first crude attempts at aircraft carriers.

Using airplanes for combat was mankind's goal even before a reliable airplane was invented. On March 28, 1898, Theodore Roosevelt reviewed the performance of an experimental model flying machine developed by Professor Samuel Langley of the Smithsonian Institution, and commented that it should be evaluated for military purposes. A month later, the Army-Navy board suggested that airplanes could serve three purposes: reconnaissance, communication, and aerial bombardment. Before these ideas could be explored, America went to war with Spain. The aviation project was shelved, although the Army gave Langley, who was never able to put a man in the air, a $50,000 grant.

In 1903, the Wright brothers, Wilbur and Orville, stunned the world with their flights at Kitty Hawk. Eventually, the Wrights sold their Flyer to the Army and to foreign countries, including France and Italy. But the Navy didn't renew its interest in the airplane for several years, despite the advances being made in aeronautical technology. The closest it came was a recommendation by the chief of the Navy Bureau of Equipment to purchase planes that could fly from a ship to carry a wireless telegraph aloft.

The next step in naval aviation happened on November 14, 1910, when civilian pilot Eugene Ely took off from a ship, the cruiser *Birmingham*, and successfully landed on shore. Three months later, Ely performed the first successful landing of an aircraft on a ship, the cruiser the *Pennsylvania*.

Tragically, Ely was killed in a crash a few months later, but he had proven the viability of landing an airplane on a ship.

(Naval Historical Center)

Civilian pilot Eugene Ely takes off from the USS Birmingham *on the first carrier-launched airplane flight in the world.*

Aviation, naval or otherwise, was the subject of intense interest in other countries, whether official or not. Germany began developing a branch of military aviation in 1909. In 1912, Japan converted the merchant ship the *Wakamiya* to carry airplanes. Britain dabbled in airplanes as well but practically abandoned the idea, much to the consternation of both American and British pilots.

The gap widened swiftly. By the next year Germany had 14 military airships, while Britain had only 1. Regardless of the lack of official support, British airmen continued to create history. On April 23, 1917, two airplanes were launched from a ship's catapult; each made a 50-mile flight. One even carried a passenger, the first time that was done on a ship as well.

Not fully utilized until World War II, the carrier group consisted of the following classes:

Fleet carrier (CV): The general model of aircraft carrier, it was designed for various missions, including engaging enemy targets in the air, on the surface, or underwater. Carriers are always the main vessel in an offensive task force. This designation was used from 1927 onward.

Large carrier (CVB): The large carrier was a fleet carrier with heavier arms and armor. This desgination was used from 1945-1952.

Attack carrier (CVA): This carrier variant evolved during the Cold War. It carried nuclear attack aircraft rather than multipurpose aircraft. The designation is primarily given to indicate nuclear capability, and was used from 1952-1975.

Light carrier (CVL): This smaller carrier carried the full range of multipurpose aircraft, but fewer of them. The CVL was designed to be a fast attack vessel. The hull design was based on that of a warship, rather than that of a merchant ship, like the other designations. Light carriers were operational from 1943-59.

Antisubmarine carrier (CVS): This carrier's purpose is to carry and deploy antisubmarine aircraft. Based on a modified CV design, they were deployed from 1953 to the mid-1970s.

Escort carrier (CVE): This smaller class of lightly armed and armored carrier was designed to escort convoys. These ships were originally designated as auxiliary (AVG) vessels, which was switched to ACV in 1942, and finally changed to CVE in 1943 until 1959.

By this time, the U.S. Navy had become interested in the airplane again and began constructing naval air stations and schools at Hampton Roads, Long Island, Miami, Pensacola, and San Francisco. A naval aircraft factory was erected in Philadelphia, and the American Naval Flying Corps was launched. By the end of World War I, it boasted 25,000 men, many of them in Europe, with more than 500 Curtiss flying boats.

Naval aviation was not perfected in time for World War I, but like much military technology, it was pushed forward by the demands of the conflict. Although airplanes were still used more as an adjunct to land campaigns, and although the perceived usefulness of the ship-launched aircraft would not be realized for 20 more years, it was still a bold step forward. It also helped set the stage for aerial combat in World War II, including Pearl Harbor.

THE END OF THE WAR

Hundreds of thousands of Americans reinforced the British and French troops in Europe, and a series of offensives soon had the combined Austrian-German forces on the run. By November 1918, a shattered Austria begged for peace. The treaty reached with the Austrians on November 3 demobilized Austrian armed forces, broke the military alliance Austria had with Germany, and forced the country to withdraw from all disputed territory.

With the alliance crumbling and its army in retreat, Germany suffered a revolution, forcing the Kaiser to flee the country. A German delegation traveled to France to discuss terms of armistice. On November 11, 1918, the armistice was signed, and all hostile action ceased at 11 A.M.

Although the Navy didn't participate in any major combat actions, its role in facilitating land operations and assisting with the defense of Great Britain was invaluable to the Allies' cause. By the time the armistice was signed, the Navy had escorted millions of tons of ships and cargo across the Atlantic and ferried almost two million American soldiers to Europe, all without losing a single transport ship or life.

American military power was seen as the deciding factor in the war, much to the worry of Great Britain, which became concerned that, if it chose to, America might expand its own borders—and with such a powerful Army and Navy, no country on earth would be able to stop it.

For the first 120 years, the Navy had no award system for gallantry because awards were thought to be a throwback to the empire America had left behind. In 1905, Theodore Roosevelt created a series of Army badges signifying participation in various campaigns. The Navy followed suit in 1908, authorizing awards to be retroactively awarded as far back as the Civil War.

Three major medals are awarded in the Navy, all of which were codified after World War I:

- **The Navy Medal of Honor:** America's oldest awarded military decoration was originally conceived by Secretary of the Navy Gideon Wells in 1861. At first the armed forces' highest honor was awarded only to enlisted men who had shown "conspicuous gallantry and intrepidity at the risk of life, above and beyond the call of duty." In 1915, legislation was passed making naval officers eligible for the award as well. In 1919 the "Tiffany Cross version was created, ostensibly for non-combat valor, and was also awarded in peace time as well. In 1942, the criteria for the award was modified, making it for combat valor only. Since the Civil War, 750 Navy sailors and officers have received the Medal of Honor.

- **The Navy Cross:** The second-highest decoration in the Navy, it is presented to a person exhibiting great heroism that doesn't justify the Medal of Honor. However, the act or execution of duty must be performed in the presence of great danger or at great personal risk. When created in 1919, the Navy Cross was the third-highest honor, under the Distinguished Service Medal. In 1942, that order was changed, and the Navy Cross has held its distinction ever since. Since World War I, 4,170 Navy personnel have received the Navy Cross.

- **The Navy Distinguished Service Medal:** The third-highest Navy award is given to Navy or Marine personnel who distinguish themselves by "exceptionally meritorious service to the Government in a duty of great responsibility." Thousands of naval personnel have been awarded this honor since it was created.

CHAPTER 12

AN UNEASY PEACE

The years after World War I fell into a pattern, with periods of naval disarmament followed by disagreement on how to keep parity among the navies of the world's strongest countries. The Treaty of Versailles was the best compromise that could be worked out among the participants of World War I, particularly in regard to the captured German fleet. While Great Britain and America agreed that sinking the ships would be in their best interests, France and Italy pushed to have the fleet divided among the victorious nations, thereby bolstering their own smaller navies.

German naval officers had other plans. On June 21, 1919, the crews of 66 ships of the defunct German Navy, consisting of 10 battleships, 5 battle cruisers, 5 light cruisers, and 46 torpedo boats, scuttled their own vessels anchored at Scapa Flow, in northern Britain, in a show of contempt. Although this was an embarrassment for the British, they and the American governments privately rejoiced, since they didn't have to worry about arming less-powerful countries now.

However, as President Wilson sailed to Europe to lobby for the creation of his international peace organization the League of Nations, countries around the world were already rearming. Wilson's points—which included total freedom of the seas for all nations—were met with skepticism among the world's politicians. Great Britain, in particular, its national pride already stung by American assistance in World War I, said it would spend every last shilling to have the world's strongest navy. But with a war-decimated economy, it was in no shape to outspend America, even when the U.S. fleet scrapped more than 400 ships, including 38 battleships, 87 light cruisers, and 300 destroyers and torpedo boats. But America also reinstated its 1916 naval building plan, which had been suspended by the war. Wilson, pushing for a repeat of the 1916 bill for 1919, told England that if it joined the League of Nations, he would cancel the new bill. London grudgingly agreed, and Wilson's dream moved forward.

But the United States Congress would not give Wilson's proposal the unilateral approval he wanted, and America did not join the league. His health shattered by the past year's efforts, Wilson ended his term a semi-invalid.

POST WORLD WAR I CONFLICT

At the same time, trouble was brewing in the Far East. Although in 1917 America and Japan had revised the Open Door Treaty, originally created by Secretary of State John Hay in 1899 so that Japanese and American interests in China would be respected by the other nation, it was just a temporary solution to a larger problem. Japan was already making plans to extend its power, and no treaty was going to stand in their way.

In October 1917, the Bolshevik Revolution began in Russia. The ruling government fought back, assisted by Allied forces in northern Russia and the city of Vladivostok in Siberia. The intervention by the Allied units in northern Russia, including a naval contingent led by Rear Adm. Newton A. McCully, ended in 1919 with the evacuation of Archangelsk and Murmansk, with no real progress made. The other involvement by the Allies was a joint British-Japanese-American effort that failed, with each side following its own agenda for the area. Great Britain wanted the Bolsheviks stopped so Russia could concentrate on the Germans. The Japanese wanted to quell the uprising, fearing a revolutionist nation so close. The United States thought Russia should settle its internal squabble alone and was there to keep an eye on the other two nations.

When Japan landed 70,000 troops at Vladivostok by October 1918, America feared the Japanese would take more Russian territory and kept soldiers in the region until 1920. But when the Americans left, the Japanese stayed, retaining control of portions of the Siberian coast and the oil-producing island of Sakhalin. The Siberian intervention created more tension among Russia, Great Britain, Japan, and the United States, and would fuel the future conflict in the Pacific during World War II.

The tension grew worse as representatives from Great Britain, France, Italy, and Japan met in America for the Washington Conference of 1921–1922, called by new President Warren G. Harding to limit the naval arms buildup. After protracted and fierce negotiation, the countries ratified several treaties in attendance, to be abided by until 1936:

- **Five-Power Treaty Number 1:** This specified the ratio of capital ship tonnage that each nation could have; it was known as the 5:3:3:1.67:1.67 ratio. For every 5 tons possessed by America, Great Britain and Japan were to have 3 tons, and France and Italy were to have 1.67 tons. The maximum vessel displacement was set at 35,000 tons; the maximum gun caliber was set at 16 inches for capital ships and 8 inches for all others. The United States and British allocations were set at 135,000 carrier tons; Japan was approved for 81,000 carrier tons, and France and Italy each were allotted 60,000 carrier tons. A moratorium also was established on the construction of capital ships for 10 years (carriers were classified as experimental ships, not capital ones).

- **Five-Power Treaty Number 2:** This extended the rules of warfare for surface ships to submarines and outlawed the use of poison gas. Although this treaty was agreed to in principle, it was never signed by France, rendering it ineffective.

- **The Four-Power Treaty:** America, France, Great Britain, and Japan all agreed to respect the other countries' bases and possessions in the Pacific Ocean, with naval defenses in the Pacific to be maintained at their current level. The United States and Great Britain also agreed not to continue fortifying holdings within striking distance of Japan.

THE U.S. NAVY TAKES TO THE AIR

Military aviation received a huge boost with a June 1919 report by the Navy's General Board advocating increased development of naval aviation that could "accompany the fleet in all parts of the world." A month earlier, Navy Lt. Cmdr. A. C. Read accomplished the first trans-Atlantic flight in the NC-4 flying boat, designed by Glenn Curtis. But to put airplanes in every corner of the globe required a ship the Navy didn't have yet: the aircraft carrier. A project had been started to convert an 11,500-ton Navy collier ship, the *Jupiter*—but the first American aircraft carrier, renamed the *Langley*, wouldn't be finished until 1922.

In June 1921, the Bureau of Aeronautics was organized, with Rear Adm. William A. Moffet chosen as its first leader. In 1922, he advocated building three smaller carriers so the United States could maximize the entire 135,000 tons of displacement allowed. Two years later, a special Board of Inquiry took the first real steps to integrating airplanes and the Navy: It allocated $20 million for an airplane-construction program and another 23,000-ton aircraft carrier, and it recommended the assignation of Navy personnel to aviation duty.

Still, it took the prodding and cajoling of Army Brig. Gen. William Mitchell (see *Alpha Bravo Delta Guide to the U.S. Air Force*) to prove the value of the airplane versus capital ships. In July 1921, after a mock test of Navy planes dropping water-filled bombs on dummy warships, Mitchell was supposed to attack the 22,800-ton *Ostfriesland*, a prize from World War I, with one live bomb at a time so that Navy observers could see the damage afterward. Instead, his squadron of Navy and U.S. Marine aircraft dropped 67 bombs, scoring 16 direct hits and sinking the ship. Although he got in trouble for his deviation from the plan, he proved that an airplane could sink a battleship.

Mitchell's demonstration changed the Navy's thinking about the strategic value of carrier-based airplanes. It was obvious that America needed true carriers, not just a floating runway. Although the *Langley* had served its purpose in training both pilots and naval engineers in the art of launching and landing planes at sea, the next step was already underway. In April and October of 1925, the carriers the *Saratoga* and the *Lexington* were launched. Once again, the U.S. Navy stood at the forefront of naval technology (see Appendix C).

From then on, the Navy also embraced aviation for its own sake. On May 9, 1926, Navy Cmdr. Richard E. Byrd claimed to be the first man to fly an airplane over the North Pole. He did the same at the South Pole on November 28, 1928 (see Appendix B).

But as advanced as the carriers were, the Navy felt it didn't have enough of them. In 1929, U.S. carrier tonnage stood at 78,700, with the Royal Navy boasting 107,550 tons and Japan wielding 67,000 tons. One area that the United States did lead was the number of aircraft it could launch, with 250 planes taking part in field exercises that year, compared to Great Britain's 150 carrier-based planes total. But international conflict and chilly relations stalled carrier fleet expansion for several years.

UNCOMFORTABLE NEIGHBORS—THE UNITED STATES AND THE REST OF THE WORLD

Relations between America and potential enemies on both coasts remained chilly throughout the 1920s. In the Pacific, the United States antagonized Japan again in 1924 by passing new laws that effectively stopped Japanese immigrants from entering the country. In 1926, the fleet held a major naval exercise in the Pacific Ocean; both developments did not sit well with Tokyo.

Across the Atlantic, the United States and Great Britain were glaring at each other not only because of the naval buildup, but also because England had staked out the majority of bases near oil resources around the world, giving it a distinct advantage in powering the Royal Navy.

In 1927, matters came to a head with a second naval conference aimed at blocking some of the loopholes in the Washington Conference treaty. This time, however, the United States and Great Britain could not agree on anything (Japan had actually suggested that everyone cease building warships altogether, which was met with predictable skepticism by America and Britain). The two countries could not agree on the cruiser issue, either in what the maximum displacement should be or how many each side should have. After more than two months of debate, the summit ended with nothing gained.

Before another attempt could be made, the Great Depression engulfed America, and its ripples spread around the world, especially in Europe, which was still dealing with rebuilding from World War I. With the crash came Herbert Hoover, who, with England's Prime Minister Ramsay

MacDonald, worked together to hold another world naval power summit in 1930. This time the United States and Great Britain solved the cruiser issue, dividing them into two classes grouped by armament (one with 8-inch guns and one with 6-inch guns). For Japan, which felt that the Washington treaty ratio had handicapped its ability to defend itself, the ratios of tonnage were set at 5:3 for the larger class and 10:7 for the smaller class. Japan also gained an equal amount of submarine tonnage to what the United States and Great Britain had. The capital ship-building ban was also extended for six more years.

Back in the States, America tightened its belt as Hoover slashed spending in every department, cutting the destroyer program in half in 1932 and suspending all naval construction for 1933.

Meanwhile, already upset at the return of Sakhalin Island to Russia and doubly stung by what was (correctly) seen as American trickery in the Washington Treaty, the Japanese began its own expansion campaign, invading Manchuria in September 1931. In January 1932, the Japanese stepped up their attacks on China, including bombing Shanghai. Although the League of Nations investigated both incidents, the toothless organization could do nothing about either.

Elsewhere in the Pacific, in a doom-laden foreshadowing of what would happen nine years later, Adm. Harry Yarnell used two carriers and several destroyers to launch a simulated and totally successful surprise attack on Pearl Harbor.

The year 1932 was tumultuous for several countries. Germany and Japan installed new governments, and a young firebrand named Adolph Hitler began his rise to power, becoming chancellor by the following year. The United States was still keeping an eye on Japan and updated its war plans accordingly, in case the necessity ever arose. In the fall, Americans chose their own next president, Franklin Delano Roosevelt.

With the new president came several changes. The Navy had been suffering as a whole since the end of World War I, hindered by presidents and secretaries of the Navy that either were against fleet expansion and upkeep, or, in the case of Hoover, were restricted by lack of funds. Because he had served as assistant secretary of the Navy—and thought much like his cousin Teddy—Roosevelt understood that America needed a sound

Navy. One of his first acts in office was to promote his "New Deal," complete with increased governmental spending. With one executive order, passed as part of the national Industrial Recovery Act of 1933, the Navy received $238 million over three years for the construction of 32 vessels. Over the next 36 months, the Navy gained 4 cruisers, 2 carriers (the *Yorktown* and the *Enterprise*), 16 gunboats, 4 submarines, and 2 gunboats. It was a promising start for the Navy, the new administration, and, although no one knew it yet, the world.

Roosevelt had a strong ally in Carl Vinson, the chair of the House Naval Affairs Committee. Vinson held the view that a fleet composed of all the technology there was to offer would prove most useful. Despite strong opposition from parties that thought a naval buildup would lead to war (much like opponents had since the Revolutionary War), Vinson spearheaded a bill that called for a system of eventual ship replacement, ensuring that America would always stay in the lead as new technology became available.

Relations between the United States and Japan remained cold. However in 1934 Japan notified the other powers that at the end of 1936, it would no longer abide by the treaty boundaries. Japan had already been violating the treaty by building ships of larger displacement than was stated in the talks. In 1937, the country began building a new class of superbattleships (the flagship of the class, the *Yamato*, weighed an astonishing 72,000 tons). The warships were to be armed with the latest innovation, the 18-inch gun, which was 30 percent more powerful than the 16-inch gun.

Despite domestic pressure to move the annual naval exercises out of the Pacific (since the Japanese might have interpreted them as a not-so-subtle warning), the Navy held its maneuvers near the International Date Line as scheduled. With the depression worsening, the last thing the U.S. public wanted was to get involved in another conflict. When the Nye report was made public in June 1935, Americans' feelings against war intensified.

In 1935–1936, hearings were held to report the findings of a committee that had been investigating alleged improper sales tactics by munitions manufacturers. What they had found was shocking. U.S. arms companies had been selling weapons systems and ammunition to foreign countries, often supplying two countries fighting each other. They had enlisted the help of governmental departments, including the War Department and the Navy, to support such foreign sales. Naval missions near South America had apparently inadvertently assisted arms dealers by being "misinterpreted by neighboring countries as support of any military plans of the nations to which they are attached," and causing those countries to purchase more arms to defend themselves, primarily from American arms manufacturers.

Disgusted by the idea that American companies were profiting from foreign wars, the nation became more isolationist. Congress provided measures to make the arms deals more difficult, granting the president power to block arms shipments to any country he deemed belligerent in 1935. Other measures were designed to reinforce American neutrality, including the 1936 act forbidding loans to belligerent countries. However, the arms dealers won a limited victory in 1937 when a law was passed allowing belligerent countries to purchase arms for cash.

In November 1937, Roosevelt rode America's uneasy feeling about the state of the world to a second term. Despite the growing qualms about war, including the outbreak of the Sino-Japanese War in October, he could not free up more money for the Navy.

Rear Adm. Harry Yarnell advised using the bases and carriers in the Pacific to slowly strangle Japan with the help of European allies. He felt that airplanes would be the key to controlling enemy traffic. On December 12, the Japanese proved him right by bombing and destroying the U.S. gunboat the *Panay*, which had been escorting three American oil tankers. Two Americans died and 30 were wounded in the attack. Back home, the outrage was real but brief. Twelve days later, the Japanese apologized for the incident, which Secretary of State Cordell Hull grudgingly accepted.

Roosevelt's attention was focused on what he saw as the larger problem—Germany. He sent Capt. Royal Ingersoll to Great Britain to begin repairing relations between the two countries, or at least the two navies. The president also tried to persuade Congress to increase naval building by 20 percent in January 1938, asking for 3 battleships, 2 carriers, 9 light cruisers, 23 destroyers, 9 submarines, and 950 naval aircraft. With conflict threatening to break out no matter what America's stance was, the bill required only minimal handling by Senator Vinson to get it passed in the House. The president signed the bill into law on May 7, just a few months before Hitler's troops took the Sudetenland. Still America watched and waited, letting Europe deal with the aggressive Germans.

CHAPTER 12: AN UNEASY PEACE

When no official repercussions came (the Munich Conference actually allowed Germany to keep the territory it had just taken), Japan stepped up its war with China. Americans observing the Far East conflict sent word that once Japan was done with its neighbor, it would most likely turn its attention to the United States, with an attack on Pearl Harbor an unlikely but distinct possibility. Two years later, this prediction came true in the most horrifying attack possible.

CHAPTER 13

WORLD WAR II

World War II was both the beginning and the end of an era for America, the Navy, and the world. It was the last war with fleet-versus-fleet combat, with the battles at Coral Sea, Midway, and Leyte Gulf showcasing the power of capital ships, particularly aircraft carriers. When it was over, America was the lone superpower standing amid the ruins of Europe, Russia, and Japan.

Yet the enemy also began and ended an era as well. Japan proved the airplane's true military power in its devastating sneak attack on Pearl Harbor. Germany reinvented land war with its mechanized *blitzkriegs* against Europe. And imperialism, already in decline, was dealt its final blow in the years after the war.

RISING FROM THE ASHES

After World War I, Germany had been severely punished by the Treaty of Versailles and reduced to a fraction of its former power. Stripped of its military and colonies, the Germans also owed reparations to other European countries, despite having no viable economy. Excluding it from the League of Nations isolated the nation further, fostering resentment in the populace. The German government was unable to rebuild, make war payments, and handle the Great Depression, which had now spread worldwide.

The country found what it thought was its savior in Adolph Hitler. A mesmerizing, power-hungry, and politically savvy Austrian, Hitler led the National Socialist German Workers Party—the Nazis. The political party remained on the fringes until the depression in 1929, when Hitler gained support by appealing to the German public's national pride while allying with businessmen, politicians, and military officers. In 1933, he was named chancellor by the ineffective president, Paul von Hindenburg.

Hitler solidified his hold on the country, nullifying articles of the German constitution and holding elections to install his own people. Passage of the infamous "Enabling Act" gave Hitler even more power, letting him pass laws without the consent of the legislative body. His rise from minor politician to dictator of Germany was almost complete.

In the mid-1930s, Germany enjoyed a rebirth in both nation and spirit. Hitler utilized the relatively untouched German lands and began many public programs, including the Autobahn, the national system of roads. He built schools in almost every town and village, and revitalized industry. Technological interest was also high, with German scientists soon leading the way in electronics, armaments, and aeronautics.

Once Germany was back on its feet, and with the majority of the populace under his control, Hitler began planning the conquest of Europe and then the world. In 1935, he announced that Germany would no longer abide by the tenets of the Treaty of Versailles. In 1936, German soldiers entered the Rhineland, which had previously been off-limits, and began fortifying it. France and Great Britain complained but wanted the United States to take the lead in disciplining Germany. But rocked by the Great Depression and sick at heart over its own warmongering arms companies (see Chapter 12), America had no interest in getting involved in another European confrontation.

In 1938, representatives of Great Britain, Germany, France, and Italy met in Munich to attempt to avert a war in Europe. England and France agreed to give the Sudetenland to Germany, opening the rest of Czechoslovakia to invasion. They hoped to contain Germany by allowing it to take portions of other countries, practicing a lesser form of *laissez-faire* politics. Hitler promised that he would not seek any more lands in Europe, which was a blatant lie. After the Munich conference, he was even more confident that the other European nations wouldn't oppose him.

In March 1939, Hitler completed his takeover of Czechoslovakia, despite that country's ignored pleas for help to both France and Great Britain. Emboldened by his success, the dictator kept going.

Before continuing his conquest, Hitler had to neutralize two potential enemies—Italy and Russia. He ordered troops into Austria, which Italy needed for its own continued survival, and forced the Italian leader, Benito Mussolini, into an unequal alliance. As for Russia, while the two countries had been at war just over two decades ago, the new governments now thought an alliance would be useful. Although both were still wary (and each planned to use the other for its own ends), Germany and Russia agreed to a nonaggression pact in 1939.

The stunning alliance could be interpreted only one way—Germany was on the warpath. As Hitler demanded the return of the "Polish Corridor," a strip of land dividing Germany that gave Poland access to a seaport at Danzig, Great Britain and France mobilized for war, telling Hitler that if he moved against Poland, they would defend it.

On September 1, 1939, Hitler's army crossed the Polish border. Two days later, Great Britain declared war on Germany. World War II had begun.

THE UNITED STATES AT THE START OF WORLD WAR II

America, partially recovering from the depression with the help of President Roosevelt's "New Deal," publicly shunned the European crisis. But the government and the Navy saw what was coming, and Roosevelt gathered support for a requested $4 billion construction plan. Adm. Harold R. Stark spoke to Congress about the necessity of such a bill, seeing the fleet strengthened by new 45,000-ton and 53,000-ton battleships, along with fleet carriers, which would enable the Navy to fight on even terms in the Pacific, should it come to that. In the end, 257 vessels were approved, including 13 battleships, 6 aircraft carriers, 32 cruisers, 101 destroyers, and 39 submarines. This was passed just a few days after Congress had approved a general increase of 11 percent in naval shipbuilding.

Roosevelt also cemented a friendship with Great Britain, increased America's ability to defend itself in the Caribbean and Central America, and sent a clear message to England's enemies all at the same time. In exchange for 50 old destroyers, the United States gained 99-year leases on bases in the Caribbean Sea and posts in Newfoundland and Bermuda. Although Britain was pleased by the deal, London wanted the U.S. to do more. The soon-to-be prime minister Winston Churchill asked America to enter the war on the side of the Allies, including posting the American fleet to Singapore as a show of strength to Japan. Roosevelt refused but did move the fleet to Pearl Harbor, Hawaii, over the objections of Chief Naval Officer William D. Leahy and commander in chief of the Pacific Fleet Adm. James O. Richardson. Both men felt that the fleet was too vulnerable to enemy attack at Hawaii. Roosevelt replaced Richardson with Adm. Husband Kimmel. His actions set up the catalyst that brought America into the war—the Japanese bombing raid on Pearl Harbor.

In the Atlantic, the sinking of the SS *Athenia* on September 4, 1939, killing 28 of the 316 Americans on board, led Roosevelt to form a naval "neutrality patrol," to sail the western Atlantic from Canada to the Azores and report any hostile action against other European vessels. Roosevelt was unable to do anything more, however, when public sentiment was still against entering the war. He declared a state of national emergency on June 27, 1940, and strengthened embargoes against aggressor countries, including cutting off machinery and fuel shipments to Japan.

In the Atlantic, U.S. military ships began to come under fire from German U-boats in 1940–1941, which grew bolder as America's fleet strength increased. Roosevelt also ordered U.S. destroyers to escort British convoys, leaving them open to U-boat attacks. The first Navy ship attacked was the USS *Kearny*, torpedoed by a U-boat on October 17, 1941. Although it was seriously damaged, the warship got to Reykjavik, Iceland. Eleven men were killed, the first American casualties of the war. On October 31, the destroyer *Reuben James* was sunk by a U-boat torpedo, killing 115 officers and sailors.

Even after these incidents, Americans didn't want to enter the war. Roosevelt, not wanting to be the aggressor, preferred to respond to Hitler's declaration of hostilities against the United States. But Hitler gave orders to spare American shipping, reasoning that as long as he didn't antagonize the United States, America wouldn't enter the war.

This didn't mean the United States wasn't preparing for conflict. The two-ocean battle plan, code-named "Plan Dog," called for a powerful force in the Atlantic, where Roosevelt and the Navy felt the greatest threat lay, and a smaller one in the Pacific to move against Japan, if necessary. On February 1, 1941, the Atlantic Fleet was officially created, under the command of Adm. Ernest J. King, and was assigned to patrol the waters west of 26° west longitude. Roosevelt also got Congress to pass the "Lend-Lease Act," which enabled him to sell, lend, or exchange war materiel to any country he felt was vital to the defense of the United States. Great Britain and Russia soon began receiving billions of dollars in supplies and vehicles.

In September 1940, Japan became the third Axis country when it signed the Tripartite Pact with Germany and Italy, stating that if one of the three countries were attacked, the other two would come to its aid. Japan also negotiated a five-year nonaggression pact with Russia in February 1941. The treaty eased Joseph Stalin's concerns (he already suspected Germany would betray him) about the possibility of fighting a two-front war against Germany and Japan.

No, Japan was after a bigger goal—sole dominion of the Pacific Ocean and Southeast Asia—but first it had to remove the U.S. presence. To do this, the Japanese Navy launched two nearly simultaneous attacks, one on the U.S. forces in the Philippines, and the second against Pearl Harbor.

AWAKENING A SLEEPING GIANT—THE ATTACK ON PEARL HARBOR

On the surface, a surprise attack by Japan seemed to be a good decision. Japan already had the largest fleet in the Pacific (bigger than the American, British, and Dutch naval forces combined), and a devastating strike against the main U.S. Navy base could cripple, if not destroy, the American presence there. It would also allow Japan to take the desperately needed oil-rich Dutch East India Islands. When the U.S. rejected Japanese overtures to lift the trade embargo and end the Sino-Japanese War in exchange for American noninvolvement in China, Japan felt it had no choice but to respond militarily.

However, the Japanese did not realize what their devastating attack on Pearl Harbor would engender. After four years of war with China, the nation did not have the resources for a protracted war, even a maritime-based one. Also, instead of remaining isolationist, America declared war on Japan in response to the raid. Nevertheless, on the morning of December 6, 1941, a fleet of six Japanese aircraft carriers—the *Akagi, Kaga, Hiryu, Soryu, Shokaku,* and *Zuikaku*—surrounded by nine destroyers, two heavy cruisers, one light cruiser, and two battleships, took their position 220 miles north of Pearl Harbor. At 5:30 A.M., a wave of 144 bombers and torpedo planes and 45 escort fighters took off, followed by a second wave of 171 planes, 54 high-altitude bombers, 81 dive-bombers, and 36 fighter planes.

At Pearl Harbor, security was surprisingly lax, despite a recent message from Washington that had opened with "This is a war warning." Although U.S. forces had successfully simulated an aerial attack on Pearl Harbor in 1928, 1932, and 1938, no one thought the Japanese had the capability or resolve to strike America first. Even when an unidentified submarine was sighted at 4:00 A.M. and another submarine was sunk by the destroyer *Ward* at 6:40 A.M., confusing reports and delayed messages did not prepare the base of the oncoming assault. At 7:00 A.M., the Opana radar base on the north side of the island reported a large "blip" representing at least 50 planes less than 100 miles away. The radar operator was told those were 12 expected B-17 bombers arriving at the nearby air base.

Lined up in the docks were nine battleships (the *Arizona,* the *California,* the *Maryland,* the *Nevada,* the *Oklahoma,* the *Pennsylvania,* the *Tennessee,* the *West Virginia,* and the obsolete *Utah,* now a training ship), three destroyers (the *Cassin, Downes,* and *Shaw*), five cruisers (the *Helena, Honolulu, New Orleans, St. Louis,* and *Raleigh*), the minelayer the *Oglala,* and the flagship the *Argonne,* along with dozens of smaller service vessels. The three carriers operating in the Pacific, the *Enterprise, Lexington,* and *Saratoga,* were all out of the harbor on different missions and missed the entire raid.

With the radio call of *"Tora, tora, tora!"* (Japanese for "tiger"), signaling that the Americans had been caught entirely by surprise, the enemy planes roared in. After two bombing and strafing runs at 8:02 and 9:00 A.M., respectively, Pearl Harbor and the surrounding air bases were in total chaos. The Japanese had sunk six battleships, the *Arizona, California, Nevada* (which had been purposely run aground to keep the harbor channel clear), *Oklahoma, West Virginia,* and *Utah;* two destroyers, the *Cassin* and the *Downes;* and the minelayer the *Oglala.* Almost all of the remaining ships, including the battleships *Maryland, Pennsylvania,* and *Tennessee;* the cruisers *Helena,*

Honolulu, and *Raleigh;* and the destroyer the *Shaw* were damaged, some seriously. The attack force had also destroyed 188 aircraft, 92 of them Navy planes. Casualties numbered 2,403 dead, among them 2,008 naval personnel, and 1,178 wounded, 710 of them from the Navy. Japanese losses had been minuscule in comparison, with 55 airmen lost with 29 planes, 1 regular submarine, and 5 midget submarines and their two-man crews.

The battleship USS Arizona's *forward ammunition magazines explode during the Japanese raid on Pearl Harbor.*

Although the strike at Pearl Harbor was an unqualified victory for the Japanese, they had not done as thorough of a job as they would have liked. The shipyards and dry docks were not attacked, and repairs to the salvageable ships began as soon as rescue operations ceased. The *California, Nevada, West Virginia,* and *Oglala* were all raised and repaired. Perhaps more important, the oil and fuel supplies for the bases were untouched. If the carrier group commander Vice Adm. Chuchi Nagumo had ordered a follow-up raid on those stores, the American forces in the Pacific would have been halted for a minimum of six months until more fuel could be sent and the facilities could be rebuilt. But despite advice to attack a third time from several of his officers, Nagumo ordered his fleet to sail west to Midway.

The attack on Pearl Harbor galvanized Americans across the nation, and the demand was clear: war. Response from Congress was swift and merciless. President Roosevelt went before the general assembly the next day to ask for a declaration of war on Japan in a brief speech that famously referred to December 7 as "a date which will live in infamy." Except for one representative, every other member of the Senate and House of Representatives voted to declare war.

On December 11th, Hitler declared war on the United States, allowing Roosevelt to respond in kind. America was in the fight at last, and military planners were faced with the nightmare they had hoped wouldn't happen: a two-front war.

After the destruction of Pearl Harbor, and knowing that the U.S. Navy would be facing engineering and construction challenges like it had never seen before, the Chief of the Bureau of Yards and Docks, Rear Adm. Benjamin Moreell, received approval for one the most famous Navy units of all time—the Construction Battalion.

Quickly nicknamed "Seabees" (for Construction Battalion), the first recruits were placed under the command of the Navy's Civil Engineer Corps. Because experience was valued more than youth, the average age of the first Seabees was 37.

Deployed mainly to the Pacific during World War II, 325,000 Seabees built airfields, bridges, roads, storage facilities, hospitals, and housing. Demobilized after the war, they were reduced to only 3,300 men on duty. After the war, they were divided into two units: Amphibious Construction Battalions (PHIBCBs) and Naval Mobile Construction Battalions (NMCBs). The Korean Conflict mobilized 10,000 men halfway around the world to Inchon, where they built causeways for the American invasion.

Since then, the Seabees have worked around the globe, during both war and peace, providing engineering and construction knowledge and experience wherever they are needed. From Vietnam, where the Seabees fought the Viet Cong beside their Navy and Marine comrades and built schools, hospitals, and infrastructure, to repairing Navy bases from Puerto Rico to Greece to Japan, the Seabees have been on the job.

In 1971, the Seabees began a 10-year project building the Navy base at Diego Garcia, an atoll in the Indian Ocean that now handles the fleet's largest ships and cargo planes; it was a vital supply point for American forces in the Middle East. During the Gulf War, more than 5,000 Seabees built camps for more than 42,000 personnel, constructed 14 galleys that could feed 75,000 people, and laid down 6 million square feet of aircraft parking apron. Wherever they've gone, the Seabees have always lived up to their motto: "Can Do!"

FRONT ONE—WAR IN THE ATLANTIC

The declaration of war was what the U-boats prowling the Atlantic had been waiting for. The operation was called *Paukenschlag* and was deadly to Allied merchant shipping. The east coast of America was so target-rich that German captains often had their pick of what to shoot. American coastal defenses were nonexistent, with brightly lit cities often silhouetting merchant vessels. From January through April 1942, U-boats sank 112 vessels totaling 927,000 tons just in American waters. A total of 303 ships—totaling more than 2 million tons—were sunk by German forces around the world in those 5 months.

By May, America had renewed the convoy system, with limited success. Roosevelt, along with Churchill, still considered Hitler the primary menace and quickly moved against Germany. In January 1942, the combined Chiefs of Staff of America and Great Britain was created to coordinate the joint war effort, allocating the forces in the Atlantic and Pacific. Germany announced unrestricted submarine warfare in June 1942, and the Atlantic Fleet went to work.

Finding a suitable method of combating the silent killers, however, took cooperation among several nations. In the end, American, British, Canadian, and Icelandic ships, radar stations, and aircraft combined to create a net over the North Atlantic to escort valuable merchant convoys and to locate, track, and destroy U-boats wherever they operated. The new invention of radar was invaluable in the war against the submarine, as was the capture of the U-110, a German submarine containing the "enigma" encryption machine, enabling the British to decode U-boat radio transmissions.

In order to bring fleet manpower up to strength, the U.S. Navy allowed women (who had also briefly volunteered in World War I) to enlist as WAVES (Women Accepted for Volunteer Emergency Service). The Navy Nurse Corps also played a valuable role during wartime, much as they had done since their inception in the early twentieth century.

In October 1942, the first of more than 86,000 women volunteered for WAVE service and reported to schools such as Oklahoma A&M College to train in essential noncombat skills to replace men who were going to war. Women learned shorthand, stenography, and typing as well as advanced courses in history and naval communication. Secretary of the Navy James Forrestal said the WAVES had released enough men for active duty "to man completely a major task force." The men available were sufficient to man 10 battleships, 10 aircraft carriers, 28 cruisers, and 50 destroyers. The Navy achieved its enlistment goal (which had originally stood at just 10,000 recruits) by 1944, and the program was stopped in 1945, but not before tens of thousands of women contributed to the war effort in their own way.

(Naval Historical Center)

WAVES trainees march in formation behind their color guard.

Despite prevailing public opinion against the idea, women were not strangers to the reality of combat. During the Civil War, Catholic nuns served as nurses on the *Red Rover,* a captured Confederate steamship outfitted as a naval hospital vessel. Nurses also cared for the sick and wounded at the Norfolk Naval Hospital in Virginia during the Spanish-American War.

On May 13, 1908, the Navy Nurse Corps was officially established, with a superintendent appointed by the Secretary of the Navy and a core of professionally trained nurses. In October 1908, the first 20, known as "The Sacred Twenty," reported for duty at the Naval Medical School Hospital (now the Bureau of Medicine and Surgery) in Washington, D.C. Since then, the Corps has grown to more than 5,000 active and reserve nurses; during war, their numbers rise even higher. In World War II alone there were more than 11,000 nurses in the Corps.

Since its inception, the Corps has gone all over the world, tending to the sick and wounded in war zones in every major engagement. Along with their wartime duties, they are also responsible for training the next generation of nurses, as well as other personnel with no previous medical experience. The Corps handles Navy health care on an ongoing basis and oversees nursing schools, clinics, and mobile hospitals all over the world.

Another precedent was set in June 1942, when the first African-American ensign, Bernard Robinson, joined the U.S. Navy. Even though African Americans had fought in the War of 1812, the Civil War, and the Spanish-American War, by the twentieth century they were relegated to menial roles, such as ship's cook Doris Miller. That all changed in 1942, however, when they were first allowed to apply for an officer's commission. The first to do so, Samuel L. Gravely from Richmond, Virginia, joined in September, knowing what he would face in the service. He persevered and became the Navy's first black vice admiral.

In the fall of 1942, the U-boats had changed their codes again and were wreaking havoc on Allied shipping, sinking 700,000 tons of merchant shipping in November alone. British cryptanalysts cracked the new code in early 1943, and the convoys were able to avoid the wolf packs again. Radar was becoming more advanced, with surface ships now able to mark the U-boats without the Germans knowing.

Once the U-boat code was broken again, the Atlantic grew safer by the month. In response, Grand Adm. Karl Dönitz revised his estimated goal of merchant shipping that needed to be sunk from 500,000 tons a month in May 1942 to 1.3 million tons a month in September. But his naval yards couldn't produce enough U-boats to replace the submarines being sunk (which was happening more often) and keep up the pressure on convoys crossing the Atlantic as well.

The Allied embrace of air cover for the convoys was the final blow to the enemy submarine fleets (due to incredible shortsightedness, the Nazi high command never allowed its Navy to have aircraft). By the summer of 1943, the U-boats had been chased into the central part of the Atlantic, where their threat was diminished. With Britain secure from the sea, preparations were begun later that year for the massive invasion Roosevelt had been clamoring for.

The first Allied push, code-named Operation Torch, was the invasion of North Africa, and it required access to Mediterranean ports in French Morocco and Algeria for success. However, the operation was handled primarily by British ships and American Army personnel in a combined effort, as the Pacific was quickly becoming the U.S. Navy's primary theater of war.

THE SECOND FRONT: BLOOD IN THE PACIFIC

On the other side of the world, the Pacific Ocean forces were reeling from a concentrated assault by the Japanese military. Hours after the attack on Pearl Harbor, and despite being prepared for an assault, Clark Field in the Philippines was bombed. The Japanese destroyed 18 of the 35 B-17 bombers, 56 fighter planes, and 25 other aircraft, losing only 7 of their own planes. Three weeks later, an invasion force headed straight for Manila, forcing the Americans to retreat to Bataan and rerouting merchant shipping farther south.

Elsewhere, the Japanese onslaught continued through Hong Kong and into Malaysia. A British army of 70,000 surrendered after being backed into Singapore. Japanese bombers and torpedo planes sank the British heavy cruiser the *Repulse* and the battleship *Prince of Wales*, neither of which had had any air support. The enemy advanced west toward Thailand and Burma and south to the Dutch East Indies, threatening Australia itself, which looked to the U.S. for help.

But America had its own problems. With the loss of Wake Island, Guam, and the Philippines, the staging points for Plan Orange, the war plans developed by the Naval War College in the 1920s would be very hard to execute.

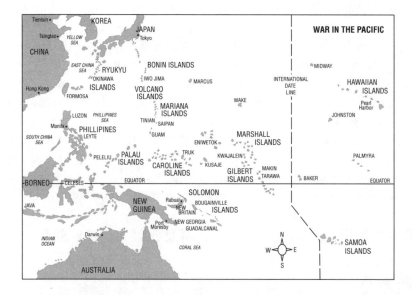

During the 20 years leading up to World War II, a joint Army-Navy board and the U.S. Naval War College designed plans involving conflict between the United States and each major country in the world, under the "Rainbow Plans" program. Plan Orange, the battle strategy for a war with Japan, was the only plan developed to conclusion, although it was never formally recognized or approved by either Congress or the president. It involved using the Navy fleet to "island-hop" across the Pacific, creating supply bases to push onward until Japan was reached. After the U.S. Navy destroyed its maritime forces, the island nation would be blockaded and bombed until it was forced to submit.

Still, the overall plan was sound, and with the increased reliance on aircraft versus capital ships, the war in the Pacific would be a fleet-based and, even more important, carrier-based campaign. Adm. Chester W. Nimitz was assigned to Pearl Harbor, replacing Admiral Kimmel, who was unjustly blamed for the damage done by the Japanese in December. Nimitz immediately began planning how to defeat the Japanese in its own backyard.

The Navy got as many ships and men into the Pacific as possible, and in some places they were already striking back at the Japanese. The U.S.

government announced unrestricted submarine warfare, and the new "gray wolves" were eager for action. American submarines claimed 50,000 tons of enemy shipping in the first months of the war, while losing just four of their own boats. At Timor, the American portion of the combined American, British, Dutch, and Australia command (ABDACOM), under the command of Vice Adm. William A. Glassford, executed a brilliant series of hit-and-run attacks when it encountered Japanese forces. Although equipped with obsolete light cruisers and destroyers, they dodged the Japanese destroyer screen and sank four transport ships and a patrol vessel, leaving only when they ran out of ammunition. The Battle of Balikpapan, the first true surface action of the Pacific campaign, would have been even more successful if the Americans had had more reliable torpedoes: Many failed to run on course, maintain their depth setting, or detonate upon impact.

CARRIER VS. CARRIER—THE BATTLE OF CORAL SEA

In March 1942, the Japanese embarked on their next campaign, a push south to Port Moresby, Papua New Guinea, only 300 miles from the Australian coast. With the establishment of a seaplane base in the Solomons and another one in the middle of a scattered group of islands known as the Louisade Archipelago, they could launch coastal attacks on Australia with ease. On April 30, the Pearl Harbor veteran aircraft carriers the *Zuikaku* and the *Shokaku* (together carrying 147 aircraft), along with the light carrier *Shoho*, 7 destroyers, 2 light cruisers, 6 heavy cruisers, 3 carriers, and 11 troop transports, began the 2,000-mile journey for the Coral Sea.

Having broken Japan's naval code early on, American military cryptanalysts intercepted enemy communiqués, and knew their destination. However, the only carriers near the area were the *Lexington* and the *Yorktown*, carrying 143 airplanes between them and assisted by an assorted group of destroyers and support ships. Although the *Enterprise* and the *Hornet* were dispatched from Pearl Harbor, they would not reach the area in time. A small British force of cruisers and destroyers would be the only other support the carriers had.

Although the dates for the battle were May 4 through May 8, 1942 (hostilities began when an American air raid on Tulagi destroyed one enemy destroyer, three minesweepers, and five seaplanes), the crucial fighting began on May 7, when Japanese patrol planes spotted the tanker the *Neosho* and the destroyer the *Sims*. Carrier-based bombers sank the destroyer, killing all but 16 men on board. The fuel ship was hit seven times but still floated, although it was dead in the water. One hundred and twenty-seven stranded crewmen were rescued by May 11, and the tanker was sunk.

The Japanese struck again with a wave of bombers attacking a group of three cruisers and two destroyers off the eastern tip of New Guinea. Concentrated antiaircraft fire drove them off without a single hit. Meanwhile, American scout planes located a group of ships 200 miles away, which turned out to be two light cruisers and several merchant ships. On the way back, the strike force spotted another fleet, which included the Japanese light carrier the *Shoho* and four cruisers and destroyers near New Guinea. Still fully armed, the planes attacked, sinking the *Shoho*. The Americans had lost only three planes, and they reported their success with the famous report "Scratch one flattop."

But the Japanese weren't done yet, and a series of dogfights between the two fleets occurred over the rest of the day. As night fell, a group of Japanese planes, confused in the darkness, spotted the lights of what they thought was their carrier. It was, in fact, Rear Adm. Frank Jack Fletcher's fleet. American gunners shot down one plane as it came in for a landing.

By the morning of May 8, the two fleets had located each other 200 miles apart, and a large strike was launched from both sides. Although the opponents were evenly matched (the Japanese had 6 destroyers, 4 heavy cruisers, 2 carriers, and 122 aircraft, while the United Sates had 7 destroyers, 5 heavy cruisers, 2 carriers, and 121 aircraft), the battle was decided by the carriers alone. The Japanese fared better this time. The *Lexington* was hit by two torpedoes and then took three hits from Japanese dive bombers, causing raging fires below deck. Although the fires were fought successfully, gasoline vapors suddenly ignited in a tremendous explosion and more fires. At 5:07 P.M., Capt. Frederick C. Sherman gave the order to abandon ship. The destroyer the USS *Phelps* fired two torpedoes into the carrier's hull and sent her to the bottom at 7:56 P.M. on May 8, 1942. The *Lexington* received two battle stars for its performance during the Pacific Campaign.

The Japanese bombers also hit the *Yorktown* and shot down 33 American planes that day, plus 36 more on the sunken *Lexington*. Meanwhile, the

Shokaku, under cover in a tropical squall, suffered only three hits, which damaged the flight deck, but was able to recover its bombers and torpedo planes.

The USS Yorktown *is hit by a Japanese torpedo at the Battle of Midway.*

The Japanese claimed victory at the Battle of the Coral Sea after sinking 1 carrier, 1 destroyer, and 1 tanker; destroying 66 aircraft; and killing 546 men. They had lost more planes (77) and men (1,074), but only one ship, the *Shoho.* Strategically, the victory was America's because it had stopped the Japanese advance toward Australia, and the loss of even one carrier taxed the already overstressed Imperial Navy. The loss of Japanese aircraft and pilots was even worse, as the *Zuikaku* was useless until replacements arrived.

It was only a matter of time until the Japanese fleet attacked again. U.S. code breakers at Pearl Harbor, led by Joseph Rochefort, perhaps the greatest code breaker the U.S. military ever had, struggled to figure out where they would strike next. Using false messages sent to the Japanese for confirmation, Rochefort told Fleet Adm. Chester W. Nimitz that the Japanese would launch a feint at the Aleutian Islands and send their main force to take the strategic Midway atoll.

SIX MINUTES TO VICTORY—THE BATTLE OF MIDWAY

Having stung the Americans in the Coral Sea, Admiral Yamamoto set a trap that he hoped would destroy the carriers that had escaped Pearl Harbor. He divided his fleet into two parts. The first was a diversionary force of four troop transports, two light carriers, three heavy cruisers, two light cruisers, and nine destroyers sent to attack the Aleutian Islands, hoping to divert American ships north. His main fleet consisted of three forces, with the carrier force containing 4 aircraft carriers, 2 battleships, 2 cruisers, and 12 destroyers. The landing force for Midway was made up of 12 transport ships, 4 heavy cruisers, and 2 destroyers, with a covering force of 2 battleships, 4 heavy cruisers, and 7 destroyers. Yamamoto would supervise the attack from the First Fleet, which was made up of 3 battleships (including his flagship, the 72,000-ton *Yamato*), 1 light carrier, 1 light cruiser, 2 seaplane carriers, and 13 destroyers. In addition, there were 15 Japanese submarines in the area. The admiral committed the majority of his country's navy to draw out the Americans.

The problem was that the plan was extremely complicated and relied on an exact timetable, including predicting how the enemy fleet would respond. When American code breakers figured out the operation, the trap was doomed before it was even started.

The American fleet was a poor opponent for the Japanese, consisting of only two carrier groups. Task Force 16, led by Rear Adm. Raymond A. Spruance, consisted of two carriers, the *Enterprise* and the *Hornet*; six cruisers; and nine destroyers. Task Force 17, commanded by Rear Admiral Fletcher, consisted of the damaged carrier the *Yorktown* escorted by two cruisers and six destroyers. The two groups were supported by 15 submarines but were still vastly outnumbered and outgunned. The only area in which the two forces were relatively even was in aircraft, with 233 American planes to 272 Japanese aircraft. This proved to be the most crucial element. There was also a multiunit force of more than 100 bombers and fighters from the

Army, the Navy, and the Marines at Midway, who would play their own parts in the battle (see the *Alpha Bravo Delta Guide to the U.S. Army* and the *Alpha Bravo Delta Guide to the U.S. Marines*).

The fight began on June 3, when Army B-17s, acting on scouting reports from Catalina PBY patrol planes, bombed the Midway occupation force, sailing 200 miles ahead of the First Fleet. Despite the B-17 bombing run and a night attack by four PBYs, only one support oiler was hit—but not stopped.

The next morning, the Japanese launched their bombing assault on Midway itself, destroying most of the Marines' fighter plane group there (17 out of 26 planes were downed), along with several supply buildings and facilities; the runways were left intact, though.

After a retaliatory attack by six Avengers and four B-26s from the island, Admiral Nagumo ordered another strike on the island to destroy the rest of its defenses. His change of plan necessitated changing the weapons on his planes from antiship torpedoes to bombs, starting at 7:15 A.M.

A Navy Catalina patrol plane spotted Nagumo's carrier force 200 miles southwest of the *Yorktown* task force. Admiral Fletcher ordered Admiral Spruance to attack with the *Enterprise* and the *Hornet*.

Meanwhile, a Japanese scout plane reported that an American force was about 200 miles from Nagumo's carriers. After 15 minutes, Nagumo ordered the bombs removed and replaced with torpedoes again at around 7:45 A.M. At 8:10, he received word that the ships were destroyers and cruisers, not carriers, but that was the least of his worries. His force was already suffering attacks from bombers at Midway. Also, an American submarine, the *Nautilus*, fired a spread of torpedoes at the carriers. The damage would have been incredible, but many torpedoes missed or didn't detonate and the sub escaped, followed by part of the destroyer screen.

At 8:20 A.M., Nagumo received the report he had been dreading: An American carrier force was in the area. The first Midway strike force, low on fuel, had returned. Against the advice of his subordinates, Nagumo didn't launch the ready planes, but put them below and took the empty planes on board.

A half-hour earlier, 37 dive-bombers had launched from the *Hornet*, heading for the Japanese carriers. However, the U.S. air group commander missed the enemy and almost immediately turned around. Most of the bombers landed at Midway or straggled back to the *Hornet*.

At about the same time, 15 TBD Devastators from the *Hornet* and 14 from the *Enterprise* found the Japanese carrier unit, the first ones at 9:25 A.M. But without fighter cover, they were easy prey for the covering Zeros. All of the planes were shot down, and only one American, George Gay, survived. The second wave suffered a similar fate, although 4 of the 14 planes made it back. No hits were scored in either attack. Another wave of 12 Devastators tried at 10:00 but all of them were shot down or ditched in the ocean.

As devastating as the assaults were to the Americans, they set up the destruction of the Japanese fleet. Although the bomb and torpedo runs had caused little damage, they had made the fleet scatter, making it easier to attack the ships separately and also preventing the launch of any planes. Finally, the low-level Devastator attacks pulled the Zeros down to intercept them, leaving the carriers with no high-level air cover.

Throughout the evasive maneuvers, the Japanese had continued to rearm and refuel their planes, leaving bombs and torpedoes lying on the deck. Minutes away from launch, two groups of dive-bombers appeared. Bomber Squadron 3 was made up of 17 Douglas SBD-3 Dauntlesses from the *Yorktown* and was led by Lt. Cmdr. Maxwell F. Leslie. The second group of 30 bombers was from the *Enterprise* and was led by Lt. Cmdr. Wade McClusky.

Leslie's group had accompanied the *Yorktown*'s doomed torpedo bombers and was now free to attack the *Soryu*. McClusky's force had been at the original position of the enemy fleet and had followed a lone destroyer that had been tracking the *Nautilus* and was now heading back to its fleet. His planes concentrated on the carriers the *Akagi* and the *Kaga*.

Only three planes bombed the *Akagi*, but the carrier took two hits at 10:26 A.M., one on the flight deck and one in the main hangar, causing major damage and crippling the ship. On fire and out of control, it was scuttled the next morning.

Its sister carrier, the *Kaga*, suffered four bombs, one near the bridge, killing the captain and command staff. The others exploded on the flight deck and in the main hangar. The *Kaga* was abandoned almost immediately and sank just before the *Akagi*.

The third carrier to go was the *Soryu*, which was hit three times, also on the hangar and the flight deck, and sank a few hours later.

In about six minutes, the Japanese Navy had been dealt a stunning blow. Admiral Nagumo had been literally carried off the bridge of the *Akagi* and was fuming onboard a light cruiser. When the location of the *Yorktown* was reported, he ordered the last carrier, the *Hiryu*, to attack. It sent out two waves, one of 18 dive-bombers and 6 fighters, immediately. Another group of 10 torpedo bombers and 6 fighters was ordered out soon afterward.

A dozen *Yorktown* Grumman F4F-4 "Wildcat" fighters provided air cover while Leslie's remaining bombers landed on the *Enterprise*. When scouts reported enemy planes inbound, the Wildcats rose to meet them and stopped 10 bombers. Of the rest, six made it through and scored three hits on the carrier, damaging the boilers and leaving it dead in the water. Repairs were made, and the ship resumed its course, but it was targeted by the second wave of torpedo planes and was hit twice, causing serious damage below the waterline and eventually a 26° list.

Captain Buckmaster ordered the crew to abandon ship. Admiral Fletcher and he both agreed that the *Yorktown* should be saved, if possible, and repair crews returned to the ship, assisted by the destroyer the USS *Hammann*. But a Japanese submarine launched four torpedoes at the two ships, sinking the *Hammann* and hitting the carrier once. The sinking destroyer's exploding depth charges further damaged the vessel. On June 7, 1942, the *Yorktown* sank in 3,000 fathoms of water. The ship earned three battle stars for its actions at Coral Sea and Midway.

But the *Yorktown* did not go down unavenged. It had launched a squadron of 16 Dauntless dive-bombers, and they located the *Hiryu* and her escorts. Joined by 24 SBD dive-bombers from the *Enterprise* (14 of these planes were actually from the *Yorktown*), the 2 groups attacked, scoring 4 hits on the enemy carrier while losing only 3 planes. Despite heavy damage and torpedoes fired from its own escort, the *Hiryu* did not sink until the morning of June 5.

But the Americans weren't finished with the Japanese yet. While Admiral Spruance's task force left the battlefield on the evening of June 4, an American submarine located a group of four heavy cruisers and two destroyers, part of the cover for the Midway landing force, in the early hours of June 5. Spotting the sub, one of the cruisers accidentally rammed another while executing an emergency turn, slowing both vessels. A flight of B-17s from Midway couldn't find them, but a marine bombing squadron located the oil slick from one and attacked, with no success. It took three more bombing runs by planes from the *Enterprise* and the *Hornet* to finally sink one cruiser, heavily damage another, and hit both destroyers.

Admiral Yamamoto still tried to salvage something from the failed operation. He sent six heavy cruisers and their destroyer escort to the last two limping cruisers, hoping to draw Spruance's fleet close enough to Wake Island to target it with his own land-based aircraft. Admiral Spruance didn't take the bait, however, and after the bombing runs on the enemy cruisers he retreated east from Midway to await reinforcements from Pearl Harbor. With his last chance gone, Yamamoto assembled the rest of his fleet and ordered a withdrawal on June 8.

Far to the north, Vice Adm. Boshiro Hosogaya led his forces against the islands of Kiska and Attu, bombing Dutch Harbor, Alaska, and "capturing" (there was almost no resistance) a weather crew, 39 Aleuts, and 2 missionaries. The diversion had failed miserably, and an overcomplicated plan, indecision, and faulty intelligence had cost Japan its main mobile air support.

The Battle of Midway was a great tactical and strategic victory for the American Navy. Even though the Japanese still had more ships in the Pacific, their top naval officers were unwilling to gamble their capital ships or remaining carriers on complicated battle plans. Admiral Nimitz and his officers had secured Pearl Harbor and Midway, providing a morale-boosting victory that enabled them to take the fight to the Japanese.

THRUST AND PARRY AT GUADALCANAL

The battle at Midway re-energized the joint Pacific forces. A combined force of Australians and Americans held off a Japanese assault on Port Moresby in Papua New Guinea.

However, flamboyant and headstrong Army Gen. Douglas MacArthur clashed with Admiral King over how to continue the offensive. MacArthur wanted the Marines, America's only true amphibious landing force, to take the major Japanese base at Rabaul, on the island of New Britain. The

Marines would be supported by two Navy aircraft carriers—half the carrier fleet in the Pacific. King retorted that the Navy would handle its own operations, not be subject to MacArthur's grandstanding. The Joint Chiefs of Staff compromised on a multibranch operation, code-named Watchtower, involving all three branches. In the planning stages, however, intelligence discovered the Japanese building an airfield on Guadalcanal, an island not marked for occupation yet. Whichever side controlled the airfield would control the air over the Solomon Islands. If the Japanese held it, they could renew their push toward Australia. The United States needed it to begin its own island-hopping drive toward Japan. The Watchtower plans were altered to include the capture of Guadalcanal, and the operation was launched in early August 1942.

Escorted by Task Force 61, now consisting of 3 carriers, 1 new fast battleship, 1 light and 5 heavy cruisers, and 16 destroyers, U.S. Marines seized the area, including the fiercely contested Tulagi and Gavutu Islands and the almost-completed airfield on August 7 and 8. Holding them, however, soon became another matter. The Japanese controlled the waters around the Solomons at night and were running the "Tokyo Express," a high-speed run through the "Slot," a channel along the island group by which they were able to reinforce at Guadalcanal and also hit any U.S. warships in the area.

Right after the Marines dug in, American forces suffered a major defeat at the Battle of Savo Island, off the north coast of Guadalcanal. Although the force had split into three groups to cover all avenues to the beachhead, a Japanese formation of two light cruisers, five heavy cruisers, and one destroyer commanded by Vice Adm. Gun'ichi Mikawa slipped in and blew apart three American cruisers—the *Astoria*, the *Quincy*, and the *Vincennes*— and one Australian heavy cruiser, the *Canberra*. The USS *Chicago* was also badly damaged, and if not for a lucky shot from the *Quincy* that hit the Japanese flagship's bridge, the enemy force might have laid waste to the entire Allied fleet in the area. Although the heavy cruiser the *Kako* was later sunk by an American submarine, the Japanese ships escaped from the engagement at Savo with only slight damage. A total of 1,270 Allied soldiers had been killed and 700 had been wounded in America's worst naval defeat during the war. Adm. Frank Fletcher, fearing another attack, removed his carriers from Guadalcanal, leaving the Marines and aircraft to defend themselves as best they could.

By the time World War II was over, more than 50 Allied and Japanese ships littered the bottom of the channel between Guadalcanal and Savo Island. The deadliest stretch of water in the Pacific came to be known as "Iron Bottom Sound."

The ocean around Guadalcanal and the Solomons soon became as hotly contested as the islands themselves, with Japanese and American forces jockeying for advantage. Admiral Yamamoto ordered Vice Admiral Nagumo to take a group of 3 carriers, 4 heavy cruisers, 2 battleships, and 168 aircraft against the American forces there. The U.S. fleet consisted of the carriers the *Enterprise*, the *Saratoga*, and the *Wasp*; the new battleship the *South Carolina*; 2 light and 5 heavy cruisers; 18 destroyers; and 254 aircraft. On August 24, a patrol plane spotted the light carrier the *Ryujo* and escort, which had been sent out by Nagumo as a diversion. Admiral Fletcher sent his torpedo planes and dive-bombers against the lone ship, just as Nagumo had hoped. Fletcher discovered the location of the larger Japanese force after his strike had taken off, and efforts to redirect them were unsuccessful. The bombers did carry out their mission, sinking the *Ryujo* and severely damaging the seaplane carrier the *Chitose*.

The Japanese attack began at 4:00 P.M. Fletcher had a defensive screen of 53 F4F fighters, which engaged the escort Zeros and also shot down 12 of the 36 dive-bombers. The remaining Vals directed their attacks on the *Enterprise* and hit her 3 times, killing 74 sailors but failing to sink the carrier. The *South Carolina*'s antiaircraft defenses shot down 14 planes, and no Japanese bombers reached the *Saratoga*. When Fletcher broke off the engagement and headed south, the battle was over, with the Americans sinking another valuable enemy carrier and downing 90 Japanese aircraft while losing only 17 planes.

Nagumo's secondary objective was to provide cover for a Guadalcanal landing force escorted by four destroyers that ran the Slot and got within 100 miles of the island on August 25. A mixed force of SBD Dauntless dive-bombers from Guadalcanal and the *Enterprise* attacked, causing heavy damage to the flagship cruiser and a transport. Rescue operations were underway when a squadron of eight B-17s launched from the air base at New Hebrides flew overhead. Their bombing was right on target, sinking one destroyer, damaging another, and canceling the landing.

Despite this loss, the Tokyo Express delivered men and supplies to the Japanese forces on Guadalcanal, with the Navy seemingly powerless to stop them. However, the momentum was turning for the Allies. The Battle of Cape Esperance marked one of the first effective uses of surface radar, with the Americans firing on and sinking one Japanese heavy cruiser and one destroyer. Unfortunately, they also sank one of their own destroyers and incapacitated another by friendly fire.

> The invention of RADAR (the acronym for radio detection and ranging) in the 1920s and 1930s was a critical advantage for the Allies. Sending radio waves across the ocean and sky and reading which ones bounced back to them off ships and airplanes allowed the fleet to cover a wider area and know when ships were attempting to sneak up on them. Although Japan was as advanced as any other nation, its forces did not utilize radar, which cost them dearly in the constant search for the enemy's location.

An American resupply effort, including the 7th Marine Regiment, tried to sail from Samoa to Guadalcanal. On the way, the escort task force, including the carriers the *Wasp* and the *Hornet*, came under fire from Japanese submarines. The *Wasp*, hit three times, was scuttled. The battleship the *North Carolina* and the destroyer the *O'Brien* also were hit but not sunk, although the *O'Brien* went down on its way back to the West Coast for repairs. The task force had done its job, however, and the 7th Marines landed on the island on September 18th, bringing with them desperately needed weapons and supplies.

The Japanese also kept coming but occasionally ran into American ambushes, like the one on October 8. A group of two light cruisers, two heavy cruisers, and five destroyers caught a Japanese force running the Slot, sank a cruiser and a destroyer, and damaged a heavy cruiser. Return fire sank a U.S. destroyer and damaged a light cruiser.

On October 18, Adm. Frank Fletcher and Adm. Robert L. Ghormley, the man in charge of Operation Watchtower, were both recalled, their progress in the Pacific deemed too slow by Nimitz and King. They were replaced by their exact opposite in temperament and aggressiveness, Adm. William Frederick Halsey Jr., who wanted to strike fear into the Japanese.

Learning that elements of the Japanese Imperial Navy (4 aircraft carriers, 4 battleships, 2 light and 8 heavy cruisers, and 29 destroyers) were on the move, Halsey's orders to 2 American carrier groups were simply: "Attack—repeat, attack!" Task Force 61 contained the *Enterprise*, the battleship the *South Dakota*, two cruisers, and eight destroyers. Task Force 17 was made up of the *Hornet*, four cruisers, and six destroyers. On October 26, 1942, in what became known as the Battle of the Santa Cruz Islands, planes from both sides took to the air, bombing whatever targets they could.

The Japanese carrier *Zuiho* and Pearl Harbor veteran *Shokaku* both sustained serious damage and had to withdraw, along with the heavy cruiser *Chukuma*. On the American side, the *Enterprise* took 3 bomb hits in 2 separate raids that killed 44 sailors and wounded 75, but didn't sink the carrier. The destroyer the *Porter* was hulled by a torpedo and eventually sank, and the destroyer the *Smith* was badly damaged when a crippled Japanese plane crashed into it.

But the aircraft carrier the *Hornet* took the most damage during the battle, suffering two enemy torpedoes, three bombs, and two airplane impacts that turned her into a fiery floating ruin. The crew was evacuated and American destroyers shot nine torpedoes into her hull, but the *Hornet* still didn't sink. The Japanese eventually finished the carrier with four torpedoes. The losses in the Battle of the Santa Cruz Islands now meant that the United States had only one operating carrier in the Pacific—the damaged *Enterprise*.

THE BATTLE OF GUADALCANAL

With both sides relying so heavily on air power, it was unusual that one of the major battles around Guadalcanal was an old-fashioned shootout at relatively close range. But in the early morning darkness of November 13, a large Japanese escort force of 2 battleships, 2 light cruisers, 2 heavy cruisers, 24 destroyers, and 2 aircraft carriers was making runs on the Tokyo Express. The United States knew it was coming, however, and waited with 5 cruisers and 8 destroyers. Outnumbered and outgunned, Rear Adm. Daniel J. Callaghan formed an old-fashioned line of battle and waited for the convoy to come to him in Iron Bottom Sound.

The Americans spotted the Japanese fleet on radar but were surprised when they sighted them visually only 20 minutes later. Although the United States had the advantage, the Japanese drew first blood by shelling the cruiser the *Atlanta* to a pulp. A close-quarters gunfight ensured. When it was over, the American side had lost four destroyers and two cruisers, and every other ship but one had been seriously damaged. On the Japanese side, two destroyers had been sunk, three had been damaged, and the large battleship the *Hiei*, which was supposed to have destroyed Henderson airfield on Guadalcanal, was badly damaged; it eventually sank after repeated bombing raids by American forces.

The Imperial navy was determined to land its troops on the island, however, and it blasted Henderson Field with a mixed group of cruisers and destroyers. After a two-hour bombardment with no return fire, Admiral Mikawa was content with his efforts. But he'd destroyed only 18 planes. Bombers and torpedo planes harassed his fleet all the way out, damaging four of his cruisers, one of which was later sunk by *Enterprise* bombers.

Meanwhile, the 12 Japanese troop transports still sailed for the island, lightly covered by air support from the carrier the *Hiyo*. Combined air attacks from Henderson Field, the *Enterprise*, and B-17s from Espíritu Santo sank eight troopships on November 14. The remaining four retreated, waiting for another fleet to shell the airfield and landing site. This group, however, consisting of one light cruiser, two heavy cruisers, nine destroyers, and the battleship *Kirishima*, ran into Rear Adm. Willis A. Lee's group of four destroyers and two battleships that night.

The lead group of one cruiser and three destroyers was sighted on radar, and Lee's ships opened fire. The Japanese responded with their deadly long-lance torpedoes. Soon two destroyers, the *Preston* and the *Walke*, were sinking; another, the *Benham*, was seriously damaged and sank the next day.

One area in which the Japanese excelled was in torpedoes. Their Type 93 "long-lance" torpedo was designed for launch from surface ships, not submarines. With a top speed of 49 knots (59 miles per hour!), a range of 22,000 feet (more than 4 miles), and a 1,078-pound explosive warhead, it was one of the deadliest weapons in the Imperial Navy's arsenal.

The Americans were inflicting damage of their own, however, damaging a Japanese destroyer so badly that it later sank. When the battleships spotted each other, the *South Dakota* suffered an electrical malfunction that took out all its systems, including steering and gunnery. Helpless in the water, the Japanese destroyers opened fire, causing massive damage to the deck but leaving its hull virtually intact (none of the torpedoes fired at the ship hit).

The other untouched battleship, the *Washington,* found the range of the *Kirishima* and used her radar-aimed cannons to damage the battleship enough that it sank the next day. Rear Adm. Raizo Tanaka, having seen his transport fleet reduced to a third of its original size, beached the last four ships and off-loaded a mere 2,500 men.

By now the Navy had achieved air superiority over the Slot and was preventing supply ships from aiding the Japanese forces on Guadalcanal. There was one final confrontation, in which American ships surprised Admiral Tanaka in Iron Bottom Sound as he attempted to throw supplies overboard to drift to the beach. Although the Americans fired first, their faulty torpedoes did little damage, while the Japanese torpedoes tore open the cruisers the *Minneapolis,* the *New Orleans,* and the *Pensacola* and sank the cruiser the *Northampton.* The Japanese retreated, and the American ships staggered to Tulagi Harbor for repairs.

It took two more months of heavy fighting, but the Marines secured Guadalcanal by February 1943. With this loss, the inexorable Japanese advance had been blocked.

THE ATLANTIC FRONT—THE END OF THE WAR VERSUS THE U-BOATS

On the other side of the world, Operation Torch, the amphibious invasion of North Africa, had been an unqualified success. With the U-boats stymied in the Atlantic, troop convoys crossed the ocean unmolested, and the invasion began in November 1942. Morocco and Algeria were liberated within days, and a firm foothold was gained on the continent.

Roosevelt and Churchill met in January 1943 to map out their future strategy. America wanted a cross-Channel invasion, but Churchill said not yet. They did agree to fight the Axis powers to complete and unconditional surrender.

On March 1, 1943, Admiral King summoned about 100 experts in anti-submarine warfare to discuss the state of the war against the U-boats. He stressed the importance of supplying Russia so it could continue the war against Germany. Almost two weeks of discussion ended with an agreement to divide the ocean into areas of responsibility for each nation. But only three days later, the U-boats struck in a flurry that rivaled their early action of the war: 122,000 tons of shipping was sunk in the next several weeks, with only one submarine lost in return.

The Allies stepped up their patrols and began sinking more U-boats as 1943 progressed. At the end of April, a convoy of 42 ships encountered a pack of 52 U-boats, and a running battle began over the next several days. The submarines sank 12 merchantmen, but then fog rolled in and the Allied ships used radar to destroy the silent killers. By the end of May, 41 U-boats had been sunk. The loss was so great that the German navy all but abandoned the North Atlantic, moving operations to the central portion of the ocean.

Although the Tenth Fleet was theoretically in command there, it was also an administrative unit with no ships of its own, run by Rear Adm. Francis Low. With the increased U-boat activity, Admiral Low stepped up the convoy escorts and antisubmarine technology, including "Fido," the new antisubmarine homing torpedo. He brought out planes, radar, destroyers, and anything else at his disposal. The U-boats were on the defensive, and from this point on, losses in merchant and warships steadily declined until the end of the war.

Trident, the second war conference, was held in Washington, D.C., in mid-May, and the Allied leaders agreed on a date to invade Europe: May 1, 1944. In July, Roosevelt and Churchill also launched the invasion of Sicily, which led to the secret surrender of Italy on September 3, 1943. The U.S. Navy forces in the Atlantic would be primarily escorting convoys until D-Day.

The Pacific theater was also dealt with by giving General MacArthur and Admiral Halsey permission to begin a pincer movement against the main Japanese base of Rabaul.

ISLAND-HOPPING IN THE PACIFIC OCEAN

First, there remained the small matter of the Japanese-held Aleutian islands of Kiska and Attu, captured in the diversionary action preceding the Battle of Midway. American forces had shelled the enemy for nine months; now it was time to remove them.

In March 1943, a small American unit with the light cruiser the *Richmond*, the heavy cruiser the *Salt Lake City*, and four destroyers stumbled into the main unit of the Imperial navy, made up of a light cruiser, two heavy cruisers, four destroyers, and two armed merchant transports. In a lopsided battle, the *Salt Lake City* took on both Japanese heavy cruisers, the *Nachi* and the *Maya*, for over three hours and survived. All of the American ships escaped what could have been a severe loss.

In a precursor to what would happen in the Pacific, the American invasion force bypassed the closer island, Kiska, and landed on Attu first, planning to cut off the Japanese on Kiska from their supply lines. However, 2,600 enemy soldiers fought 11,000 Americans for more than two weeks, halting the advance. The Japanese finally launched a heedless charge against the enemy lines, often blowing themselves up with hand grenades, killing 600 American soldiers and wounding more than 1,200.

Determined not to make the same mistake, the Navy bombarded the Kiska emplacements for more than two months before landing 29,000 men, including 5,000 Canadians, on August 13. They searched the island for a week before admitting that the Japanese had evacuated during the shelling. But with the Japanese, total attention could be brought to the rest of the ocean, where the main action was.

DEATH IN THE TROPICS

The spring of 1943 also brought an unexpected stroke of luck to the U.S. forces in the Pacific. Discovering that Admiral Yamamoto was visiting forward bases, Nimitz approved a plan to intercept his air unit. On April 18, 18 P-38 fighters intercepted the 2 Betty bombers escorted by 6 Zeros and shot down both Bettys and 4 Zeros, losing only 1 of their own. Although Yamamoto's chief of staff survived, the architect of the Pearl Harbor raid and one of Japan's greatest strategic minds did not. When Adm. William "Bull" Halsey heard of the successful mission, he said, "Sounds as though one of the ducks in their bag was a peacock."

(Naval Historical Center)

Fleet Adm. Chester W. Nimitz, commander in chief of the U.S. Navy in the Pacific during World War II.

The twin offensives approved by the Allies began on June 30, 1943. MacArthur's troops attacked in Papua New Guinea, and Halsey's forces invaded the central Solomon Islands. The Army would take a land route to the Huon Peninsula at Papua then hop to the island of New Britain. The Navy and Marines would be responsible for taking enough of the Solomons, including the large northern island of Bougainville, that bombers could reach Rabaul.

The Japanese were just as determined to stop them, and they concentrated their defenses on the Navy, resulting in a series of brief, vicious battles. The Japanese revived the Tokyo Express to resupply their Solomons bases, and a game of search and destroy ensued. In the Battle of Kula Gulf on July 6th, the sides were evenly matched: 10 Japanese destroyers coming down the Slot versus 3 American cruisers and 4 destroyers. Although the Americans sank two Japanese warships, they lost a cruiser to the feared long-range enemy torpedoes, and they also failed to prevent the reinforcement of the men at New Georgia Island.

The next duel, the Battle of Vella Gulf on August 6 and 7, was a certain American victory. Using superior technology, 6 U.S. destroyers met 4 Japanese destroyers and sank 3 of them, killing 1,800 soldiers and sailors.

The next action was two months later, when the Japanese made an attempt to rescue 600 men on the island of Vella Lavella. Nine destroyers and four submarine chasers tried to reach the island but were intercepted by three Navy destroyers. Outnumbered four to one, the Americans sank one enemy ship while taking heavy damage. One U.S. destroyer was lost, and the other two were hit by enemy guns and collided, putting them out of action for a few months. The Japanese got their men and withdrew, elated over their success. It would be their last.

It was time for Halsey to begin leapfrogging along the Pacific Islands as had been done in the Aleutians. The first time the Navy tried this in the South Pacific, it was at the island of Bougainville, the critical staging point for the Navy half of the Rabaul pincer.

When four Imperial cruisers and six destroyers sailed out from Rabaul on November 2 to attack the U.S. ships providing fire support, the American force of four cruisers and eight destroyers sank one enemy cruiser and destroyer and drove off the others without losing any of their own in the Battle of Empress Augusta Bay. The landing force had been protected, and the Marines continued their advance, eventually cutting off the Japanese garrison.

Although the battleship was becoming obsolete for ship-to-ship combat, it still played an important role in shore bombardment before a ground invasion. The 16-inch guns mounted on the *Iowa*-class battleships the *Iowa*, the *Missouri*, and the *Wisconsin* were the most powerful the United States had ever developed.

The Mark 7 fired two types of ammunition, a 2,700-pound armor-piercing round, which could penetrate 32 feet of concrete or 14.5 inches of armor at a range of 8 miles ("point blank" penetration is a staggering 32 inches!), and a 1,900-pound high-capacity shore-bombardment round. Each shell used a 660-pound powder charge, broken down into three silk bags.

To load one of the three guns in a turret, the shell and propellant were hoisted up from the powder room and shell deck into the gunroom. The shell then was moved into the breech, followed by the powder bags. The breech was ratcheted shut, and the gun was ready to fire.

During Operation Desert Storm, the USS *Missouri* and the USS *Wisconsin* fired more than 1,000 rounds of 16-inch ammunition. Targeting enemy bunkers, ships, and artillery sites, they proved there was still a role for the big gun in modern warfare.

With repeated air raids turning Rabaul into a crater, Nimitz put his plan into action. On November 20, Marines landed at Tarawa; they took the island three days later, despite incredible resistance.

The Navy was growing by the week. Halsey's two task forces had been reinforced by Task Force 50.3, made up of three carriers (the *Essex*, the *Bunker Hill*, and the *Independence*) and nine destroyers. Halsey upped the air raids against Rabaul even further, destroying what remained of the Imperial fleet there and neutralizing the 90,000-man garrison.

Task Force 58, commanded by Rear Adm. Mark Mitscher, was formed in the Pacific in January 1944. This huge fleet consisted of 36 destroyers, 6 cruisers, 8 fast battleships, and 12 carriers carrying an immense 750 airplanes.

From there, it was on to the Gilbert Islands, then the Marshall Islands, and the important Kwajalein atoll and its sister islands, Roi and Namur. With four carrier groups able to attack at once, the Japanese defenders had no chance. The island fell in four days.

Pleased with the string of successes, Nimitz ordered the fleet to continue to Truk, which Admiral Yamamoto had selected as the Japanese Navy's operational base. His replacement, Adm. Mineichi Koga, had been fighting a losing battle against the superior American forces for several months. When he learned that the Marshall Islands had fallen, he withdrew the majority of his fleet 900 miles west to the Palau Islands. On

February 17 and 18, 1944, American bombers and battleships destroyed the remaining ships (three light cruisers, eight destroyers, and several miscellaneous warships) and hundreds of planes at Truk.

Plans for the invasion of Europe were firming up, as were the plans for Operation Forager, the occupation of the Marianas. Both operations called for almost 400 combat ships and 7,000 landing craft of various types carrying more than 300,000 soldiers. Incredibly, both major offensives began on the same day: June 6, 1944. While the Navy's role in the D-Day invasion was secondary to the Army's, in the Pacific the situation was almost the opposite, with the Navy providing invaluable support to the Army and Marines.

OPERATION OVERLORD—THE NORMANDY INVASION

With the bulk of the fleet in the Pacific, older battleships were assigned to fire support during the invasion of the Normandy region of France. These ranged from the *Nevada*, repaired since the bombing at Pearl Harbor, to the heavy cruiser the *Tuscaloosa*, and down to the World War I battleships the *Texas* and the *Arkansas*. At 4:45 A.M. on June 6, 1944, they and hundreds of other Allied ships began bombarding the German coastal defenses at the Utah and Omaha beaches. As the fleet engaged the gun emplacements, 200,000 men swarmed aboard amphibious landing craft that set out on the roiling waves soon afterward, heading for the beach.

At Utah, resistance was light. Gen. Omar Bradley's 1st Army gained a foothold almost immediately, with 21,000 men hitting the sand with 1,700 vehicles and thousands of tons of supplies.

Omaha, however, was more heavily fortified and by the end of the day had gained the nickname "Bloody Omaha." The Navy ships shelled the concrete gun turrets for hours, but a freshening wind made the ocean too choppy to get tanks ashore. The Germans there also received reinforcements from a nearby army division. It seemed that Bradley's force might be swept off the beach, so the warships pulled in as close to shore as possible and continued their bombardment, hitting artillery, tanks, bunkers, and anything else in range. By evening, the beach was secure and the first of millions of men and hundreds of thousands of tons of supplies and vehicles were being off-loaded.

The Navy's losses during D-Day were relatively light, consisting of the following ships destroyed:

3 destroyers (sunk by mines)

2 destroyer escorts

2 transports

2 minesweepers

1 submarine chaser

1 seaplane tender

4 LSTs (Landing Ship, Tank)

9 LCIs (Landing Craft Infantry, Large)

1 LCF (Landing Craft, Flak)

24 LCTs (Landing Craft, Tank)

8 LCMs (Landing Craft, Mechanized)

1 LCS (Landing Craft, Support)

81 LCVPs (Landing Craft, Vehicle and Personnel)

17 LCAs (Landing Craft, Assault)

7 LCPs (Landing Craft, Personnel, Large)

However, a huge storm three days later wreaked havoc on the ships offshore, destroying or damaging more than 300 small craft and, more important, destroying one of two artificial harbors (known as Mulberries) that been started there.

The Allies turned their attention to Cherbourg, France, which the Germans had originally thought would be the invasion target. General Bradley marched elements of the 1st Army to the city by June 25. A naval force of 3 battleships, 4 cruisers, and 11 destroyers under the command of Vice Adm. Morton Deyo was assigned to destroy the harbor's coastal defenses. In fierce shelling, the 280-mm German guns hit four destroyers and the *Texas*, but only one ship was damaged severely. Two days later, the city fell to the Army. Deyo's force sailed to help in Operation Dragoon, a second-front operation that involved taking the French port of Marseilles and preventing elements of the German army from flanking Gen. George Patton's 3rd Army. With a patched-together fleet of American, British,

French, and even Greek ships, the invasion commenced on August 15, with Navy ships again bombarding coastal defenses. Planes spotted for destroyers and kept an eye on the Germans, who soon retreated in the face of the troops coming ashore. Ten days later, the Allies were in Paris.

Navy technology helped the troops inland as well. When a crucial bridge over the Rhine River at Remagen was destroyed, the Navy dispatched LCVPs overland to ferry troops and equipment across the river. Without the Navy, the job simply couldn't have been done in Europe. And in the Pacific, this fact was even more apparent.

GOING THE REST OF THE WAY

While the U.S. Navy had been battling its way across the Pacific, General MacArthur had been doing the same thing (see *Alpha Bravo Delta Guide to the U.S. Army*). On June 13, 1944, Vice Admiral Mitscher began bombarding the Mariana Islands. Saipan was invaded two days later, covered by seven battleships, five cruisers, and seven escort carriers close to shore. Adm. Raymond Spruance commanded the Fifth Fleet farther out, made up of seven fleet carriers, seven fast carriers, and seven fast battleships.

Nimitz's plan to end up in the Mariana Islands had been working perfectly, but the string of relatively easy victories changed at Saipan, with faulty intelligence underestimating the enemy. Although air raids destroyed aircraft and artillery, much of the island's defenses remained intact. The invading Marines were in for another real fight: Elements were drawing together on the ocean for the final showdown between the American and Japanese fleets.

THE BATTLE OF THE PHILIPPINE SEA, OR "THE GREAT MARIANAS TURKEY SHOOT"

The First Mobile Fleet had been lying in wait for much of 1943 and the beginning of 1944, hoping to meet and destroy the U.S. Navy in one grand naval battle. When the Japanese force entered the Philippine Sea on June 13, it consisted of 5 fleet carriers and 4 light carriers, carrying a total of 430 airplanes and supported by 7 battleships and 13 cruisers. Commanded by Vice Adm. Jisaburo Ozawa, the fleet had planned to fight the Americans at the Caroline Islands, but when intelligence said that U.S. carriers were in the Marianas, Ozawa was ordered to find them.

Admiral Spruance reacted to the news of the approaching Japanese fleet with concern. Even though he had overwhelming numbers on his side (15 carriers carrying 891 airplanes, 7 battleships, 21 cruisers, 69 destroyers, and 26 submarines), he had problems. The bloody Saipan invasion had still not been finished. If he pulled out to meet the Japanese, the support near the island would be all the Marines had, leaving their transports vulnerable. Spruance ordered the rest of the waiting Army troops ashore and had the transports pull back.

By June 18, Ozawa knew approximately where the Americans were. Not wanting to fight at night, he waited until the next morning to attack. The admiral expected much of the American air force to have been destroyed by raids from aircraft based in the Mariana Islands. But U.S. attacks had crippled both air bases, leaving hardly any planes to send.

Spotting the American fleet at 7:30 A.M., Ozawa sent 2 waves of fighters and bombers, 69 in the first wave and 128 in the second wave launched a half-hour later. Having gone through the majority of their skilled pilots in earlier battles, the Japanese were no match for the experienced Americans. Add to this the new F6F "Hellcat" fighter, which could outrace, outclimb, and outdive the Zero, and the enemy force was doomed. The Japanese lost 42 planes in the first attack and 98 in the second (although only about 70 were actually downed by American pilots). A third wave with the remains of the Japanese air force, 82 planes, was also intercepted, with 73 of them shot down. All told, the Japanese lost more than 300 aircraft in one day's fighting, with 243 of them downed by carrier-based aircraft. The lopsided battle was dubbed "the Great Marianas Turkey Shoot." But that wasn't the only problem the Japanese had that day. American submarines also sank two aircraft carriers, the *Taiyo* and the *Shokaku*.

On June 20, the American fleet located the Japanese, who were retreating to refuel. Knowing they were outside the American airplanes' maximum range, Admiral Mitscher ordered a counterattack anyway. The swarm of 215 planes sank another carrier, the *Hiyo*, and two oil tankers; damaged three other carriers and one battleship; and shot down 80 more Japanese aircraft, bringing the total lost to more than 400. Ozawa gathered the battered remains of his fleet and retreated to Okinawa. Mitscher would have pursued, but he was busy recovering the planes that had run out of fuel and were ditching into the ocean all around his fleet, if they weren't crash-landing on the carriers. Spruance would have pursued the Japanese as well, but he felt he had to stay and protect the ground forces on Saipan.

Regardless, this battle crippled the Japanese air force. For the rest of the war, all enemy operations were without sufficient air support: They had just seven carriers left, and many planes were used to defend air bases on other islands, such as Formosa and Luzon.

ON TO THE PHILIPPINES

The U.S. advance continued, with the successful operation to capture the rest of Guam stretching into August 1944. At the end of July, President Roosevelt met with General MacArthur and Admiral Nimitz to finalize plans to reach Japan. Nimitz wanted to encircle and cut off the Philippines by bombing Luzon to the North and having MacArthur's mixed force capture Mindanao in the South. With both sides taken, they could then combine and invade the island of Formosa.

MacArthur took a contrary view as usual and said that any offensive action should include the Philippines. The Japanese would not be able to reinforce the islands easily, the local population was ready to revolt, and liberating the islands would be important for future U.S.–Philippine relations. Nimitz grudgingly agreed and sent Admiral Halsey to relieve Admiral Spruance with the Fifth Fleet, now renamed the Third Fleet. Mitscher's Task Force 58 was now called Task Force 38.

Halsey sent Mitscher's three task groups to Formosa, where the carrier aircraft would go up against a hastily assembled group of more than 1,000 planes. But the novice Japanese fighter pilots were outmatched by the battle-hardened Americans. In more than 1,300 sorties October 13–16, Allied forces shot down more than 500 planes and bombed ships, hangars, and fuel depots and ammunition dumps all over the island. The U.S. lost 79 planes and 64 airmen altogether. A heavy cruiser and light cruiser were also damaged, but both were quickly repaired and returned to action.

LAST CHANCE FOR THE JAPANESE: THE BATTLE FOR LEYTE GULF

Overjoyed by their success, the Americans moved up invasion of the Philippines two months. On October 20, 1944, MacArthur famously waded ashore and told the Filipinos, "I have returned!" He was standing at the head of the 6th Army, which consisted of 200,000 men and was backed by the largest one-nation invasion fleet in the world: 842 ships, with 261 warships.

By this time, the bulk of the Japanese navy consisted of some 64 warships of various kinds. The fleet sailed to the Philippines praying for a miracle—and almost got it.

The Japanese plan was similar to the one they had tried and failed with at Midway: to use part of the fleet as a diversion to divide the enemy, and then attack and destroy the separate units. The rest of the once-proud Imperial navy split into three forces, each one to approach Leyte Gulf from three directions: east, west, and south.

Although the Japanese forces came from three different directions, Navy documents call them the "Northern," "Center," and "Southern" fleets, which is how they will be referred to from here on.

The diversionary Northern force, led by Vice Admiral Ozawa, who had lost at the Philippine Sea four months earlier, consisted of one carrier, three light carriers, two battleships, three light cruisers, and eight destroyers. He was to lure as much of the American forces away from the island group as he could.

The Center group, led by Vice Adm. Takeo Kurita, would coordinate its 5 battleships, 10 heavy cruisers, 2 light cruisers, and 15 destroyers with the Southern group, made up of 2 battleships, 3 heavy cruisers, 1 light cruiser, and 11 destroyers, and led by 2 vice admirals, to launch simultaneous attacks from 2 directions on the main American force.

They faced a huge American force. The Seventh Fleet alone contained 6 battleships, 18 escort carriers, 4 heavy carriers, 5 light carriers, 83 destroyers, 25 destroyers' escorts, 11 frigates, and 44 torpedo boats. The Third Fleet consisted of 16 fleet carriers, 6 battleships, 6 heavy cruisers, 9 light cruisers, and 58 destroyers, all divided into 4 battle groups based on 4 or 5 carriers apiece.

Numerically, it should have been an easy victory. But whereas U.S. forces had the intelligence to forecast the Japanese Navy's movements, this time the enemy's plan worked much better. Also, although the U.S. forces had come together, they were still commanded by two different men, with

MacArthur controlling the Seventh Fleet and Halsey in charge of the Third Fleet. Admiral Nimitz's orders to Halsey—to cover the forces in the southwest unless the opportunity arose to attack a major portion of the enemy fleet, which would then become his primary assignment—were sufficiently vague to be interpreted a number of ways. Halsey's controversial decision, however, almost made the victory at Leyte a stalemate—or worse.

The Battle of Leyte Gulf actually consisted of four actions, each of which is detailed in the following sections.

Opening Moves—The Battle of the Sibuyan Sea

The fighting started well on October 23, 1944, when two U.S. submarines located the Center Force and attacked. They sank two heavy cruisers, one of them Vice Admiral Kurita's flagship, and damaged another heavy cruiser so badly that it withdrew.

Notified of where the Center Force was, Halsey had arranged his four carrier groups in an arc to cover the San Bernadino Strait between the islands of Samar and Luzon. Before his fleet could move, they were attacked by three waves of 50 bombers each from Luzon. The Hellcats and AA gunners drove them all off except for one plane, which hit the carrier the *Princeton*. Fires from the bomb spread to the torpedo storage hold, causing an explosion that gutted the carrier and heavily damaged a cruiser next to it. The *Princeton* was sunk that evening by an American cruiser.

Another carrier group of the Third Fleet had launched two attack waves on the Center Force, concentrating on one of the largest battleships in the world, the 65,000-ton *Musashi*. Twenty-one bombs and one torpedo later, the super-battleship rolled over and sank, taking at least 1,000 men with it. The air strikes hit three other battleships but didn't stop them, and they damaged a heavy cruiser enough that it had to turn back. Vice Admiral Kurita sent the rest of his force toward San Bernadino Strait again. An hour later, he received attack orders from the commander in chief of the Combined Fleet, Adm. Soemu Toyoda.

Meanwhile, the Southern Force was preparing to attack through the Surigao Strait at the southern end of the island group. Rear Adm. Thomas Kinkaid had foreseen an attack there and was preparing a suitable welcome for the Japanese.

At 3:40 P.M., scout planes from the Third Fleet spotted Ozawa's battle-ships and found his carriers an hour later. They reported this information back to Halsey, who felt they were the major threat. Wanting to decisively crush the Japanese carriers, he took the rest of his fleet and headed north to engage the diversionary force. Halsey didn't even radio the commanders of the Seventh to let them know his plans. Instead, Kinkaid intercepted a transmission that said three of the carrier groups were moving out. He assumed that a task force was staying behind to guard the strait, which was not the case. With his fourth group already engaged against the Center Force, the San Bernadino Strait was now unguarded, leaving the unaware Seventh Fleet wide open.

Between the Navy and a Hard Place—the Battle of Surigao Strait

The Japanese had divided their Southern force into two groups at Surigao. The vanguard, commanded by Vice Adm. Shoji Nishimura, consisted of two battleships, one heavy cruiser, and four destroyers. It proceeded first, fol-lowed by the rearguard, made up of two heavy cruisers, one light cruiser, and seven destroyers. Facing them were 6 battleships, 4 heavy and 4 light cruisers, 26 destroyers, and 39 torpedo boats, all led by Rear Adm. Jesse B. Oldendorf.

The advance unit entered the strait at approximately 10:30 P.M. on the night of October 24. Patrol Torpedo (PT) boats—fast, agile, 80-foot watercraft—began making hit-and-run attacks on the advancing force without much success. Their position reports, however, were invaluable, for they allowed the destroyers to set up on either side of the advancing line of ships and fire their torpedoes right down the middle. The two lead battleships were both hit—one sank and one continued. Three of the four destroyers were also hit; two sank and the third was forced to retreat.

All that was left to engage the American battleships and cruiser force lined up at the head of the strait in perfect raking fire formation were one battleship, one heavy cruiser, and one destroyer. The *T* was crossed to per-fection. The battleship and the cruiser were both destroyed, but the dam-aged destroyer almost escaped; it was later sunk by the PT boats.

The main Southern Force, commanded by Vice Adm. Kiyohide Shima, also ran into the PT boats, which torpedoed a light cruiser and forced it to withdraw from the formation, leaving only two heavy cruisers and seven destroyers. When Vice Admiral Shima encountered the burning hulk of the battleship sunk earlier, he ordered a retreat. His flagship then promptly collided with the still-burning wreck of a cruiser, damaging his vessel severely. Shima's force was harassed all the way back by the speedy American PT boats.

But while the Navy was repelling the Southern Force, the Center Force had sailed down San Bernadino Strait and right toward the unprotected Seventh Fleet.

Caught by Surprise—the Battle of Samar

With Halsey taking three quarters of his fleet to pursue the diversionary force, Vice Admiral Kurita's force advanced on the Seventh Fleet, whose primary mission was to provide air and antisubmarine support for the Leyte beachhead. The unit was not equipped or trained to combat an enemy fleet.

The early dawn on October 25 was peaceful until 6:45 A.M., when one of the six escort carriers of Task Unit 77.4.3 picked up a radar contact. Two minutes later, a pilot from another carrier spotted a large force of 4 battleships, 8 cruisers (6 heavy, 2 light), and 12 destroyers. Task Group 77.4.3 was commanded by Rear Adm. Clifton Sprague, who thought the Third Fleet still guarded the north entrance. The rest of the Seventh was 100 miles to the south, leaving the small force all alone. Besides the carriers, his force contained seven destroyers, which Sprague knew wasn't a match for the enemy fleet he'd found. Sprague ordered his fleet to get underway, but by 6:58 A.M., the Japanese were close enough to begin firing.

At 7:01, Sprague broadcast a call for assistance to the rest of the force as his group sailed east at 17 knots, almost their top speed. The Imperial navy ships could easily make 27 knots and were redeploying into an anti-aircraft formation when they sighted the U.S. fleet. In what later turned out to be a mistake, Vice Admiral Kurita ordered a "General Attack," letting each ship engage on its own without any oversight. The maneuvering ships struggled to get in a semblance of order to annihilate the enemy.

With huge Japanese battleships and heavy cruisers bearing down on them, Sprague sent his carriers into a nearby rain squall for cover and then circled them around to the southwest, hoping they would be able to launch aircraft. At 7:16 A.M., he ordered three destroyers, the *Heermann*, the *Hoel*, and *Johnston*, to attack. The trio sailed into almost certain death without hesitation, fearlessly engaging the superior enemy. The four escort destroyers also joined in, along with whatever aircraft Sprague could launch from his carriers as they left the area. For the next two and a half hours, the waters near Samar Island were a chaotic mass of shells, bombs, smoke, and flames.

> A crucial engagement in the first minutes of battle was the destroyer the *Heermann* versus the super-battleship the *Yamato,* Kurita's flagship. The *Heermann* launched a spread of four torpedoes at the massive vessel, which took frantic evasive action to get out of the way. As a result, the huge ship found itself cruising away from the battle at top speed, flanked on either side by a pair of American torpedoes, making it impossible to change course. By the time he shook his "escorts," Kurita's ship was well away from the main battle, preventing him from bringing his huge 18-inch guns into play during the fight.

Although the U.S. destroyers should have been blown out of the water, the lack of Japanese air support evened the odds. The planes repeatedly bombed the Center Force, making it constantly take evasive action. Three destroyers, the *Hoel,* the *Johnston,* and the escort the *Samuel B. Roberts,* were sunk. The escort carrier the *Gambier Bay* was also hit numerous times and sank at 9:07 A.M.

The Americans inflicted heavy damage on the enemy as well. Three of the Japanese heavy cruisers were sunk, primarily by the bombing raids, and most of the other ships had taken some damage as well. But although the *Yamato* was out of action, the Center Force had enough firepower to crush the task force and was on the verge of doing so when, incredibly, Vice Admiral Kurita ordered a withdrawal at 9:11 A.M. Out of sight of the action, he made his second mistake and assumed that the U.S. forces had escaped, just when the rest of his cruisers were on the verge of obliterating the battered task force. Admiral Sprague could hardly believe it when the remaining Japanese warships turned and left.

The main element of the Seventh Fleet was also coming under attack by this time, with a new twist—*kamikaze* fighters. The suicidal attacks focused on the first task force covering the Leyte beachhead and Sprague's group as well. One Zero impacted the *St. Lo,* damaging it severely enough to eventually sink the escort carrier. Four other *kamikaze* attacks damaged but did not sink four separate carriers.

Overwhelming Force—the Battle of Cape Engano

The rest of Halsey's fleet—13 carriers, 6 battleships, 12 cruisers, and 42 destroyers—moved at full speed to catch the Japanese carriers. Along the way, they split into two groups, one a task force of the new "fast battleships" led by Rear Adm. Willis Lee, and the rest of the fleet, commanded by Halsey. Halsey planned to send airplanes in first and then pursue with his warships.

At 4:30 A.M. on October 25, Admiral Mitscher had his planes readied on deck. He had launched his first attack group of 180 planes before they had visual confirmation of the Northern Force, and he was simply waiting to unleash them. When the first sighting came at 7:10, he got his chance.

The bombs began falling at 8:00 and lasted all day. With a little more than 100 planes total among his carriers, and pilots so inexperienced that they could barely take off from a carrier deck, Ozawa's fleet provided little resistance. When it was over, his flagship, the *Zuikaku* (which had struck Pearl Harbor), a destroyer, and two light carriers were sunk. All of the other ships had taken damage as well.

Twenty-two minutes into the offensive, urgent messages began coming in from the Seventh Fleet requesting help from Halsey. The admiral knew his forces could not get back to help in time. Unaware that Kurita's Center Force had not been stopped, he thought he was fighting the greatest threat to the Seventh Fleet. Therefore, he didn't send any ships down until he received the following message from Admiral Nimitz at 10:00 A.M.:

"WHERE IS RPT (repeat) WHERE IS TASK FORCE 34 THE WORLD WONDERS"

The last three words were meaningless jargon to confuse enemy code listeners, but the radioman who was supposed to remove them when he delivered the message to Halsey didn't. The admiral took the message as a grave insult and sent Task Force 34 back to Leyte Gulf, accompanied by a carrier group for air support. Rear Admiral Lee got the order to move out right when his ships were approaching within cannon range of the enemy. To his dying day Halsey claimed he had made the right decision, that the carriers were the biggest threat. The debate over his actions has continued since the end of the war.

With the fast battleships on their way back, a force of four cruisers and nine destroyers was detached to continue escorting the rest of the carriers in the Third Fleet. Around 2:25 P.M., Mitscher ordered this group to pursue the retreating Northern Force. It sank the already damaged last carrier and another destroyer. At 11:10 that evening, a U.S. submarine torpedoed the light cruiser the *Tama*, finishing the last action of the Battle of Leyte Gulf.

While still a decisive American victory, Leyte Gulf should have been an overwhelming one. Halsey's decision to leave San Bernadino Strait unguarded—and, even worse, not tell anyone—contributed to the loss of 1,500 American sailors and the sacrifice of 2 destroyers and a destroyer escort, along with the loss of 3 small carriers. The Japanese losses were much higher, including 10,000 men killed in action and the sinking of their 4 carriers, 3 battleships, 10 cruisers, and 11 destroyers. Their gamble had failed. The fleet was all but decimated afterward and was not a factor for the rest of the war.

With the Imperial navy out of action, MacArthur secured the Luzon and Mindoro islands and then moved on to the dozens of smaller islands that made up the rest of the Philippines. The massive land, air, and sea operation continued for three months, hampered by the *kamikaze* strikes from Japanese planes.

Translated from Japanese, *kamikaze* means "divine wind." It was a method used late in the war by the Imperial military not only to destroy U.S. Navy ships, but also to psychologically discourage the American military by showing how dedicated the Japanese were to their nation. Inexperienced young pilots volunteered to fly their planes into enemy ships, believing they were doing their duty for their emperor and Japan.

The escort carrier the *Ommaney Bay* was sunk by a *kamikaze*, as carriers and cruisers were both targets of these devastating assaults. The worst of these happened on January 6, 1945, during Vice Admiral Jesse Oldendorf's shore bombardment of Luzon before the invasion. His Fire Support Unit of 6 battleships, 6 cruisers, and 14 destroyers came under attack by *kamikaze* planes, which hit 1 battleship, 3 cruisers, and 4 destroyers and sank 1, the *Long*. A plane impacting the bridge of the flagship the *New Orleans* killed the ship's captain and two British military representatives. The next day, Japanese planes dove from the skies again, hitting two more destroyers and forcing another destroyer to fall back for repairs.

The Luzon invasion began on January 7 and was largely successful because Oldendorf's fleet was suffering most of the *kamikaze* attacks. On January 8, however, the Japanese targeted the 40-mile-long convoy, forcing a carrier to turn back and hitting the flagship of the group as well. But the assault continued and Luzon fell, as did the rest of the Philippines in savage, bloody fighting (see *Alpha Bravo Delta Guide to the U.S. Army*). From there on, the Navy's role primarily was what it had been during D-Day: providing fire support and escorting troop transports from island to island, now always watching the skies for *kamikaze* attacks.

THE END OF THE WAR

In Europe, the invasion had been successful. The German army had been caught in a pincer movement of its own making. Hitler's two-front land war had failed. The last German offensive, at Bastogne, Belgium, in mid-December 1944 through January 1945, had been decisively repelled with heavy losses to the crumbling Third Reich in the Battle of the Bulge.

The Allied leaders met in Yalta in February 1945 to discuss plans for Europe and to finish the war against Japan. Roosevelt called upon Stalin to send men to the Asian front. Stalin said he would comply as soon as Germany surrendered.

Before the Nazis could be finally defeated, the world was rocked by two deaths. On April 12, 1945, Franklin D. Roosevelt died of a cerebral hemorrhage. On the afternoon of April 30, Adolph Hitler, broken and insane, killed himself while Russian troops sacked Berlin.

Command of the remains of the German military passed to Adm. Karl Dönitz, who was unaware at the time that Hitler was dead. Dönitz and Adm. Hans von Friedeburg immediately began negotiating the terms of a cease-fire agreement with the Allies. On May 7, the Germans signed the treaty with Allied representatives; the next day, they signed again in front of the Soviets. May 8, 1945, became the anniversary of the victory in Europe.

Japan, however, was another matter. In March, the Marines took Iwo Jima. In April, Okinawa was invaded, beginning a two-month campaign. (See *Alpha Bravo Delta Guide to the U.S. Marines.*) The *kamikaze* pilots were still a thorn in the fleet's side, sinking dozens of ships at the two islands and killing almost 5,000 men. But the Americans kept moving forward.

During the struggle to capture Okinawa, the last Japanese super-battleship, the 65,000-ton *Yamato,* armed with nine 18-inch guns, headed to its final battle. Assigned to help fight the naval forces at Okinawa, the vessel's orders included beaching itself as an instant fortress, if necessary.

Two hundred miles from the island, the battleship was spotted by American patrols. A large air force, over 350 planes total, took off to sink the last symbol of the Imperial navy. With no air cover, the outcome was predestined. At 2:23 P.M. on April 7, the mighty warship slipped beneath the waves and took with it the last vestiges of the Japanese naval presence.

In 1985 and 1999, the *Yamato*'s remains were located in 1,000 feet of water and were examined. The once great ship now lies in two parts, a bow portion and a main battery clustered together, and the midships and stern section lying overturned nearby. More than anything else, the *Yamato* represented the pride and overconfidence of the Japanese navy in World War II.

With the staging point for an invasion of Japan secure, the plans were put into effect, including overwhelming air raids on the Japanese islands. Under pressure in China as well as in its holdings in the Pacific, and fighting on beyond all hope or reason, the Japanese government still didn't surrender. Then new President Harry S. Truman revealed the American secret weapon: the atomic bomb. Testing had proved its ability, and Truman immediately released the Potsdam Declaration on July 26, which delineated the surrender terms for the Axis and set up the organization of the United Nations.

Truman was, in effect, calling for Japan's immediate and unconditional surrender. But it was not to be. It took two atomic bombs on Hiroshima and Nagasaki to force the government to concede defeat. Still, it took an order from Emperor Hirohito himself to make many military officers accept that they were beaten.

On September 2, 1945, representatives of the emperor, including the prime minister, came aboard the USS *Missouri,* Fleet Admiral Nimitz's flagship, to sign the armistice terms. Six years after the war had begun, and four years after the United States had become involved, World War II was over.

CHAPTER 14

PEACE AND THE COLD WAR

The peace brought about by the alliance between the United States, Great Britain, and Russia didn't last long. As early as 1947, the United States and the USSR were adversaries again. The United States remembered the Soviet Union's broken promises to leave Poland alone and its promotion of communist governments in countries such as Bulgaria, Czechoslovakia, Romania, Yugoslavia, and East Germany, and Middle Eastern countries such as Afghanistan. The world was on the edge of a cold war, not of offensives and invasions, but of atomic and later nuclear brinksmanship.

Amid all this, the U.S. Navy found its successes in the Atlantic and Pacific overshadowed by two atomic bombs. With the dawn of the nuclear age and no other navy that could even hope to face America's fleet, the inevitable cutbacks began. The naval budget for 1947 was chopped from $5.1 billion to $4.1 billion. By 1948, as had traditionally happened after war, the Navy had been reduced 75%, to just 267 combat ships.

One of the high points of the post–World War II era was Admiral Nimitz's creation of the Blue Angels, a squadron of precision-flying aircraft and pilots that would "enhance Navy recruiting and credibly represent Navy and Marine Corps aviation and the armed forces of America as ambassadors of good will."

Formed in 1946, the Blue Angels were first led by Lt. Commander Roy Voris and flew the Grumman F6F Hellcat. By August, they were using the F8F Bearcat and created the famed "diamond" formation, with four planes flying just a few feet apart from each other at hundreds of miles per hour. Since then, the Angels have gone through several planes, including the F9F-5 Panther, the F9F-8 Cougar, the F11F-1 Tiger, and the F-4J Phantom II. In 1974, they moved to the McDonnell Douglas A-44F Skyhawk II and were renamed the Navy Flight Demonstration Squadron. In 1986, the Blue Angels celebrated their fortieth anniversary and unveiled their new fighter, the McDonnell Douglas F/A-18 Hornet. Since 1946, the Angels have flown for more than 260 million spectators and still put on 70 performances a year during the show season.

This is not to say that the shrinkage didn't happen without a fight. Navy secretary Frank Knox had died in office in mid-1944 and was replaced by James V. Forrestal, who had served in the secretary's office since 1940. Suspicious of the Soviet Union, he wanted the United States to maintain its presence around the world, especially in maritime affairs, and knew that isolationism wouldn't work anymore. He fought tooth and nail for every budget dollar, saying that although the atomic bomb was powerful, it still needed carrier-based aircraft for delivery.

Forrestal and Navy leaders began re-engineering the fleet for the future. Under the guidance of Rear Adm. Harold B. Salada and Adm. Marc Mitscher, a new kind of aircraft carrier was proposed to carry long-range bombers as soon as a smaller atomic bomb was developed (the original weapons each weighed 10,000 pounds). Only the largest carriers could currently handle a 45,000-pound (including one bomb) long-range bomber.

The leaders of the Navy were also looking for a way to watch the burgeoning submarine fleet the Soviet Union was putting into the water. From 1945 to 1950, the USSR launched 350 submarines, outnumbering the U.S. fleet by 2 to 1. Looking to even the odds, the Navy examined using nuclear energy to power a ship instead of a bomb. To do this, they needed a genius, and they found one in Adm. Hyman G. Rickover (see Appendix B).

The Navy was fighting a two-front war as well; the new opponent was the newly created United States Air Force. The old Army Air Corps had demanded all aviation, land or sea-based, be assigned to the new department. The USAF, created under the National Security Act of 1947, continued its unsuccessful lobbying for two more years.

With the traditional keeper of the seas, Great Britain, razed by World War II, America was the only choice left to maintain a worldwide naval presence. In 1947, the Mediterranean Naval Force was established, the precursor to the powerful Sixth Fleet. Also that year came the first in a series of major operations into both Antarctica, under the command of polar explorer Adm. Richard E. Byrd, and the Arctic as well.

In March 1948, Russia tried to force the Europeans and Americans out of West Berlin by blockading the city, leaving only the airports open. Air Force Major Gen. Curtis LeMay informed the government that he would need 3,500 tons of supplies per day, along with 1,000 tons of coal per day in winter. The new Air Force couldn't supply enough planes, so two Navy transport squadrons were sent. In a matter of days they were outflying the Air Force, supplying the city with more than 6,500 tons of cargo in their first two weeks on the job. Soon the Navy squadrons led the entire effort in total cargo, efficiency, and gross tons per aircraft. In April 1949, the two squadrons brought in more than 23,500 tons of food and supplies and showed no sign of stopping. By May, the Russians had stopped the blockade, but the Navy squadrons were still on duty until August of that year.

Cold weather was replaced by cold war as friction grew between Russia and the former Allies. In 1948–1949, China entered into a civil war between the nationalists, led by Gen, Chiang Kai-Shek, whom the United States had been supporting since the late 1930s, and the Communist party, led by Mao Tse-tung. The nationalists had been declining for years, and in 1948 President Truman cut off U.S. funding. Less than a year later, Nanking and Shanghai had fallen, and by October 1949, China was completely communist.

The year 1949 was a pivotal year in other areas of the world as well. America joined with Great Britain, Belgium, Canada, Denmark, France, Iceland, Italy, Luxembourg, the Netherlands, Norway, and Portugal to form the military alliance known as the North American Treaty Organization, or NATO. That was also the year that the Soviet Union announced that it had detonated an atomic bomb. The National Security Council responded that America's military must keep parity with the USSR's forces. The arms race had begun, and the temperature of the cold war dropped several degrees.

By this time James Forrestal was the secretary of defense, but he lasted only two years in the position and died in May. His replacement, Louis

Johnson, thought future battles would be fought by ground soldiers and nuclear bombers. He made his stance clear by canceling the newest aircraft carrier, the *United States*, begun on April 18 and scrapped five days later. The Navy protested, culminating with the resignation of Secretary of the Navy, John L. Sullivan, and of CNO Adm. Louis E. Denfeld. But just when it seemed that naval aviation (and perhaps the Navy itself) was on the verge of extinction, the Korean conflict reinforced the importance of the aircraft carrier in combat.

BLOOD AND SNOW—THE KOREAN CONFLICT

In 1945, part of the Japanese surrender included giving up Korea, with Russia accepting the northern half's surrender (above the thirty-eighth parallel) and the United States accepting the southern half's. The Soviet Union consolidated another communist government in the North, repressing the populace and refusing to allow free elections. In 1950, the U.S.S.R. launched an invasion of South Korea, overrunning its ill-prepared forces and capturing the capital city of Seoul. The North Korean forces pushed the Americans back to the southernmost tip of the peninsula. President Truman ordered Seventh Fleet cruisers to blockade the coast and shell enemy positions while carrier-based planes flew support for the soldiers.

Although the U.S. government was willing to defend South Korea, President Truman had to ensure that the conflict wouldn't grow to involve Communist China, which might have used the distraction to attack remaining nationalists on Taiwan. Receiving a resolution from the United Nations to organize a multinational force to stop the invasion, Army and Navy men and ships were scrambled to the area. After a daring amphibious landing at the tidal flats of Inchon led by General MacArthur, American forces retook Seoul, cutting off the North Koreans near Pusan. MacArthur gained approval to take the offensive north. He sent another force ashore at Wonsan, despite the presence of 3,000 mines in the harbor, which were cleared by the Navy with the loss of two minesweepers.

Despite warnings from China that it would respond militarily, the American advance continued north. Near the Yalu River, the two separate U.S. armies ran into 180,000 Chinese troops. The U.S. forces were forced back to the thirty-eighth parallel, and around 105,000 soldiers and Marines were evacuated from the port city of Hungnam, which would have been impossible without the Navy's control of the seas around Korea. In all, five ships were lost—the two previously mentioned and three others, two mine-sweepers and a fleet tugboat—from mines. The majority of ship damage came from shore batteries at Wonsan, Songjin, and Hongwon, on the North Korean coast.

The Army dug in at the thirty-eighth parallel, MacArthur was replaced, and peace talks went on for two years while sporadic fighting continued. At last a truce was negotiated in July 1953, setting the border between the two nations at the thirty-eighth parallel—exactly where it had been three years before.

Once again a war had come to the Navy's rescue. Conventional war strategy, tactics, and technology were still a vital component of America's military, and the Navy was the best way of getting troops and planes to a war zone. Johnson was dismissed, and the Navy budget mushroomed from $4 billion in 1950 to $16 billion in 1952. The carrier the *United States* was started again (and finished this time), and provisions were made for an additional carrier every year until the 1960s. More men were kept on duty, and for the next two decades the personnel rosters remained steady at about 600,000 officers and sailors.

In 1952, President Truman lobbied for a five-year, $50 billion program to upgrade the U.S. military. The Navy's cut financed 173 new ships, the refitting of 291 existing vessels, a second aircraft carrier, and a nuclear submarine. The nuclear arms race continued between the United States and Russia with the development and detonation of the hydrogen bomb in 1953, the same year Gen. Dwight D. Eisenhower was elected president.

The next generation of aircraft carriers arrived in 1954 with launch of the USS *Forrestal*. This was also the year that the U.S. Navy, the last to abandon sail power in the nineteenth century, became the first to embrace nuclear power in the twentieth, launching the world's first nuclear-powered submarine, the USS *Nautilus*.

But the Navy wasn't done yet. Under the command of Adm. Arleigh Burke, a program was begun to install nuclear-tipped missiles on nuclear submarines. The first of these ballistic-missile submarines, the 350-foot *George Washington*, was commissioned in 1959, with the first missile test launch on July 20, 1960.

The first supercarrier, the USS Forrestal, *underway in 1987.*

During this time, President Eisenhower promised aid to any country that felt threatened by the communists—and backed up his promise on several occasions, often with the Navy. In 1958, elements of the Sixth Fleet staged a landing in Lebanon to support its president against Syrian-backed Muslims and as a warning to pro-Soviet, anti-Western forces that had just taken over Iraq. The unopposed landing was peaceful, and America's point about defending other countries was made.

In August 1958, the nationalists and communists in China were arguing over possession of the Quemoy Islands in Amoy harbor. When the mainland government blockaded the port and began bombarding the island, Eisenhower sent the Seventh Fleet to reinforce his announcement that the islands would not be taken over. A task force consisting of the carriers the *Midway* and the *Essex*, five attack carriers, and an antisubmarine carrier, two heavy cruisers, several destroyers, and amphibious ships patrolled the strait between Taiwan and the Quemoy Islands. By October, the Chinese had worked it out among themselves, and the crisis ended. Eisenhower had twice shown the world America's resolve without firing a shot, and he let the Chinese and the Soviet Union know he was serious about protecting world interests.

THE 1960S—THE COLD WAR FREEZES SOLID IN CUBA AND VIETNAM

In 1960, John F. Kennedy rose to the presidency partly by claiming that Eisenhower had let a "missile gap" grow between the United States and the USSR. His administration spent billions increasing and modernizing the nuclear missile program. The Navy received its first nuclear-powered aircraft carrier and frigate in 1961 and gained a nuclear-powered cruiser and an extended-range Polaris missile in 1962. The next-generation of missile submarines appeared in 1963.

From February 16 to May 10, 1960, the nuclear submarine the *Triton*, commanded by Capt. Edward L. Beach, sailed around the world completely submerged except in two short instances. What had taken the sloop the *Vincennes* two years to accomplish in 1829–1830 had been achieved in 12 weeks just 130 years later.

Kennedy, however, didn't back up his words against the Soviets like Eisenhower had. Incidents such as the April 1961 Bay of Pigs fiasco— in which Cuban exiles trying to overthrow dictator Fidel Castro were slaughtered as they entered the harbor while the carrier the *Essex* and five U.S. destroyers watched off the coast, forbidden to interfere—revealed the U.S.'s unwillingness to get involved.

Castro requested and got increased Soviet protection, which led directly to the Cuban Missile Crisis of 1962. When the American government learned of 42 missile sites on the island, it was furious. Only 150 miles off Florida, Soviet Intermediate Range Ballistic Missiles (IRBMs) could target the East Coast with impunity. Kennedy announced a maritime quarantine of Cuba and demanded that the missiles be removed. A large portion of the Atlantic Fleet (183 ships, including 8 carriers) was mobilized into the Caribbean Sea, supported by vessels from NATO, Argentina, the Dominican Republic, and Venezuela. Kennedy gave the Soviets 36 hours warning before enacting the quarantine on October 24, 1962. The test came soon, as 25 Soviet supply-bearing ships were already en route to the island.

Early on October 24, the Navy challenged two merchant ships with a submarine escort. They stopped, and other subs in the area surfaced as well; oncoming transports either stopped for boarding and inspection or turned away. Four days later, the leader of the USSR, Nikita Khruschev, announced that the missiles would be returned to the Soviet Union, ending a stalemate that could have led to a nuclear exchange. But even as America and Russia locked horns over the Caribbean, another conflict 17,000 miles away was about to drag America into 10 years of conflict both abroad and at home.

FIGHTING THE DOMINO EFFECT—AMERICAN INTERVENTION IN VIETNAM

The United States had always had a vested interest in Vietnam since the French (supported by America) had been defeated by the Viet Minh in the early 1950s. A 1954 peace treaty divided the nation into two countries, North and South Vietnam, at the Seventeenth Parallel. South Vietnam elected a president and tried to run a democratic government, while the North turned hard-line communist, always with an eye toward "persuading" its southern neighbor to unite.

Fearing that if Communism wasn't checked in Vietnam it could spread throughout Southeast Asia (American advisors theorized that one country after another would fall in the feared Domino Effect), the government took increasingly aggressive steps to help South Vietnam in the early 1960s. First came military advisors—685 in 1960. By Kennedy's assassination in 1963 there were 16,700. Kennedy had also authorized the use of bombers to attack the Viet Cong.

After winning the election, new President Lyndon Johnson's first goal was to make sure Vietnam didn't become another China. After the Gulf of Tonkin incident, Johnson was given the power to send troops to Vietnam without an official declaration of war.

The Gulf of Tonkin, a stretch of water between North Vietnam and China, had been the site of dozens of torpedo boat raids from both sides. In February 1964, Secretary of Defense Robert McNamara ordered U.S. destroyers to patrol and monitor the gulf. On August 2, the USS *Maddox* was attacked by a North Vietnamese vessel. Two days later, the *Turner Joy* reported being fired upon, although aerial witnesses did not see any North Vietnamese boats in the area.

On August 7, 1964, Congress passed the Gulf of Tonkin Resolution, giving the president the power to "take all necessary measures to repel any armed attack against the forces of the United States and to prevent further aggression."

Johnson increased the U.S. presence off the coast of Vietnam from the two carriers of Task Force 77 (the *Ticonderoga* and the *Constellation*) to several procured from fleets in both the Atlantic and Pacific oceans. As North Vietnam had no navy other than coastal patrol boats, the fleet had nothing to fear on the open sea. The carriers were divided into two groups, with one operating at "Dixie Station" off the coast of South Vietnam, providing air support for ground operations. The other group, at "Yankee Station" in the Gulf of Tonkin on the North Vietnam coast, was responsible for finding and bombing targets in enemy territory.

In the early months, America just tried to drop enough bombs on North Vietnam to make the government negotiate for peace. Due to the heavy defenses arrayed against the fighters and bombers, including enemy MiG fighters, anti-aircraft guns, and surface-to-air missiles, the air war resulted in many American planes getting shot down. More than 400 Navy planes were downed from 1965 to 1968, with 450 airmen killed or missing in action. When the bombing didn't achieve its goals, the U.S. upped its involvement in the mission dubbed "Market Time," which involved, among other aspects, a blockade of Vietnam, including the shallow rivers and tributaries that flowed into the Mekong River delta. To patrol these areas, the Navy revived a unit that hadn't been seen since the Civil War: the riverine force. Fighting alongside were the Navy SEALS.

The most elite unit in the Navy traces its roots to the Naval Construction Battalion (SeaBees) in World War II, when volunteers were recruited to scout ahead and clear beach hazards for invading soldiers. The special units were instrumental in clearing obstacles at Omaha and Utah beaches on D-Day, and they were reorganized into Underwater Demolition Teams (UDT). UDTs operated in Korea as well and assisted in the redeployment of the UN forces there by conducting reconnaissance and infiltrating enemy guerilla units.

In January 1962, the first SEAL teams were commissioned out of the UDTs for unconventional warfare, counterguerilla warfare, and clandestine operations in all maritime environments. Instrumental during the Vietnam Conflict, SEAL teams did everything from set up listening posts or ambushes, to rescue prisoners of war.

Since then, they have performed missions around the world, from Grenada to Panama to the Persian Gulf. The men who comprise the two SEAL units, one stationed in the Atlantic Ocean and one in the Pacific Ocean, are among the most highly trained in the world. Often working in tandem with two other special Navy units, the Special Boat Squadrons (SBSs) and the Swimmer Delivery Vessel Teams (SDVs), the SEALs can be inserted, complete their mission, and be picked up from a combat zone, often without anyone even knowing they were there.

During the early months, the riverine forces suffered from a lack of capable boats, supplies, and trustworthy intelligence about the delta. In 1965, the Navy borrowed a flotilla of 82-foot-long patrol boats, which they armed with machine guns and mortars. They were soon joined by aluminum-hulled fast patrol craft, letting the Navy go anywhere the Viet Cong were. In the two years of Operation Market Time, from June 1966 to June 1968, Navy forces inspected more than 400,000 small craft and vessels.

The riverine forces also attempted to stem the flow of men and supplies moving through the Mekong Delta itself, primarily by patrolling the main river and inspecting boats sailing up and down the tributaries. Army platoons were later added for search-and-destroy missions against Viet Cong guerilla outposts upriver. Sometimes these plans backfired, as in the ambush against 18 U.S. boats in September 1967 that killed 5 men and wounded 77.

Toward the end of 1968, Adm. Elmo Zumwalt enacted Operation Sea Lords, a two-year blockade and patrol of the rivers and canals between Vietnam and Cambodia to stop more soldiers and equipment from entering Vietnam. Operation Sea Dragon was another antishipping program that extended boarding patrols to the Twentieth Parallel and into the Demilitarized Zone.

In 1968, Richard Nixon was elected president and planned to withdraw from Vietnam and turn over the fighting to the South Vietnamese Army. By the middle of 1970, America was leaving, with the nuclear carrier the *Enterprise* covering the last helicopters evacuating people from the beleaguered country in 1975.

Morale in the military was at an all-time low, with many wondering why the United States had fought a war that to them didn't seem to have any impact on America at all. Unlike previous conflicts, the United States was not in danger from a tiny country halfway around the world. The stress and dissatisfaction manifested in other ways as well. In October 1972, almost 200 men aboard the carrier the *Kitty Hawk*, frustrated by eight months of constant duty and no support back home, rioted. When it was over, 60 men were injured, 4 so seriously that they were treated at hospitals.

Tensions were also inflamed by the late 1960s riots in American cities. In the same year as the *Kitty Hawk* riot, 144 sailors, African Americans and whites both, protested aboard the carrier the *Constellation*. That incident ended without violence, and although President Nixon wanted every participant dishonorably discharged (the only Navy statute they had broken was to be a few hours AWOL, hardly a cashiering offense), Admiral Zumwalt ignored the impossible order. Nevertheless, the turbulent times did not speak well of the seemingly disorganized, chaotic Navy.

The fleet had victories and failures during this period, from the savage infighting between military branches after World War II to the upswing it received from the Korean War. Then came the steady build-up during the cold war, including the creation of the first nuclear vessels during the 1950s and 1960s, to the futile effort to save South Vietnam from Communism and that fallout afterward. The swelling peace movement would hit the military hard in the 1970s, and the Navy would be no exception.

During the first years of the Vietnam Conflict, American fighter pilots were getting shot down more frequently and weren't destroying the enemy as they had in World War II and Korea. To combat the situation, Capt. Frank Ault recommended forming a graduate-level training program dedicated to aerial combat.

Established at the Miramar Naval Air Station in 1969, the first "Top Gun" course was a four-week program simulating real combat conditions. More than 30 years later, the Top Gun program reports directly to the Chief of Naval Operations and still trains the best Navy and Marine pilots in the latest in aerial tactics, dogfighting, and technology. Each student must study an exhaustive curriculum as well as fly against instructors flying "enemy" aircraft. A graduate is expected to pass on his knowledge to his squadron. The program also teaches carrier-based air wing tactics for the F-14 and F/A-18 fighter planes.

In 1997, the program was transferred to Falloon Naval Air Station near Reno, Nevada, and became part of the Naval Strike Warfare Center. Today, Top Gun continues training the best pilots in the world how to be even better.

CHAPTER 15

SUPPORT AROUND THE WORLD

After Vietnam, the American public's faith in the country and the military were severely shaken. Despite the best efforts of people like Chief of Naval Operations Adm. Elmo Zumwalt, whose progressive programs were supposed to improve the fleet, the Navy entered a period of serious decline in the late 1970s. Although President Gerald Ford put forward a five-year construction plan for 156 ships, he was occupied with rebuilding American morale after the Vietnam conflict as well as the Watergate political scandal.

Nuclear power was still popular, and three new aircraft carriers, the *Nimitz*, the *Dwight D. Eisenhower*, and the *Carl Vinson*, were still moving toward construction at a cost of $2.5 billion each. Zumwalt's CNO replacement, Adm. James Holloway III, also proposed a nuclear cruiser for escorting carriers and antiship missile defense.

In 1976, Jimmy Carter took office and the Navy suffered even more. Even though he was a former Navy man, Carter tried to cut funding for almost everything, including the nuclear carrier and cruiser programs. Congress disagreed, and the battle over naval appropriations raged on Capitol Hill.

THE FLEET RACE CONTINUES

While the U.S. Navy was shrinking, the Soviet Union's navy grew at an alarming rate. By 1978, the USSR had 740 warships to the America's 436 ships. As the Navy had scrapped its elderly destroyer fleet, it had replaced them with dozens of frigates and missile patrol boats. The nuclear submarine program was healthy, containing 41 ballistic-missile boats and 68 conventional nuclear submarines. The Soviet Union had a submarine fleet of 294 vessels, although more than 100 of them were non-nuclear. Rickover and Zumwalt concurred that the Russian sub fleet was a potential threat.

The United States had a comfortable lead in aircraft carriers, possessing 21 to the Russia's 3 helicopter carriers, but it was behind in every other class of ship. Two supercarriers had been completed, although four years late; the *Carl Vinson* was only half built by 1978, and the fourth proposed carrier was scrapped along with 86 vessels from Ford's proposed shipbuilding plan.

The cycle of build and reduce had come full circle, and much like the contempt fostered by the rest of the world toward the outmoded American fleet during the 30 years after the Civil War, the disorganized, bickering Navy of the late 1970s became a laughingstock all over again.

Matters came to a head in 1979 with the revolution in Iran. President Carter ordered a carrier fleet to the Arabian Sea in March. There were rumblings about the Soviet Union planning an invasion of Afghanistan, but Carter's attention was on Iran, and he didn't seem to notice. In early November, Iranian militants broke into the U.S. embassy and took 66 personnel hostage. The Navy reinstated the canceled supercarrier, and Carter approved it this time, also ordering another carrier group to the Arabian Sea. When some of the hostages were released, a third group was sent over in late November because the show of force seemed to be working. But by the end of the year, the remaining 53 captives were still in Iran. Also, despite American warnings, Russia moved troops into Afghanistan, beginning a decade-long war in the country. The Carter administration appeared helpless against these depredations.

The U.S. military tried to rescue the hostages in 1980. Eight Marine helicopters from the *Nimitz* were supposed to rendezvous with Air Force transports from Egypt, but the aircraft couldn't handle the desert sand. Three of them turned back with mechanical difficulties, and another collided with a transport plane, killing eight crewmen and aborting the mission. The failed mission helped seal Carter's fate as a one-term president.

AMERICA VERSUS THE "EVIL EMPIRE"

America and the Navy were both ready for a change, and it came with President Ronald Reagan and his Secretary of the Navy, John Lehman. Both were promilitary and pro-Navy, and they looked to reverse the decline of the fleet and the men serving in it. Lehman publicly stated the Navy he wanted: 600 ships, with 15 carrier groups, 100 nuclear missile submarines, and 4 surface groups based around a battleship, including 4 renovated World War II warships (see Appendix C).

The reinvigorated Navy would need a lot of cash to rebuild after five years of cuts. The Reagan administration was happy to comply, boosting the Navy's budget from $6.6 billion to $11.6 billion.

> With the increase in spending came a corresponding decrease in oversight. Reporters learned that the Navy was paying outrageous sums for everyday items, including $659 for an ashtray and $436 for a hammer. When the story broke, Secretary of the Navy Lehman acknowledged the problems and took steps to fix the spending issue, but the Navy still endured a fair share of jokes at its expense.

The first potential trouble spot in 1981 came when the Navy jets shot down two Libyan fighters over the Gulf of Sidra, challenging Colonel Muammar al-Qaddafi's claim to the entire gulf (even international waters) as Libyan territory. Faced with the undeniable show of power, Qaddafi did not press his claim any farther.

Fleet elements were active in America's backyard as well. A communist revolution in El Salvador in 1983 was brought to the attention of the United States, which supplied advisors and 1,000 soldiers, similar to the Vietnam build-up two decades earlier. Carrier groups flanked both coasts of Nicaragua, and a SEAL covert operations team leader was assassinated in El Salvador, becoming the first American casualty in the area. With the shadows of Vietnam still in the American public's mind, the government didn't push for a full-scale commitment, and the region remained unstable through the 1980s.

Two other incidents defined military action in 1983. First, the bombing of the Marine barracks in Beirut on October 19 killed 241 men and wounded 105, many of whom were airlifted to the USS *Iwo Jima*, part of the Sixth Fleet patrolling offshore.

The second was the military coup that occurred in Grenada four days earlier. Hard-line communists had taken over the government and executed the Marxist prime minister. With 1,000 American medical students trapped there, a 12-ship task force with 1,900 Marines was sent immediately. On October 25, Vice Adm. Joseph Metcalf Jr. received orders to take Grenada. A multipronged assault by SEALs and Marines landed at several points and took the entire island by October 26. Casualties included 18 killed and 116 wounded. Further investigation revealed a definite military alliance with the Soviets. When the American forces left, a new, pro–U.S. government had been set up.

In 1985, America got involved in the war on terrorism. On October 7, the ocean liner the *Achille Lauro* was hijacked by Palestinian terrorists demanding the release of 50 of their imprisoned brethren in Israel. The vessel was quickly spotted and followed by the U.S. missile cruiser the USS *Scott*. When the terrorists tried to escape to Egypt, they were intercepted by American F-14s from the *Saratoga*. Their plane was forced down in Rome, where the terrorists were taken into custody.

At home, Lehman was just getting started. Instead of following the accepted policy of containing the Soviets at the naval defense line running through Greenland and Iceland, the secretary of the Navy pushed for war plans that involved carrier groups sailing to and attacking Russian bases. Detractors claimed that the weather and plans to attack the USSR in its own backyard would just cost the Navy ships and men. Fortunately, the plan never had to be put into effect, so the outcome will never be known.

Lehman also wanted to overhaul naval aviation. The secretary denounced the December 1984 air strike on Syria, in which the Navy lost two reconnaissance planes and two bombers, as an obsolete plan. He pushed for night raids, which brought some objections because of the increased risk involved. But when the night attack was put to the test, it worked just fine.

In January 1986, America had been building up forces near Libya and skirmished with missile corvettes and military installations of that country.

On April 10, an air raid was mounted against the Libyan capitol of Tripoli and the military air base of Benina, 450 miles away. Despite heavy ground defenses, the raid was carried out with the loss of only one plane. Lehman took this as conclusive proof that his tactics had worked (despite the fact that the French embassy and several neighborhoods in Tripoli had been accidentally hit by missile shrapnel during the raid) and saw the raid as validation that the 600-ship Navy was called for.

By this time, the previous seven years of almost unbridled naval spending was beginning to take its toll on Congress. While on target for the 600-ship goal (in 1987, the Navy boasted 509 vessels), more people were questioning the true need of such a large fleet. The costs associated with such a Navy were also spiraling out of control. The Gramm-Rudman Act, designed to balance the budget and curb military spending, caused Lehman to lodge his ultimate protest: He resigned on April 11, 1987.

The modern version of the amphibious assault force has its beginnings in World War II, when the Normandy invasion caused military strategists and planners to rethink the current means of placing men on a beach. Today the U.S. Navy and Marines have a joint amphibious assault force designed especially for littoral landings and swift coastline incursions, precisely the type of operations today's Navy is expected to carry out.

Based on a landing helicopter dockship such as the USS *Wasp* (LHD-1), the 'Gator Navy—so-called because of its amphibious speed and ferociousness—can launch a multipronged assault to almost anywhere in the world. Missions vary, performing everything from crisis response, special operations, rescue evacuations, humanitarian operations, and disaster relief. Recent assignments have included Operation Enduring Freedom in Afghanistan, assisting the Philippine military in combating terrorism, and a stopover before heading home in Rota, Spain.

Using landing craft, including hovercrafts (Landing Craft, Air Cushioned, or LCAC) cargo haulers (Landing Craft, Utility, or LCU) and venerable troop/vehicle transports (Landing Craft, Mechanized, or LCM) whose basic design dates from World War II, the Marine force takes the assigned beachhead and offloads tanks, artillery, trucks, and supplies while a mixed force of AH-1W Sea Cobra helicopters and AV-8B Harrier jets provide air support as needed.

In the future, the 'Gator Navy will contain the new *San Antonio* class of amphibious ship, with improved offensive and defensive capabilities and increased maneuverability, along with more cargo space and improved living quarters.

MORE TENSION IN THE PERSIAN GULF

The Navy's failure to upgrade its smaller vessels as Admiral Zumwalt wanted and Secretary Lehman ignored proved fatal in March 1987. A *Perry*-class frigate, the USS *Stark*, was patrolling in the Persian Gulf when it was hit by two Exocet antiship missiles launched from an Iraqi fighter, killing 35 sailors. Although the *Stark* carried the most sophisticated anti-missile detection systems, the missiles had gone undetected until impact. Iraqi leader Saddam Hussein apologized to the United States, then on friendly terms with him, and claimed the fighter thought the frigate was an Iranian oil tanker.

The incident increased tensions with Iran, and a series of attacks and reprisals ensued over the next several months. The U.S. Navy launched several assaults on Iranian oil platforms in response to missile attacks on Kuwaiti and American tankers.

The constant American presence led Iran to seek more peaceful relations with the West, but not before a terrible accident occurred on July 3, 1988. The USS *Vincennes*, an *Aegis*-class missile cruiser and the most advanced warship in the world, shot down what it had identified as an Iranian F-14—but it was actually a civilian airliner carrying 290 people, all of whom were killed in the incident. While Lehman claimed the tragedy could have been avoided if the cruiser had had air cover, the truth was that the warship was simply not designed for the mission it had been assigned.

THE COLLAPSE OF COMMUNISM

In 1989, the unthinkable began to happen. Communism, the long-held enemy of the free world, was dying. Except for China, North Korea, and Cuba, the Iron Curtain began to open across Eastern Europe. A new era dawned, with Soviet warships visiting Norfolk in July—for the first time. American ships paid a return visit to Vladivostok later that year, and on November 9, the ultimate symbol of the cold war, the Berlin Wall, was torn down, uniting Berlin and Germany.

It couldn't have happened at a worse time for the Navy. A strong defense against communism had been its battle plan for the past 44 years. With no superpower to worry about anymore (China's emergence was on the horizon yet), the "peace dividend" translated directly into military budget cuts.

The Navy, along with the rest of the armed forces, would have to retool itself for a new age.

In 1990, an article by Adm. Carlisle Trost, Chief of Naval Operations, was published in *United States Naval Institute Proceedings*. In it he listed the core principles of naval force: deterrence of a potential enemy, forward defense, mobilization of a force rapidly to a conflict area, and alliances with like-minded countries to present a strong, unified front. Trost covered all aspects of maritime forces, from the reinstituted battleships to the Coast Guard, Marines, aircraft, and the Soviet Navy. His main point was that the U.S. Navy would always be the enabler of U.S. involvement in combat around the world. Smaller crises and conflicts like the ones the Navy had been involved in throughout the 1980s would still happen, and a healthy Navy would be the first and best line of defense against them. And just because communism had collapsed did not mean the Russians were scrapping their armed forces, either. Instead, they were reducing and modernizing for efficiency.

The article drew response and comment from every quarter, with the majority agreeing with Trost's ideas. Nevertheless, cuts were made, although not as deep as they could have been. The Navy budget was trimmed from $100 billion to $97.7 billion in 1989; $1.9 billion was restored in 1990, and the budget remained steady into 1991. The secretary of defense also compacted the fleet, retiring the *Iowa* and the *New Jersey*, and scheduling the decommission of two nuclear cruisers and five nuclear submarines over the next four years.

However, the Navy was not entering a dark age, as had happened so many times before. One hundred sixty-eight vessels were under construction at the time, and all would be completed. New minesweepers, submarines, and aircraft carriers bolstered the fleet to 546 ships—not the 600-vessel Navy of Lehman's dreams, but more than enough for the present. The primary defense concerns were the Pacific Ocean, the Middle East, the Caribbean Sea, and Southwest Asia. Almost before the world could comprehend the sweeping changes of the past year, an emergency developed that would test the new peace and reinforce the necessity of a strong Navy.

OPERATION DESERT STORM: WAR IN THE PERSIAN GULF

On August 2, 1990, Iraqi leader Saddam Hussein sent the fourth-largest army in the world to conquer the neighboring oil-rich country of Kuwait. Fearing a possible invasion of ally Saudi Arabia, the United States initiated Operation Desert Shield, airlifting 18.3 million tons of equipment and supplies for the forces deployed there. A 33-nation military coalition watched as a peaceful solution was sought for the next six months. During this time, a naval blockade cut off Iraq from valuable military supplies.

The U.S. military poured men and material into the area through Saudi Arabia. On January 17, after warning Hussein to withdraw from Kuwait, President George Bush launched Operation Desert Storm, a multination assault to liberate Kuwait.

The Navy, already in position for the embargo, sailed into action. The battleships the *Missouri* and the *Wisconsin* launched Tomahawk Land Attack Missiles (TLAM) against ground defenses. Their massive 16-inch guns were also fired (for the first time since the Korean Conflict), with each ship eventually unloading more than one million pounds of ordnance against the Iraqi forces. In their last wartime action, the venerable battleships eliminated enemy coastal defenses in preparation for an amphibious invasion. They also provided a distracting cover fire on February 24, the night of the major ground offensive.

The U.S. Navy uses a variety of ship-launched missiles in everyday operations. Here are the most common types:

- **AGM-84D Harpoon:** The Navy's primary antiship missile can be launched from bombers, submarines, and surface ships. With a range of 60 nautical miles and a 488-pound high explosive warhead, it can be fired from "over the horizon" at an enemy vessel.

- **RIM-116A Rolling Airframe Missile (RAM):** An infrared-guided missile used against enemy antiship munitions, this system is carried on amphibious ships, cruisers, and destroyers. It travels at supersonic speed and carries a 25-pound conventional explosive warhead.

- **RIM-7M Sea Sparrow:** This is a surface-to-air radar-guided antimissile and aircraft weapon with a speed of 2,660 miles per hour and a 90-pound fragmentation warhead. In 2003, the Sea Sparrow will be tested with the *Aegis* fire-control system.

- **SM-2 Standard:** Carried on *Ticonderoga*-class cruisers and *Arleigh Burke*-class destroyers, the *Standard* can be fired from the MK 41

Vertical Launch System (VLS) or the MK 26 Guided Missile Launcher System (GMLS). The latest version, the SM-2 Block IV Extended Range, can travel up to 200 miles, home in on a target using radar, and detonate its blast fragment warhead on contact.

- **Tomahawk Cruise Missile:** The Navy's primary long-range cruise missile can be launched from surface ships and submarines. With a range of 1,000 miles, the Tomahawk travels at 500 miles per hour and can follow a programmed evasion path. The latest version, the Tactical Tomahawk, can be reprogrammed to hit one of 15 alternate targets in midflight using Global Positioning System (GPS) technology. It also can carry a camera so that officers can survey battle damage and redirect the missile, if needed.

- **Vertical Launch Antisubmarine Rocket (VLA):** Also carried on cruisers and destroyers, the VLA is a three-stage antisubmarine warfare missile that can carry a 98-pound warhead or launch an MK 46 MOD 5 torpedo.

- **Trident Fleet Ballistic Missile:** The primary nuclear missile of the Navy, it is a three-stage missile with a range of more than 4,600 miles. The Trident II, deployed in 1990, can travel more than 3.7 miles *per second* and carries Multiple Independently Targetable Reentry Vehicles (MIRV) for warheads.

(Naval Historical Center)

The USS Wisconsin *fires a broadside to port from its 16-inch and 5-inch gun batteries.*

Naval aircraft were based on the *Independence,* the *Saratoga,* the *John F. Kennedy,* and the *Dwight D. Eisenhower.* Coalition airplanes flew more than 100,000 sorties against enemy targets, with U.S. Navy and Marine forces accounting for one third of those. They targeted national command and control centers, communications outposts, air defense systems, power-generation sites, oil-refining installations, airfields, and enemy aircraft. Remote-controlled drones and decoys were used to fool the Iraqis into launching surface-to-air missiles. Along the way, two F/A-18 Hornets shot down two Iraqi MIG-21s. Eventually, the Iraqi Air Force left the combat zone, unable to compete with the U.S. technology and firepower. The naval aircraft also sought and destroyed dozens of Iraqi patrol boats as they tried to retreat.

As the Army and Marines moved toward confronting the Iraqi army, the Navy launched an attack on Iraqi-held oil platforms being used as observation posts. The guided-missile frigate the *Nicholas* and a Kuwaiti fast-attack craft used a combination air and surface assault to destroy two of the platforms. They also captured the first prisoners of war and found a large cache of surface-to-air missiles, which were destroyed. The *Nicholas*'s helicopters saw action again on January 22, when they engaged and defeated four Iraqi patrol boats operating near the Kuwaiti coast.

During the war against Iraq, two other situations developed that required the Navy's assistance. In August 1990, a unit of amphibious ships rescued 2,690 people from the civil war–torn city of Monrovia, Liberia. A joint Marine–Navy operation airlifted American, Liberian, Italian, Canadian, and French nationals to safety for four months.

In the strife-ridden nation of Somalia in early January 1991, another embassy rescue happened when street fighting broke out in the capital city of Mogadishu. Two hundred sixty citizens from 30 nations were taken out of the city to safety aboard U.S. ships involved in Desert Shield.

The Navy also discovered that Iraq had laid mines in international waters. To combat this threat, the U.S. Mine Countermeasures Group was created, with the specific task of clearing the waters around Kuwait. Three minesweepers and one mine countermeasures ship cleared a 15-mile long path along the Kuwaiti coastline. While moving toward shore, the sweepers were tracked by Iraqi radar linked to Silkworm missile sites in Kuwait.

The group was evacuated while the radar sites were located. During this time, two mines hit two American ships.

In mid-February, as the ground forces prepared for their major offensive, elements of the Navy prepared a staged "invasion" near Faylaka Island off the coast of Kuwait. The battleships the *Missouri* and the *Wisconsin* provided a thunderous distraction. While 80,000 Iraqis waited for a sea-borne invasion that never came, the Army and Marine units under Gen. Norman Schwarzkopf circled around the enemy. Thirty-six hours later, the Iraqi army was in ruins and the fighting was all but over.

The victory cost the Navy 6 killed and wounded 12, with 6 planes shot down. In return, the Navy and other forces had eliminated the Iraqi navy; cut the enemy air force in half; claimed 4,200 tanks, armored personnel carriers, and artillery pieces; and killed, wounded, or captured at least 100,000 Iraqi troops.

The Navy had lived up to Admiral Trost's three tenets of an effective Navy, deterring the Iraqi forces from committing to a full-out attack on the fleet, rapidly deploying to the combat area, and working with the navies of allied nations to provide a unified front. Almost as if he had asked for it, Operation Desert Shield/Storm was the perfect venue to prove the worth of the modern Navy.

PEACE IN OUR TIME

Operation Desert Storm was the last major Navy operation of the twentieth century. Several other smaller incidents occupied the fleet's attention, particularly an aviator's convention in 1991 that caused the Navy to re-evaluate its stance on men and women in its force.

In 1991, with thousands of naval aviators returning from the successful Gulf War, the annual Tailhook Convention was held in Las Vegas. The Tailhook Association is a private group of active and retired Navy and Marine pilots, defense contractors, engineers, and other military aviation personnel.

During the convention, Lt. Paula Coughlin reported being forced to run the "gauntlet," a hallway lined with drunken Navy pilots who grabbed at her and tried to remove her clothes. Coughlin filed formal charges, but when no action seemed forthcoming, she went public with her experience. The Naval Investigative Service was called in and eventually reviewed 140 cases of misconduct, including incidents in which senior officers had tried to cover up evidence of the event. Among those implicated as being near the hotel floor where the incident had taken place was current Secretary of the Navy Lawrence Gannett III and the Chief of Naval Operations and four-star admiral Frank Kelso. Gannett resigned his position, and Kelso was permitted to retire with his rank intact after a disagreement in the Senate. Coughlin's superior, Rear Adm. John Snyder, who had apparently dismissed her complaints, was also relieved of duty. Three more admirals were censured for failing to put a stop to the misbehavior. Thirty other admirals had letters of caution placed in their files, and almost 40 other officers were fined or disciplined with letters of reprimand or censure.

As for the trial, Coughlin claimed she was able to identify her main assaulter, a Marine, but there were no corroborating witnesses to support her story. The fallout from her charges put a cloud over the Navy's public image, and hampered innocent officers' careers for years. Coughlin's career ended as well, and she resigned from the Navy in 1995. Stung by the criticism of their policies toward women, the Navy took steps to equalize the fleet. Federal laws were changed allowing women to pilot combat aircraft in 1992, also to let women serve on combat ships, with the *Dwight D. Eisenhower* to be the warship to have women serve on board.

During the early 1990s, the Navy was involved in several peacekeeping missions in various areas around the world. In 1991, the communist nation of Yugoslavia disintegrated, with former provinces Croatia and Serbia declaring their independence. Fierce fighting began among ethnic groups in neighboring Bosnia, particularly a three-way war among Bosnians, Serbians, and Croats. President Clinton sent a carrier group to the Adriatic Sea to implement a maritime embargo and provide a base for Navy and Marine pilots. Bombing runs were also made over Bosnia from land bases in Italy. The limited intervention continued until 2000, when the U.S. government admitted no progress was being made and scaled back the operation after 109,000 sorties had been made. Today the area remains unstable.

On June 2, 1995, Air Force F-16 pilot Scott O'Grady was shot down while on patrol over Bosnia. U.S. Navy Adm. Leighton Smith ordered a Marine helicopter team from the amphibious assault ship the USS *Kearsage* into the area to get the pilot back, telling the Bosnian commanders to "stay out of my way." After a tense six days, during which O'Grady evaded enemy patrols and survived on grass and rainwater, the Marine unit successfully recovered him on the morning of June 8.

In December 1992, the Navy sent a SEAL team ashore at Mogadishu, Somalia, to support nation-rebuilding and humanitarian programs begun by the UN the year before. The Navy and later Marines were to occupy the U.S. embassy, secure ports and airfields, and confiscate weapons from the indigenous population. Despite a truce reached by the two main warlords in the region, friction between neighboring clans intensified and anti-American sentiment rose. The Marines came under fire, and the program was in danger of collapsing. In October 1993, the U.S. forces began to withdraw, leaving the program to be run by the United Nations. Although the multinational force continued its efforts for another year, the rest of the UN forces were pulled out in 1995. Eighteen American soldiers were killed during the mission. Both of these interventions proved that without a stable government or political party in power, peace couldn't be attained by force and technology alone.

In 1993, the shadow of Saddam Hussein still loomed over the Middle East. Although he had been defeated in the Gulf War, U.S. forces hadn't taken the war into Iraq, leaving the dictator in power. During the summer, a plot was uncovered to assassinate former president George Bush during his planned visit to Kuwait. When the plan was confirmed, President Clinton authorized a cruise-missile attack on Iraq's capital city of Baghdad. A Navy cruiser and destroyer launched a total of 23 Tomahawk missiles at the military headquarters in the city. Three missiles went off course and impacted in civilian neighborhoods, killing eight. The attack was used as propaganda by Hussein's regime against the United States.

NAVY ACTION IN THE NEW MILLENNIUM

Since the 1990s and into the dawn of the twenty-first century, the U.S. government and its military have been carrying out a war against terrorism. In 1998, President Clinton authorized a widespread missile strike against known training bases and a pharmaceutical plant of Islamic terrorist Osama bin Laden. In 2000, terrorists struck back with an attack on the destroyer the USS *Cole* on October 12, which killed 17 crewmen and injured 39.

In 1999, the U.S. Navy was part of a joint NATO bombing campaign over Kosovo and Serbia to stop "ethnic cleansing" in the area carried out by then–Serbian president Slobodan Milosevic. A carrier group returned to the Adriatic Sea and ran sorties from March 24 to June 10. The Navy's main contribution was providing E-2C "Hawkeye" surveillance planes to coordinate strikes against targets. Milosevic was defeated in the 2000 elections and was forced to step down.

On September 11, 2001, terrorism hit home in America. Two airliners impacted both towers of the World Trade Center in New York City, and another jumbo jet slammed into the Pentagon building in Washington, D.C. Among the 142 Pentagon casualties were 42 Navy Department personnel. Four retired Navy officers and one employee were also killed on Flight 77, the airplane that hit the Pentagon and impacted the area containing the Navy Command Center. Within hours the hospital vessel the USNS *Comfort* and the fast sealift ship the USS *Denebola* were en route to New York to provide assistance.

The U.S. immediately targeted international terrorism groups in Afghanistan. The aircraft carriers the *Enterprise* and the *Carl Vinson* headed to the Arabian Sea, to be joined later by the *Kitty Hawk* as the point ships in a fleet that converged on Afghanistan to launch planes and ground forces against the local Taliban government, which was harboring al Qaeda terrorists.

A strike force launched cruise missiles against military targets and terrorist-training camps on October 7, 2001. Navy pilots joined with Marine and Air Force bombers to drop 18,000 individual munitions. By November 8, more than 50,000 Americans were deployed in the area, roughly half of them aboard Navy vessels. When the operation began, 80 percent of the nation was Taliban-controlled. Approximately 78 days later, the ruling government had been toppled, Qandahar airport and several major cities had been secured by U.S. forces, and an interim government had been established.

All through 2002, joint-operation forces continued working against the remains of al Qaeda and Taliban networks in and around Afghanistan. A Navy carrier group still remains offshore, ready to provide support and mobile bases when and where necessary.

In the last quarter century, America carried out the mission it had started after World War II, policing the world and fighting the enemies of freedom wherever they struck.

CHAPTER 16

THE FUTURE OF THE FLEET

As the Navy moves into the first decade of the millennium, it, too, is already shifting its priorities to keep pace with the changing face of war today. Ships, submarines, and technology are all combining to make tomorrow's fleet even more capable and effective when the need arises.

A PLAN FOR TOMORROW: SEA POWER 21

In October 2002, Chief of Naval Operations Vern Clark set forth his vision of the Navy of the future. Integrating new technology with an updated and redesigned force, it is based on three main ideas: Sea Strike, Sea Shield, and Sea Basing.

The first aspect, Sea Strike, is the catchall term for how the Navy will deploy in combat situations: pulling together reconnaissance and on-site gathered intelligence to analyze enemy capabilities, threat level, and weaknesses, and tailoring a strike plan to fit the situation. Clark stresses that electronic and psychological warfare will play an equally important role in the Navy's ships, planes, and equipment.

Sea Shield, the second aspect, will provide comprehensive protection both for America and nations abroad. This will include the identification, tracking, and interception of threats long before they approach American borders. Elements of the Navy will be integrated with federal law-enforcement and military forces to protect the United States and its allies. An important aspect of this concept is the ability to penetrate a potential battle space and control the engagement area, thus being ready for the enemy. The Navy is also planning to extend its overland reinforcement capability, with new weapons (an improved Tomahawk missile) and aircraft (updating the E-2 Hawkeye's radar suite) and coordination with land forces in a unified front on land, sea, and air.

The final aspect is Sea Basing, which is the dispersal and location of maritime units near areas where conflict is likely. These units, consisting of aircraft carrier groups, multitask destroyers, and submarines with Navy SEALs or Army Special Forces aboard, would then be on-site and available, eliminating the planning and logistics of scrambling and sending out a task force. The Navy forces stationed in the area would coordinate with other military forces and be a prepositioned receiver of troops and equipment.

These three facets would be connected through a program called ForceNet, a completely integrated system linking intelligence, hardware, and forces both at home and deployed. The vital information for an operation will be available to all personnel involved. Strategy and tactics will utilize every bit of information from all available sources. The first steps of ForceNet are already happening, with the upgrade of data-gathering equipment and command and control systems. With advances in technology, a fully integrated Navy is on the horizon and getting closer every day.

Admiral Clark's "Global Concept of Operations" envisions a Navy able to deploy a submarine, surface strike group, or carrier strike group anywhere in the world from elements that are already onsite. To do this effectively, a fleet of 375 ships will be needed, which could be formed into 12 carrier strike groups, 12 expeditionary strike groups (guided missile frigate-, destroyer-, and cruiser-based forces), and multiple surface action groups (amphibious assault forces) and nuclear Trident submarines. Clark claims that a force of this size could supply deterrence in four possible theaters of war, simultaneously fight two enemies at once (decisively defeating one of them), and still provide homeland defense.

THE FUTURE OF THE FLEET

The Navy is working hard today be the best fleet in the world. One way to continue to do this is with the use of new and advanced technology. Here are some of the ships that will be seen in the Navy of tomorrow.

Destroyers—DD (X)

Plans for the next generation of destroyer were begun in 1991 with the start of the SC 21 (Surface Combatants 21st Century) Program. The DD 21 program had progressed to capability studies and even bids submitted by two military contractors.

In May 2001, the program was suspended pending military studies on feasibility and fleet requirements. By November, the program was retooled and designated DD (X), focusing on prototype technologies that could be used in a wide variety of land- and sea-based platforms. The systems designed for the DD (X) destroyer must be able to be incorporated with other future Navy vessels, including the Littoral Combat Ship (LCS), designed for coastal operations, and the air-dominance Cruiser CG (X).

Although still in the planning stages, this new generation of destroyer will incorporate the most advanced technology in all areas, from hull design and integrity to radar, fire control, and armament. The DD (X) will feature the following improvements:

- Dual-band radar for better stealthy target acquisition and performance in adverse weather.

- A bow-mounted undersea warfare system with high-frequency active sonar for antisubmarine and mine warfare missions and automatic adaptability to the tracking environment.

- A Total Ship Computing Environment (TSCE) that will automate many manned positions in the control room, reducing crew size. Sensors, weapons, and ship-control systems will all be tied to and controlled from the bridge.

- An integrated deckhouse and aperture, giving off a reduced signature to enemy radar while incorporating new antiblast technology as well as electromagnetic pulse protection.

- The Tumblehome hull, a new split-keel, radar-resistant hull.
- A new propulsion system, either a permanent magnet synchronous engine or an advanced induction motor. The system will be expandable and reconfigurable, and will run more quietly and reliably than conventional engines.
- The Peripheral Vertical Launch System (PVLS), which, if hit, will isolate the blast and shrapnel from the rest of the ship. The missile system is compartmentalized to provide greater access to weapons in the event of a hit. It also provides a greater chance of ship survival after impact.
- An unmanned deck gun system, currently known as the Advanced Gun System (AGS), an unmanned precision-guided weapon platform with increased fire capability, range, lethality, and sustainability. The AGS will also fire a new projectile, currently classified as the Long Range Land Attack Projectile (LRLAP), which will use Global Positioning System for guidance.

The DD (X) program is currently into the engineering model phase, so there will probably not be a prototype until 2010 or later.

Aircraft Carriers

Construction of the next generation of carrier, currently named the CVNX 1, is scheduled to begin in 2006 and will have an operational life of 50 years. The CVNX 1 would also incorporate advanced technology:

- The Electromagnetic Aircraft Launch System (EMALS) and an Electromagnetic Aircraft Recovery System (EARS), improving launch and recovery ability and efficiency. The EMALS and EARS will be designed to work with the next generation of fighter planes.
- A new nuclear propulsion unit requiring fewer operators and generating increased electrical power for future system upgrades, including energy weapons systems.
- Automatic weapons-reloading systems to rearm aircraft.
- A smaller command center containing multifunction arrays with increased detection range and decreased signal for enemy radars to spot.
- A redundant electrical grid and advanced damage-control systems, to increase survival and operational ability after sustaining damage.

The new generation of carrier is expensive: The first model would cost around $10 billion from research and development to commission. After a possible delay of the construction date for a year, which would add $400 million to the total cost, needed funding was procured. As of 2003, the CVNX was on track for production.

Submarines

The Navy's submarine program took a hit when the *Seawolf* program, the newest blue-water nuclear submarine, was scrapped after the end of the cold war rendered it obsolete by the time the first boat hit the water. With that program gone and the fleet reduced to around 55 vessels, the Navy had to come up with a plan to keep its sub force going.

The new *Virginia* program satisfies the Navy's requirements for a nuclear attack submarine while saving Congress money. The new boats, the first of which (the *Virginia*) will be launched in 2004, cost about $3.4 billion. By the fifth one, however, the price will have dropped to $1.54 billion, compared to $2.8 billion for each *Seawolf*-class submarine.

The *Virginia* class can perform multiple missions in a coastal environment, and it has been designed with this objective and in mind. These are among the missions the ship could carry out:

- Attacking inland targets with Tomahawk cruise missiles (much like the subs of today did in Operation Desert Storm)
- Locating and destroying hostile submarines
- Locating and destroying hostile surface ships
- Performing covert intelligence gathering and surveillance
- Laying, detecting, and clearing minefields, both friendly and enemy
- Providing support for Carrier Strike Force/Amphibious Strike Force
- Performing insertion/recovery of special forces teams

The *Virginia* class has also been upgraded in just about every area. Its new sensor array will be able to locate the most stealthy of submarines. It will also contain a sonar suite that specifically searches out mines. Even the old-fashioned mirrored periscope is being replaced with "photonics masts" that will transmit images to onboard display screens. Its "life of the ship" reactor means that the nuclear core will never have to be replaced.

The *Virginia* will carry a complement of 38 weapons, from the latest Tomahawk missile variant to Underwater Unmanned Vehicles (UUVs, used for reconnaissance and mine identification) to the prototype "super-cavitating" torpedo.

> The current torpedo used by the U.S. Navy, the MK 48 Advanced Capability (ADCAP) torpedo, has a maximum range of 27 nautical miles at 60 knots. However, an experimental program had produced a prototype torpedo that goes 15 km in *10 seconds*! The supercavitating torpedo is initially powered by a rocket motor. Then a chemical reaction in the nose cone creates a sheath of air bubbles or water vapor around the fuselage, reducing water drag and allowing the torpedo to reach speeds of hundreds of miles per hour. The remaining difficulty is keeping the water vapor/air bubble around the torpedo while it changes course.
>
> The Soviet Navy has already developed the *Shkval,* a torpedo that travels at 230 miles per hour, and sold it to France, China, and Iran. Unconfirmed reports claim that a malfunctioning supercavitating torpedo was the cause of the *Kursk* submarine sinking in August 2001. In America, researchers at the U.S. Naval Undersea Warfare Center launched a test model that broke the sound barrier.

The *Virginia* will also have a configurable torpedo room to handle weapons or a SEAL team. The SEALs will have available a 55-ton minisub, which the *Virginia* will be engineered to support.

The use of "smart-ship" technology, first seen on the *Aegis* ships, may reduce the number of control room personnel by as many as 15. The new system will allow the ship to be piloted and operated by three people—the pilot, copilot, and relief pilot—eliminating such positions as officer of the watch, diving officer, helmsman, planesman, and others.

Aircraft

With the introduction of the F/A-18 E/F Super Hornet in 2002 (see Chapter 1 for more details), the Navy has filled its need for a new multi-role attack plane. However, the Joint Strike Fighter (JSF) program will give the Navy its next generation of jet fighters. By introducing a base-model fighter plane with variants for three branches of the U.S. military (Air Force, Marines, and Navy), the military will minimize its costs and maximize service integration.

The Navy's model, called the X-35C, is designed for carrier assignment. It has larger wing and control surfaces than the other two models for stability and ease of flight at sea. Its internal structure has also been reinforced for the punishing carrier landings. It carries almost twice the fuel as the standard F-18C Hornet. Currently in final test flights, the X-35 is expected to be deployed in 2008.

Other Possible Future Ships

With new innovations and technologies being created all the time, it is hard to predict what the Navy will come up with next. Recent proposals have included these:

- The Littoral Surface Craft–Experimental (LSC-X), a high-speed descendant of the World War II torpedo boat, designed with a hydrofoil hull and used for interceptor duty, antisubmarine warfare, and high-speed insertion/extraction of special forces units

- The Manta, a design for a 50-ton unmanned submarine that would launch off of and operate as part of a conventional sub as a scout vessel, minefield clearer, and antisubmarine combat vehicle

- The Sea Archer, an unmanned catamaran-hulled ship carrying 7-ton unmanned aircraft called Sea Arrows, which would be used to swarm an enemy target

- The Mobile Offshore Base (MOB), a huge interconnected series of modules as long as 2 km, which would serve as a dock for ships and a temporary home for up to 3,000 troops, hundreds of tons of space for supplies, and storage of 10 millions gallons of fuel

READY TO RESPOND

No matter what technology the United States Navy adopts for the future, there can be no doubt that it is poised to react wherever and whenever it is needed, whether in forward deployment, surface force reinforcement, coastal and inland bombardment, or aerial or naval surveillance.

In its 238-year history, the Navy has weathered adversity ranging from indifferent leaders to adverse public opinion to political infighting. Like all military branches, it has experienced adversity and downsizing, yet it has always recovered its stride, often regained the lead in naval technology, and maintained its core values and beliefs—honor, courage, commitment—whenever possible.

As America moves into the twenty-first century, it is sure that the Navy will be at the forefront, in the oceans, and on the coastlines of the world, ready to defend the United States and its allies when called upon.

CLASSIFICATION OF NAVY SHIPS

Nuclear-powered aircraft carrier: CVN

Aircraft carrier: CV

Nuclear-powered ballistic submarine: SSBN

Nuclear-powered attack submarine: SSN

Missile cruiser: CG

Nuclear-powered missile cruiser: CGN

Antiaircraft warfare missile destroyer: DDG

Antisubmarine warfare destroyer: DD

Antiaircraft warfare missile frigate: FFG

Antisubmarine warfare frigate: FF

Coastal minehunter: MHC

Amphibious assault ship: LHD/LHA

Dock landing ship: LSD

Fast combat assault ship: AOE

FAMOUS U.S. NAVAL OFFICERS

Capt. John Barry (1745–1803)

Born in 1745 at Ballysampson in County Wexford, Ireland, John Barry followed in his uncle's footsteps and took to the sea as a cabin boy, eventually working his way up to mate. His first command was aboard the ship the *Barbadoes*, out of Philadelphia.

When the Revolutionary War began, Barry was given command of the 16-gun brig the *Lexington*. He immediately captured the tender the *Edward*, the first British prize taken by an American frigate on the open ocean.

In 1776, he was assigned to the 32-gun *Effingham*, still under construction in Philadelphia. Before Barry could take command, he was forced to scuttle the ship when the British attacked the city. Undaunted, he gathered a motley assortment of small boats together and conducted guerilla assaults on the Delaware River.

In 1778, Barry took command of the 32-gun *Raleigh*. Spotted by two British frigates on his first cruise, Barry led the two enemy vessels up the coast to Maine, where his ship was dismasted. Barry planned to burn the *Raleigh* and escape with his crew, but he was foiled by a turncoat sailor. Although his warship fell into British hands, he got 88 of his men to safety.

He was next assigned to the 32-gun *Alliance*, in which he defeated two British ships, the 16-gun sloop the *Atlanta* and the 14-gun brig the *Trepassy*, and destroyed the 28-gun frigate the *Sybil* in the last action of the war.

Afterward, Barry opened trade relations with China and the Far East. In 1794, the Navy was reinstated as a permanent institution, and Barry was appointed senior captain of the federal Navy. He led the Navy during the quasi-war with France, created a standardized signal book, and also suggested creating the post of Secretary of the Navy.

Barry remained the head of the U.S. Navy until his death on September 12, 1803. He was buried two days later with full military honors in Philadelphia's Old St. Mary's Churchyard.

Capt. John Paul Jones (1747–1792)

Born in 1747 in Kirkcudbrightshire, Scotland, to John Paul, a gardener, and his wife, who was part of the MacDuff clan, John Paul Jones was apprenticed aboard the ship *Friendship* at age 13. He rose through the ranks to become a merchant captain, commanding the ship *John* at age 21.

Five years later, while Jones was commanding the merchant ship the *Betsy* anchored in the West Indies, a crewmember disobeyed orders and tried to go ashore. In the ensuing scuffle, the man attacked Jones with a truncheon, forcing the captain to run him through. He wanted to turn himself in to face trial, but friends advised him to leave, so he traveled to America.

Receiving a lieutenant's commission in the Continental Navy, Jones was appointed captain of the *Providence* in 1776. He captured several British ships and destroyed at least two others during a two-month cruise.

In November 1777, Jones was charged with bringing Benjamin Franklin to France again. While commanding the man-of-war the *Ranger*, he captured the British frigate the *Drake*. This led to his receipt of the *Bonhomme Richard*, upon which he sailed into immortality.

Jones' life after the Revolutionary War was much less glorious. When the Continental navy disbanded, he signed on as a rear admiral with the Russian navy in the service of Empress Catherine the Great, hoping to leverage that position into a higher command if America ever established a permanent navy. Jones resigned after not receiving promised commissions, and he returned to France in 1790. Offered a military position by President George Washington, he declined the position and died on July 18, 1792.

Jones was buried in St. Louis Cemetery, then part of the holdings of the French royal family. After a search for his remains that lasted for more than a century, John Paul Jones was interred at the chapel in the United States Naval Academy in Annapolis, Maryland, on January 26, 1913, where he rests to this day.

Capt. Thomas Truxton (1755–1822)

Born on February 17, 1755, near Nassau, New York, Truxton, like so many of his contemporaries, took to the sea at an early age. He served as an apprentice at age 12 and even served a brief stint in the Royal Navy in 1771 at age 16. He worked on merchant ships in the years leading up to the Revolutionary War, during the conflict and he commanded several privateer vessels, including the *Independence*, the *Mars*, and the *St. James*.

Appointed to captain by Henry Knox in the U.S. Navy in 1794, Truxton trained his men meticulously, had his officers study naval tactics, and kept detailed records of his ideas and methods. He also wrote several papers on ships and the sea, including an improved system of a ship's rigging, a treatise on celestial navigation, and the first manual of signals for the U.S. Navy in 1797. He oversaw the construction of the 36-gun USS *Constellation*, which was launched on September 7 of the same year; shortly afterward, the ship got a chance to prove itself in battle not once, but twice.

Truxton served his country and his Navy for many years before his retirement. He died in Philadelphia on May 5, 1822.

Capt. John Rodgers (1772–1838)

Born near what is present-day Harve de Grace, Maryland, on July 11, 1772, John Rodgers began his career in the Navy as a second lieutenant in 1798. Assigned to the first voyage of the USS *Constellation*, he participated in the capture of the French privateer *L'Insurgente* in 1799 and sailed her back to America as prize master. In 1801, he transported the ratified treaty with France across the Atlantic.

When the Barbary Coast conflict began, Rodgers was captain of the *John Adams* and was sent with the fleet to enforce American sovereignty against Tripoli. In 1805, he was appointed Commodore of the Mediterranean Squadron. After that tour of duty, he returned to help enforce the unpopular Embargo Act of 1807 by patrolling the Atlantic coast with the New York flotilla.

In 1811, Rodgers, commanding the *President*, defeated the *Little Belt*. During the War of 1812, he captured 23 prizes and helped oversee the defense of

Baltimore. After the war, he headed the Board of Navy Commissioners until he retired in 1837. Rodgers died in Philadelphia, on August 1, 1838.

Capt. Stephen Decatur Jr. (1779–1820)

The son of noted naval officer Stephen Decatur, the second generation was born in Sinnepuxent, Maryland, on January 5, 1779. He took to the sea early, traveling with his father by age eight. At 17, he was hired as a Navy agent and was sent to New Jersey to supervise the production of the keel pieces of the frigate *United States*. Decatur also served aboard the ship as a midshipman, aided by a warrant from John Barry.

During his tenure on the *United States*, Decatur pushed himself to become an exemplary sailor. After subduing a group of deserting sailors by dueling their leader, Decatur was promoted to lieutenant in 1799. He was briefly assigned to the 18-gun *Norfolk*, and later came back to the *United States*.

When hostilities with the dey of Algiers broke out (see Chapter 3), Decatur joined the 46-gun *Essex* as first lieutenant. He then commanded the 12-gun schooner the *Enterprise* and sailed with the fleet to the Barbary Coast, where he led the expedition to destroy the *Philadelphia*.

Decatur commanded the *United States* in the War of 1812, when he defeated the *Macedonian*. He was then transferred to the *President*, which was captured by four British frigates. Decatur and his crew were later exchanged for English prisoners-of-war.

Afterward, Decatur helped negotiate peace with Algiers (see Chapter 5), as well as the leaders of Tunis and Tripoli, ending the power of the Barbary Coast nations. He returned home to serve on the Navy Board of Commissioners, where he was instrumental in designating Norfolk, Virginia, as the Navy's primary Atlantic base.

While serving on the Board of Commissioners, he had recommended that Commander James Barron not receive command of a ship-of-the-line. Insulted, Barron challenged him to a duel years later. Now retired, Decatur tried to demur, but on March 22, 1820, the two men met at Bladensburg, Maryland. Decatur said he would shoot his opponent in the hip and did so. Barron's shot struck Decatur in the abdomen; he was taken to his home, where he died a few hours later.

Capt. Isaac Hull (1773–1843)

Born in Connecticut on March 9, 1773, Hull was the nephew of Gen. William Hull, who adopted him after his father, Joseph Hull, died. At 14, he began his maritime career as a cabin boy on a merchant ship of one of his uncle's friends. When the ship was wrecked during a voyage 2 years later, the 16-year-old saved his captain's life. At age 21 he commanded a merchant ship that traded with the West Indies. When the Navy was officially started, Hull entered the service as a fourth lieutenant in recognition of his sailing abilities.

He served on the USS *Constitution* as first lieutenant and then was promoted to master commandant on the brig the *Argus* in 1804. After sailing with Commodore Edward Preble's fleet to the Barbary Coast, he was given command of the USS *Constitution* in 1806.

When war broke out, Hull was hampered by orders commanding him to join Commander Rodgers's fleet, which was preparing to sail from New York. On the way there, he ran into five British warships and outran them in a three-day chase. Three days after the surrender of Fort Detroit on August 16, 1812, Hull redeemed his family's honor by destroying the *Guerrière*.

After these exploits, Hull relinquished command of the USS *Constitution* in 1813 and received orders to head up Portsmouth Naval Shipyard and construct America's largest warship. Hull battled incompetent builders, red tape from Congress and the Navy, the constant threat of British attack, and even the weather to rebuild the shipyard and complete the 74-gun *Washington*.

He also served as a member of the naval board and commanded squadrons in both the Pacific Ocean and the Mediterranean Sea. After his retirement, he settled down with his family in Philadelphia. Hull died on February 13, 1843, and was laid to rest in the Laurel Hill cemetery.

Master Commandant Oliver Hazard Perry (1785–1819)

Born on August 23, 1785, in South Kingston, Rhode Island, Perry entered the service as a midshipman at age 13 on the sloop-of-war the *General Greene*, which was commanded by his father. He also served during the Barbary Coast conflict. Perry earned the rank of lieutenant in 1805 at age 20 and supervised the building of coastal gunboats. Afterward, he was given command of the 14-gun *Revenge* and patrolled the upper half of the American coast.

At the beginning of 1811, Perry accepted a mission to survey several Rhode Island harbors. Inclement weather and bad piloting caused the *Revenge* to run aground. Perry requested an investigation into the incident and was cleared of any wrongdoing.

When the War of 1812 began, Perry, now a master commandant, was in charge of 12 gunboats at the harbors of Newport and New London. When nothing happened there, he requested a transfer to either the high seas or the Great Lakes. When Commodore Isaac Chauncey received Perry, he sent him to Erie, Pennsylvania, to oversee the construction of the fleet there.

When his fleet sailed out to engage the British, they did so underneath a flag bearing James Lawrence's defiant last words, "Don't Give Up the Ship." Perry was the first American naval leader to defeat an entire enemy squadron and take all of the captured vessels as prizes.

After his heroism on the Great Lakes, Perry captained the frigate *Java* in 1815 and patrolled the Barbary Coast again. In 1819, he was ordered to take the frigate *John Adams* to Venezuela on a diplomatic mission. Although his mission was successful, Perry contracted yellow fever there and died near Trinidad on August 23, 1819. Although he was buried in Trinidad with full military honors, his body was exhumed and reinterred at Newport, Rhode Island, where a monument to him was erected by the state.

Capt. Thomas Macdonough (1783–1825)

Born in Delaware, Macdonough was the sixth of ten children and the son of a physician and major in the Revolutionary War. After the death of both his parents by age 11, Macdonough secured a midshipman's commission in the Navy with the help of friends of his late father.

His first taste of action was under Capt. Alexander Murray aboard the USS *Constitution* during the Barbary Coast conflict. During one battle with a Barbary pirate ship, he broke his cutlass while boarding. Not pausing for a moment, he grappled with an enemy sailor and then took his pistol and shot the man dead. He also accompanied Stephen Decatur on the mission to destroy the *Philadelphia* and was promoted to lieutenant afterward.

When war broke out with Great Britain, Macdonough was given a division of gunboats to command. In September 1812, he was sent to Lake Champlain to take over the fleet there—all two gunboats and three transport vessels of it.

With the help of shipwright Noah Brown, Macdonough was ready for the British when they arrived. After his overwhelming victory, Macdonough was honored by the United States government and was even bequeathed a farm by the population of Plattsburg, Vermont.

The Battle of Lake Erie was Macdonough's crowning achievement. Afterward, he suffered from tuberculosis and was limited to land positions due to his increasing illness. He commanded the *Constitution* briefly but gave up the post because of his poor health. MacDonough died on November 10, 1825.

Capt. David Porter Jr. (1780–1843)

Born in Boston on February 1, 1780, David Porter Jr. was the son of Capt. David Porter, who had commanded Continental navy ships during the Revolutionary War.

In 1798, he entered the service as a midshipman on the USS *Constellation* and participated in the battle against the French frigate the *L'Insurgente*. Promoted to lieutenant in 1799, he was assigned to the West India station, where his schooner the *Experiment* escorted merchant ships and fought pirates. Later in his tour, he captured the French 14-gun schooner the *Diane*.

Porter then accompanied the U.S. Navy to the Barbary Coast, where he participated in the defeat of the *Tripoli* by the *Enterprise*. His next ship wasn't so lucky: Porter was captured with the rest of the crew of the *Philadelphia* in 1803.

Released in 1806, Porter was given command of the *Essex* and sailed to the Pacific Ocean in 1812, where he began a one-ship war against the British whaling trade. In February 1814, his ship was severely damaged by two British vessels, the *Phoebe* and the *Cherub*. Porter was sent home with his crew and later wrote an account of the *Essex*'s voyage, which was published in 1815.

After the war, Captain Porter served on the board of Navy Commissioners from 1815 to 1823; then he resigned to head up the West Indies Fleet, or "Mosquito" fleet. Suspended for rescuing another Navy officer at Puerto Rico, Porter resigned in disgust and took a position with the Mexican navy in 1826.

He returned to the United States in 1829, when President Andrew Jackson appointed him consul general to the Barbary Coast nations. Later he became the minister resident at Constantinople, where he negotiated the first trade treaty with Turkey and the Ottoman Empire in 1831.

Porter died in 1843; his remains were returned to the United States and buried at the naval asylum in Philadelphia. His two sons, William David and David Dixon, both served in the Union navy during the Civil War.

Capt. Robert "Fighting Bob" Field Stockton (1795–1866)

Born to Richard "The Duke" and Mary Stockton on August 20, 1795, Robert Stockton studied at the College of New Jersey when he was 13 years old. He left school to enter the Navy in September 1811, securing a midshipman's commission on the frigate the *United States* under Commodore John Rodgers. During the War of 1812, he acquired the nickname "Fighting Bob" for his cool head in battle. The *United States* helped defend Baltimore and Alexandria,

Virginia, where Stockton was promoted to master's mate; he was promoted to lieutenant on September 9, 1814.

After 16 years in the Navy, he returned home to his ancestral home in Princeton, New Jersey. He became active in national politics, supporting Andrew Jackson's presidential bid. Captain Stockton sailed to the Mediterranean again in December 1838, commanding Isaac Hull's flagship the *Ohio*. Recalled to the United States in 1839, he was offered the post of secretary of the Navy by the victorious President John Tyler. Stockton turned down the position and built a steam warship for the Navy instead. That ill-fated vessel was the *Princeton*.

Afterward, Stockton headed west, first to Texas, and then to the California territory, where he made his mark in history. After gaining control of upper California, he began running the territory as acting governor; he published the first English and Spanish newspaper, the *Monterey Californian*, and made preparations for a local government.

After the arrival of Commodore William Shubrick, who relieved him of his duties, Stockton headed back to New Jersey, where he resigned his commission in the Navy and served as a state senator. Stockton died on October 7, 1866, and is memorialized today by the town of Stockton, California.

Commodore Matthew Calbraith Perry (1794–1858)

Born to Christopher and Sarah Perry in South Kingstown, Rhode Island, on April 10, 1794, Perry was the younger brother of the War of 1812 hero Oliver Hazard Perry. At age 15, he entered the Navy as a midshipman, first serving on his brother's ship the *Revenge* and then transferring to the frigate *President*, which destroyed the sloop *Little Belt* in May 1811. When war erupted in 1812, he was aboard the *United States*, which spent most of the conflict stuck behind a British blockade of New London.

Afterward, Perry spent 10 years (1833–1843) at the New York Navy Yard, which culminated in his commanding the *Fulton II*, the first practical U.S. Navy steam vessel. He then oversaw the completion of the *Mississippi*, one of two steam frigates commissioned by the Navy. Perry earned the rank of captain in 1837 and was given command of the New York Navy Yard in 1841. He also spent two years (1843–1844) commanding the African squadron.

When the United States created the Mexican War, Perry replaced Commodore David Connor in the Gulf of Mexico. He assisted Gen. Winfield Scott's assault on Veracruz and defeated pockets of Mexican resistance along the coast.

He was then assigned his most delicate mission by President Millard Fillmore: to open the long-closed ports of Japan. With a squadron of seven vessels, including two steamships, Perry sailed into Edo Bay and presented the local magistrate a polite letter from President Fillmore to the Emperor of Japan, promising to return for an answer the following spring. In 1854, the emperor agreed to America's minor trade and hospitality requests, including letting U.S. ships purchase coal from Japan and "most favored nation" trading status for the United States.

For his diplomatic achievements, Perry was awarded $20,000. Almost four years after his crowning glory, he died on March 4, 1858.

Rear Adm. John A. D. Dahlgren (1809–1870)

John A. D. Dahlgren was born on November 13, 1809, the son of the Swedish consul in Philadelphia, Pennsylvania. He began his maritime service as an ordinary sailor and then joined the Navy in 1826 as a midshipman. From 1834 to 1837, he worked for the Coastal Survey, putting his skills as a mathematician to good use.

After many years of service, he was assigned to the Ordnance Department in 1847, where he began studying the construction of cannons. Shocked into action by the explosion of the Peacemaker on board the *Princeton* in 1844, Dahlgren was put in charge of developing a better cannon. His experiments led to the most powerful weapon made at the time, the Dahlgren gun.

When the Navy Yard commander left for the Confederacy in 1861, Dahlgren was promoted to captain by special congressional act and was made chief of the Bureau of Ordnance. In July 1863, he was promoted to rear admiral and received command of the South Atlantic Blocking Squadron. He took Charleston harbor and helped Sherman capture Savannah, Georgia, in 1864.

After the war, Dahlgren commanded the South Pacific Squadron and then came back to the Bureau of Ordnance. He returned to the Washington Navy Yard in 1869, where he served until his death on July 12, 1870.

Capt. Raphael Semmes (1809–1877)

Born on September 27, 1809, in Charles County, Maryland, Semmes was orphaned at age 10 and was admitted to the Navy in 1826 by a presidential appointment through his uncle, Benedict Semmes. After five years sailing in the West Indies and Mediterranean, Semmes returned to the Navy Yard and graduated at the head of his class. He gained the rank of midshipman and studied law during the next three years.

Semmes returned to sea in 1846 as first lieutenant on the *Porpoise*, part of the Vera Cruz blockade. His account of this time was published in 1851 as *Service Afloat and Ashore During the Mexican War.*

Promoted to commander in 1855, he spent the next five years heading the bureau in charge of lighthouses until the Civil War. Immediately resigning his commission, Semmes headed south to help with the war effort.

Semmes was appointed a commander in the southern navy in April 1861, and he captained the steamship *Sumter,* which took 18 prizes in 6 months. In January 1862, a Union fleet at Gibraltar forced him and his crew to abandon the ship.

Semmes headed to England, where he was given command of the just-completed *Alabama.* Over the next two years, he captured almost 60 merchant vessels and fought and sank the USS *Hatteras.* All told, he captured or destroyed $6,000,000 of cargo and ships.

In June 1864, while anchored at Cherbourg, France, the USS *Kearsage* found Semmes. After a short duel on June 19, the *Alabama* sank and Semmes was rescued by a British yacht and taken to England. He went back to America and rejoined the Confederacy until the South surrendered.

In December 1865, Semmes was arrested and put on trial for not giving himself up to the *Kearsage.* Acquitted of all charges, he lived the rest of his life as a civilian; he wrote and published his autobiography and practiced law. He spent his last years as a prominent member of Mobile, Alabama, and died August 30, 1877.

Adm. David G. Farragut (1801–1870)

Born James Farragut on July 6, 1801 in Knoxville, Tennessee, he was the son of Jorge Farragut, who served in both the Revolutionary War and the War of 1812.

Farragut formed a close relationship at a young age with the Porter family, stemming from an incident in which his father rescued David Porter Sr. When his mother died in 1808, the elder Porter offered to take in James and his sister. James changed his name to David, as was the custom of the times, and went to sea at eight years old; he received a midshipman's appointment when he was nine and a half. He served with Porter during the cruise and capture of the *Essex.*

Farragut spent the next few decades hunting pirates in the Caribbean, patrolling the Gulf of Mexico, and returning to the South American coast again, but never in command of his own ship. That changed during the Mexican War, when Farragut was made the commanding officer of the 20-gun *Saratoga* in 1847. Afterward he returned to the Norfolk Navy Yard, where he remained until 1855, when he was finally promoted to captain of the steam sloop the *Brooklyn.* After a peaceful five-year tour, he returned to Norfolk.

When the Civil War began, Farragut stayed with the Union and fought in the Mississippi River campaigns with his stepbrother, David Dixon Porter. For his bold capture of New Orleans, Congress created the position of rear admiral and bestowed it to Farragut on July 16, 1862.

In 1864, he achieved everlasting fame in the battle of Mobile Bay, Alabama. Sailing into a mine-laden harbor, Farragut issued the immortal orders, "Damn the torpedoes. Four bells (full speed ahead), Captain Drayton." The fleet followed the admiral and won the battle.

Returning to New York a national hero, he was made the U.S. Navy's first admiral in 1866. Admiral Farragut died on August 14, 1870. His funeral procession included 10,000 sailors and soldiers, and was led by President Ulysses S. Grant.

Adm. David Dixon Porter (1813–1891)

Born on June 8, 1813, in Chester, Pennsylvania, Dixon began life with impossibly large footsteps to follow: He was the son of Commodore David Porter, one of the heroes of the War of 1812. But David Jr. carried on the family tradition with pride, first serving in the Mexican navy and then joining the U.S. Navy as a midshipman in 1829. His posts were many and varied, including duty in the Mediterranean Sea, in Brazil, and at the Hydrographic Office in Washington, D.C. He was promoted to lieutenant in 1841 and commanded his first ship in the Mexican War.

After the war, he left the Navy to work in the private sector before returning to service in 1855. In 1861, frustrated by the entrenched officer hierarchy and lack of command opportunities, he almost resigned again when the Civil War broke out.

After a brief stint blockading Mobile Bay, Porter joined up with his stepbrother, David G. Farragut, to assault New Orleans.

Afterward, he was temporarily relieved of duty due to his irascible nature, but he was called to duty again by no less than President Lincoln himself. Placed in charge of the Mississippi Squadron, Porter worked in concert with his equal on land, Ulysses S. Grant, to transport thousands of Union troops across the river and bring about the fall of Vicksburg. For his part in the Vicksburg campaign, Porter was made the Navy's second rear admiral in 1863.

He later led the North Atlantic Blockading Squadron and helped capture Wilmington, North Carolina.

After the war he served as superintendent of the Naval Academy, where he enacted sweeping changes to the curriculum, increased funding, and improved the grounds. Promoted to vice admiral in 1866 and admiral in 1870, he was the naval advisor to Ulysses S. Grant's administration. Porter died on February 13, 1891.

Rear Adm. Alfred Thayer Mahan (1840–1914)

Born on September 27, 1840, in West Point, New York, Mahan was the son of an engineering professor at the West Point military academy. He studied for two years at Columbia University before enrolling in the Naval Academy, graduating in June 1859.

Mahan's Civil War years were spent on blockade ships, followed by duty patrolling the South American coast aboard the obsolete steam-sloop the *Wachusett*. In 1885, he joined the Naval War College's faculty. Here he laid the foundation for his seminal volume *The Influence of Sea Power Upon History 1660-1783*, published in 1890.

In the summer of 1893 Mahan was ordered back to naval duty and captained the cruiser the *Chicago* on a European tour. Received as a hero in Europe, he was bestowed honorary degrees from Cambridge and Oxford and, upon his return home, from Harvard, Yale, and Columbia.

Promoted to rear admiral, Mahan retired in 1896 and kept writing; he published several more naval volumes. He died on December 1, 1914.

Rear Adm. George Dewey (1837–1917)

Born on December 26, 1837, to Julius Yemans Dewey, a wealthy physician, George Dewey was the third of four children. He enrolled in Norwich University when he was 15. After 2 years, he was appointed to the Naval Academy, where he was one of the 15 graduating students out of a class of 60 "acting midshipmen."

His first assignment was on the *Wabash*, the flagship of the Mediterranean Squadron. After two more cruises, Dewey passed his lieutenant's examination and was commissioned in April 1861, just before the start of the Civil War. Assigned to the steam frigate *Mississippi*, Dewey rose to executive officer at age 25 and fought in the Battle of New Orleans. He was next assigned to the *Monongahela*, Adm. David Farragut's flagship.

Afterward, Dewey spent time at a variety of assignments, including teaching at Annapolis and tours all over the world. In 1885, he took command of the steam sloop the *Pensacola*, which sailed to Europe as Rear Adm. Samuel F. Franklin's flagship. When his tour ended in 1889, Dewey accepted the position of chief of the Bureau of Equipment and Recruiting, approving such innovations as electric searchlights and a modern engine telegraph. After that he was placed in charge of the Board of Inspection and Survey, which was responsible for evaluating every Navy warship.

Dewey was promoted to the rank of commodore in 1896. In 1897, he became the commander in chief of the Asiatic Squadron. Several months later, war broke out between Spain and the United States, and Dewey was ordered to the Philippines, where he demolished the Spanish fleet in the Battle of Manila Bay. Promoted to rear admiral, he continued his blockade of Manila Bay until reinforcements arrived.

After his return to America, Dewey was persuaded to run for president in 1900; he abandoned this after a month and a half. He was then chosen as president of the General Board of the Navy, where he served for the next 16 years. He also served as chairman of a joint Army-Navy board, holding both positions until his death on January 16, 1917.

Adm. William S. Sims (1858–1936)

Born on October 15, 1858, in Port Hope, Canada, Sims entered the U.S. Naval Academy and graduated in 1880. He then began a 17-year stint serving on various ships during the Navy's decline. Afterward, he served as an American envoy in St. Petersburg and Paris for three years, where he reviewed foreign countries' navies and technology.

During this time, he saw the "continuous aiming system" demonstrated, which kept a gun automatically aimed at the target and achieved an 80 percent hit rate. Its inventor, Capt. Percy Scott, had also developed telescopic sights and used crosshairs instead of antiquated notched sights; Sims wanted the Navy to adopt all of this as soon as possible.

Sims wrote directly to President Roosevelt in 1902; his comments got him placed in charge of target practice. Sims overhauled the entire training program, creating competitions among the various gun crews for the greatest accuracy. He also used an actual moving target rather than the inefficient buoy system, which forced observers to guess where a shell would have hit an enemy vessel. His theories were proven when the old battleship the *Indiana* achieved 48 hits out of 48 shots on a moving target. From then on, gun crews in every ship studied Sims's rules and procedures.

Promoted to captain in 1911, Sims taught at the Naval War College for two years and became its president in 1917, the year after he was promoted to rear admiral. During World War I, he implemented the convoy system as a way to protect shipping from German submarines, and he recommended that antisubmarine forces be sent to Europe. He also enacted the North Sea mine operation, which attempted to prevent the U-boats from entering the area to prey on merchant shipping.

After the war, he returned to the Naval War College and retired from the Navy in 1922, after a 42-year career. In 1930, he was promoted to admiral and died in Boston on September 25, 1936.

Adm. Bradley Allen Fiske (1854–1942)

Born on June 13, 1854, in New York City to Rev. William Allen and Susan Bradley Fiske, Bradley Allen Fiske was appointed to the U.S. Naval Academy in September 1870 and graduated in 1874. He then took a year to study electricity and its application to naval vessels. Along the way, he invented a telescopic gun sight, an optical range finder, an electrical gun turret, and an electric range finder used at the battle of Manila Bay. Along with fighting in the Spanish-American War, he served on the Army-Navy Joint Board and at the Naval War College.

When the airplane was invented, Fiske became one of its strongest proponents. In 1910, after civilian pilot Eugene Fly flew a plane off the deck of a ship, Captain Fiske not only flew a plane off a ship, but also landed on it. Convinced of the importance of this new invention, he created and patented plans for a torpedo plane and organized the Department of Naval Aviation.

In 1913, he was appointed head of the U.S. Navy and created the position of Chief of Naval Operations, the senior flag officer in the Navy. Although some of the greatest men in the Navy would serve in this position, the man who created it never would. Blocked by Secretary of the Navy Josephus Daniels, Fiske watched as William S. Benson became the first CNO.

When World War I began, Fiske, now an admiral, crossed swords with Daniels again over U.S. involvement. Finding the secretary's neutral stance untenable, he resigned his commission in May 1916.

Fiske continued his service as president of the U.S. War College until 1923, where he is credited with developing the war game. He also wrote many articles on the state of the Navy, including his popular autobiography, *From Midshipman to Admiral,* published in 1919. He died in New York City on April 6, 1942, and was buried in Arlington National Cemetery.

APPENDIX B: FAMOUS U.S. NAVAL OFFICERS

Adm. Richard E. Byrd (1888–1957)

Born on October 25, 1888, to Richard E. Byrd Sr. and Marie Byrd in Winchester, Virginia, Richard Byrd entered the U.S. Naval Academy at 20 and was commissioned in 1912. He served four years on battleships until an ankle injury removed him from active duty. His love affair with the airplane was kindled during pilot training in World War I, and he graduated as a naval aviator in 1918.

Byrd pioneered several aspects of early flight, including making night landings on carriers and navigating at sea with no landmarks. His experiments with navigational instruments drew attention from the Navy, which put him in charge of sending four flying boats across the Atlantic in 1919. Only one made it, but the NC4's flight was successful.

In 1924, Byrd began planning a private expedition to fly to the North Pole. Two years later, he and his pilot, Floyd Bennett, claimed to have flown over the North Pole on May 9, 1926. Upon their return to the United States, both men were awarded the Medal of Honor.

Byrd continued flying, first crossing the Atlantic and then conquering the South Pole in November 1929. When World War II broke out, he returned to active duty and served as the Chief of Naval Operations. Byrd spent his remaining years in the Navy as head of the United States Antarctic Programs. He died in Boston on March 11, 1957, and was buried in Arlington National Cemetery.

Ship's Cook First Class Doris Miller (1919–1943)

One of the most celebrated heroes of World War II was Ship's Cook First Class (one of the few positions open to men of color at the time) Doris Miller, an African American serving on the battleship the USS *West Virginia*. When the attack happened at Pearl Harbor, Miller, the ship's heavyweight boxing champion, was ordered to carry wounded sailors to safety. When the ship took more damage, he was ordered to assist the mortally wounded captain. After that, he manned a .50-caliber machine gun and helped fight off the attacking Japanese.

For his heroism, Miller was commended by the Secretary of the Navy Frank Knox and was awarded the Navy Cross, which was presented to him personally by Admiral Chester W. Nimitz. He returned to duty on the USS *Indianapolis* until November 1943, when he transferred to the escort carrier the USS *Liscome Bay*. During Operation Galvanic, involving the taking of the Makin and Tarawa atolls in the Gilbert Islands, the *Liscome Bay* was torpedoed by a Japanese submarine, detonating the aircraft bomb magazine. The warship went down in just a few minutes, taking 646 members of the crew with her, including Doris Miller.

The frigate the USS *Miller*, commissioned on June 30, 1973, was named after Doris Miller. In addition, a bronze commemorative plaque is dedicated to Miller's memory in the Miller Family Park at the U.S. Naval Base at Pearl Harbor.

Adm. Ernest J. King (1878–1956)

Born in Lorain, Ohio, on November 23, 1878, King read about the Navy as a young boy, stimulating his interest in the sea. In 1897, he received an appointment to the Naval Academy from an Ohio representative of the fourteenth district.

King's service began when he served on the USS *San Francisco* during the Spanish-American War. Graduating in 1901, he was commissioned an ensign on June 7, 1903. His first cruise took him literally around the world. Returning to America in 1906, he served as an ordnance and gunnery instructor at the Annapolis Naval Academy. During World War I, he worked on Admiral H. T. Mayo's staff and then headed the Naval Academy's Postgraduate School. He was then assigned to the submarine fleet, overseeing the recovery of the sunken USS S-51.

In 1926, King became the senior aide on the staff of Commander Air Squadrons for the Atlantic Fleet. The next year, he went through naval aviation training and graduated in May 1927. He headed up the Scouting Fleet in 1928 and the Naval Air Station at Norfolk, Virginia, in 1929. In 1930, he was given command of the USS *Lexington* for a two-year cruise. Afterward, he studied in the senior officer course at the Naval War College and achieved the rank of rear admiral in 1933.

In February 1941, King was promoted to admiral as commander in chief of the U.S. fleet. That December, Roosevelt also gave him the position of Chief of Naval Operations; he was one of only two officers to ever hold both positions simultaneously. King updated the Atlantic Fleet and coordinated U.S.–British efforts in cracking the German U-boat codes. He also lobbied for more resources for the Pacific campaign.

In 1944, King was present at the Normandy invasion. Afterward, he watched his political and naval power erode. After the war, Secretary of the Navy James Forrestal made him accept an advisory position to the secretary's office. King also served as president of the Naval Historical Foundation. He died in the Naval Hospital at Portsmouth, New Hampshire, on June 25, 1956.

Fleet Adm. Chester William Nimitz (1885–1966)

Born in landlocked Fredericksburg, Texas, on February 24, 1885, Nimitz first tried to get into the Army but couldn't gain an appointment to West Point. He entered Annapolis in 1901. A highly intelligent student, he graduated seventh out of a class of 114 and then joined the USS *Ohio* on a tour of duty to the Far East. In 1907, he was commissioned an ensign and was given command of the gunboat the *Panay*. After that, he took command of the USS *Decatur* and ran her aground, for which he was court-martialed; he managed to rise above that incident.

The next phase of his career was in the fledgling submarine fleet, where he served up to and during World War I. He commanded three submarines and then led the Atlantic Submarine Flotilla for a year. In 1917, he went to COM-SUBLANT (Commander, Submarine Force, U.S. Atlantic Fleet) as the aide and chief of staff.

Afterward, Nimitz served on several ships, including the USS *South Carolina*. He studied tactics at the Naval War College in 1922 and then served as chief of staff to the commander of battle forces and later the commander in chief of the U.S. Fleet, Adm. S. S. Robinson.

Nimitz was the first professor of naval science and tactics at the newly created ROTC program at the University of California–Berkley. He also returned to submarines in 1929 as the commander of Submarine Division 20 for two years. For the next eight years, he alternated duty in the Bureau of Navigation with commands of cruiser and destroyer battalions. Nimitz was appointed commander in chief of the Pacific Fleet and Pacific Ocean areas on December 31, 1941.

On December 19, 1944, he was promoted to Fleet Admiral. When Japan formally surrendered on the USS *Missouri*, Nimitz himself signed the armistice document. Afterward, he served as Chief of Naval Operations for two years, and continued to advocate the Navy and the nation, including a position as assistant to the secretary of the Navy in the Western Sea Frontier. Admiral Nimitz died on February 20, 1966.

Fleet Adm. William Frederick Halsey Jr. (1882–1959)

Born in Elizabeth, New Jersey, on October 30, 1882, William Frederick Halsey Jr. inherited his love for the sea from his father, Navy Capt. William Halsey. He was appointed to the academy by President William McKinley himself in 1900. After graduating in 1904, he completed his mandatory two-year hitch at sea and then sailed with the Great White Fleet around the world in 1907.

He spent most of the next quarter century on destroyers, earning command of the USS *Dupont* in 1909. When World War I broke out, Halsey was in the Queenstown destroyer force with two ships under his command. He was moved to Destroyer Division 32 for the remainder of the war and then went to the Office of Naval Intelligence.

Afterward, he returned to the sea and his destroyers in the 1920s. In 1932, Halsey attended the Naval War College; he then went to the Naval Air Station at Pensacola, Florida, for flight training. Designated a Naval Aviator in 1935, he was never a full-time pilot due to his eyesight and seniority. Interested in carriers, Halsey was given command of the *Saratoga* for two years. In 1940, he was promoted to the rank of vice admiral of the Commander Aircraft Battle Force.

In April 1942, Halsey became commander of Task Force 16 and escorted Jimmy Doolittle's bombers to their Tokyo raid. Later he was made commander of the South Pacific Forces, battling around Guadalcanal and working with General MacArthur in implementing the "island-hopping" campaign.

In June 1944 he was given command of the Third Fleet, which he operated mostly successfully, except for his actions at Leyte Gulf, for which he was chastised by President Roosevelt. Halsey also sailed the fleet into two hurricanes with heavy losses, but was protected from punishment by Admiral King. After the war, Halsey was assigned to the office of the secretary of the Navy. On December 11, 1945, he became the fourth and final officer to achieve the rank of Fleet Admiral.

Retiring in 1947, he became an honorary vice president of the Naval Historical Foundation. Halsey died on August 16, 1959, at Fishers Island, New York.

Adm. Hyman G. Rickover (1900–1986)

Born in Makow, Poland, Rickover emigrated with his parents to Chicago when he was six years old. In 1918, he entered the Naval Academy and was commissioned as an ensign in 1922. He served on two surface vessels and then finished his Master's degree in electrical engineering. In 1929, he received his first assignment in the submarine services, commanding the boats S-9 and S-48; he captained his last, the USS *Finch*, in 1937.

During World War II, he was the head of the Electrical Section at the Bureau of Ships. In 1946, Rickover was assigned to an atomic plant in Tennessee to learn about nuclear energy. He returned to the Navy as its leading expert in the field and was made the head of both the Nuclear Propulsion Division of the Bureau of Ships and the Naval Reactors Branch of the Atomic Energy

Commission. His primary assignment: to build a working nuclear reactor for ship propulsion.

Working with a limited budget and incredible engineering problems, Rickover and his staff did just that. His tireless efforts and persistence paid off when the world's first nuclear submarine, the USS *Nautilus*, got underway for the first time on January 17, 1955, with Rickover on the bridge.

After a struggle Rickover was promoted to rear admiral, and oversaw development of the Navy's nuclear fleet. He served as head of the nuclear program for almost 40 years, exempted from mandatory retirement by congressional mandate due to his irreplaceable role. Rickover retired in 1982 and died on July 8, 1986.

Adm. Arleigh G. Burke (1901–1996)

Born near Boulder, Colorado, Arleigh Burke decided early in life that he wasn't going to be a farmer. Unable to finish school due to a flu epidemic, he received an appointment to the Navy in 1919 and graduated seventy-first in his class of 413 in 1923.

Burke served on a variety of ships, including the battleship *Arizona* and several fleet auxiliary vessels. Afterward he completed his degree in ordnance and engineering and served two tours in the Bureau of Ordnance. Promoted to lieutenant commander in 1938, he took command of the destroyer the *Mugford* the year after.

When World War II started, Burke was working at the Naval Gun Factory and didn't see action until he was given command of Destroyer Division 23, the first of four divisions he would command in 1943. He participated in the Pacific campaign and destroyed almost 20 Japanese ships and 30 aircraft.

In March 1944, Burke teamed up with Vice Adm. Marc Mitscher, head of Task Force 58, for the rest of the war. He participated in all major naval battles until May 1945, when the two men were sent back to the United States Burke stayed with the admiral until his death in 1947.

Assigned to the Naval Operations section, Burke was involved in the "Admiral's Revolt" concerning the approval of a new supercarrier versus the Air Force's B-36 bomber program. He was promoted to rear admiral in 1950, just in time for the Korean Conflict.

After the war, Burke was selected ahead of 99 more senior officers to become the Chief of Naval Operations. During his three terms, he established the Special Projects Office and backed research into a ballistic missile development program. He was also instrumental in developing the nuclear-powered Navy, with carriers, cruisers, and battleships built during his tenure. He oversaw the conversion of guided missile cruisers and helped establish the Atlantic Fleet Antisubmarine Defense Force. Burke died on January 1, 1996.

Adm. Elmo R. Zumwalt Jr. (1920–2000)

Born in San Francisco, California, to Drs. E. H. and Frances Zumwalt on November 29, 1920, the young man who would hold the Navy's highest posts entered the service at 19. After graduation, he served several tours of duty on destroyers in World War II. He participated in the Battle of Leyte Gulf and, in 1945, commanded a captured Japanese gunboat on a mission to disarm elements of the Japanese military at Shanghai, China.

He continued on destroyers until the Korean Conflict, when he transferred to the USS *Wisconsin*. Afterward, he served in the Bureau of Navy Personnel and the office of the assistant secretary of the Navy.

Zumwalt was then awarded command of the first guided missile cruiser, the USS *Dewey*, in 1959. In 1961–1962, he studied at the Naval War College and then was assigned to the office of the assistant secretary of defense. From 1963 to 1965, he served as executive assistant to Secretary of the Navy Paul H. Nitze.

In 1965, Zumwalt was the youngest officer promoted to rear admiral (he was 44). The following year, he took over as director of the Chief of Naval Operations Systems Analysis Group, which evaluates and analyzes the Navy on an ongoing basis. In 1968, Zumwalt became Commander of the Naval Forces, Vietnam, and Chief of the Naval Advisory Group in the U.S. Military Assistance Command, Vietnam, where he helped direct naval operations during the Vietnam Conflict.

In 1970, President Nixon nominated him for Chief of Naval Operations, a position he held until 1974. After his Navy career, Zumwalt ran for senator and served as president of the American Medical Building Corporation in Milwaukee, Wisconsin. He died in Durham, North Carolina, January 2, 2000.

FAMOUS SHIPS OF THE UNITED STATES

The USS *Constitution:* "Old Ironsides"

The oldest ship still in service today, the *Constitution* was launched on October 21, 1797. It first patrolled the West Indies and captured privateers during the quasi-war with France. Upon returning to the States, the ship was partially overhauled, sent to tour Europe, and then brought back just before the War of 1812 to the Washington Navy Yard, where maintenance was completed. On the next voyage, Capt. Isaac Hull and his crew escaped five British war ships in a three-day chase. On August 19, the *Constitution* defeated the *Guerrière* in single combat and then fought the 38-gun frigate the *Java* on December 29, 1812. The *Constitution*'s most famous battle was the defeat of the 34-gun frigate *Cyane* and the 21-gun ship-sloop *Levant*.

After serving in the Mediterranean Squadron from 1821 to 1828, the *Constitution* was removed from active duty. An evaluation report (which was erroneously published) gave the impression that the *Constitution* was to be scrapped. However, public outcry convinced the Navy to have the ship refurbished in 1835. For the next 20 years, the *Constitution* served in the Mediterranean, Pacific, and African squadrons.

In 1855, the *Constitution* was removed from active duty and spent five years at the Navy Yard at Portsmouth, New Hampshire. It became a training ship for the next 10 years. By 1871, the ship needed major repairs for the 1876 centennial.

Thirty-five years later, the *Constitution* was falling apart but was saved by another public show of support. In March 1930, the *Constitution* sailed out of dry dock completely renewed, and from 1931 to 1934 it toured the United States, traveling 22,000 miles and visiting 90 port cities. Since then, "Old Ironsides" has undergone another two major refurbishings, one from 1972–1975 for America's bicentennial, and another in 1992, when it was brought back to its original appearance. The *Constitution* was the ship of honor from July 21–23, 1998, when tall ships from around the world gathered in Boston Harbor to pay tribute to one of the first and most famous of America's warships.

Statistics:

Cost (in 1797 dollars): $302,718

Power: Sail (42,710 square feet on three masts)

Length: 204 feet

Beam: 43.5 feet

Mast height: Foremast: 198 feet, mainmast: 220 feet, mizzenmast: 172.5 feet

Displacement: 2,200 tons

Top speed: 13 knots (approximately 14.95 miles per hour)

Crew: 450, including 55 Marines and 30 boys

Armament: Thirty-two 24-pound guns, twenty 32-pound carronades, two 24-pound bow chasers

Date deployed: October 21, 1797

The USS *Princeton:* A Vessel Ahead of Its Time

The tragic accident aboard the *Princeton* delayed the American steam program for years. While the only thing remembered about Robert Stockton and John Ericsson's vessel is the explosion of the *Peacemaker,* the ship also incorporated several innovative design aspects that made it the premier warship of its time.

The *Princeton*'s white oak hull was much thicker that any other warship's. Driven by screw propeller, it was powered by anthracite coal–burning engines that lay completely below the waterline, protected from damage and enemy guns. The smokestack could be lowered to hide the fact that the ship was powered by steam, if necessary. With the clean-burning anthracite coal, the *Princeton* could move with her sails furled and without revealing her steam-powered engines.

More advanced concepts were used for the weapons systems and fire control. Ericsson had already invented a range-finding device and complemented that with a mechanism that allowed an entire side of the ship's 42-pound cannons to fire a devastating broadside at the same elevation. Each of the two main deck guns could be fired independently on its own swivel.

The massive wrought-iron cannon designed by Ericsson was known as the *Orator*. It used 50 pounds of black powder and could throw a 225-pound projectile more than 5 miles. The Swedish inventor also developed a new system of securing the guns against recoil. The "friction recoil" mechanism he invented was the forerunner of the systems still used in ship-mounted armaments today.

The accident relegated the *Princeton* to a footnote in history rather than the flagship of a new ship class that would have had unchallenged mastery of the world's oceans. The ship's own end was ignominious as well. When Stockton resigned from the Navy in 1851, the steamship was condemned. But when Stockton accepted a Senate seat, the Navy rebuilt the *Princeton*, whereupon Stockton himself spurned the new vessel. The new *Princeton* was in service for only a short time before it was scrapped for good, with much of her technology, including Ericsson's marvelous engines, disappearing into history. Because of this, there is no information about the technical specifications of the ship.

The CSS *Hunley:* The Confederate Submarine

The CSS *Hunley* was a true submarine, designed to travel underwater armed with a mine that would detonate upon contact with an enemy ship. Designed by Horace Lawson Hunley, James R. McClintock, and Baxter Watson, it was built in Mobile, Alabama, out of a steam boiler that had been cut in half and widened by adding a 1-foot-wide strip of iron to each side and tapering the ends. The *Hunley* used water and iron weights for ballast; in a pinch, the weights could be dropped from the bottom of the hull to increase buoyancy. Propulsion was provided by eight men turning a hand crank that powered the propeller, while a ninth man controlled the rudder. A long pine boom was attached to the front of the submarine, with the mine at the end.

With only rudimentary controls, the *Hunley* was difficult to operate during the best of times. During tests at Charleston Harbor in South Carolina, crew mistakes caused the submarine to sink twice, the first time killing five sailors and the second time killing all eight aboard, including Hunley himself, who had commanded the cruise.

Despite these tragedies, the *Hunley* was raised again and a volunteer crew took it out on February 17, 1864. Their target: the USS *Housitonic*, an 11-gun sloop-of-war that was part of the Union blockade of Charleston harbor. The *Hunley* approached to 100 yards when it was spotted by a lookout. The Union ships tried to avoid the submarine, but the mine detonated, sinking the *Housitonic* and killing five men.

Although the *Hunley* seemed to escape injury and headed back toward Charleston Harbor, it disappeared that same night. The wreck of the *Hunley* was located off Sullivan's Island in May 1995. On August 8, 2000, it was raised and prepared for restoration.

Statistics:

Hull: ⅛-inch iron plate

Power: 8-man hand crank

Propulsion: Single 3.5-foot diameter propeller

Length: 40 feet

Beam: 3.5 feet

Height: 4 feet

Top speed: About 4 knots

Crew: 9 total—1 helmsman, 8 on the crank

Air supply: About 3 hours

Armament: 1 90-pound mine

Date launched: July 1863

The *Indiana* (BB-1), the *Massachusetts* (BB-2), and the *Oregon* (BB-3): Building a Naval Backbone

The *Indiana*, the *Massachusetts*, and the *Oregon* incorporated the latest shipbuilding design and construction. All three vessels incorporated coalbunkers in their hull design, enabling them to cross an ocean without refueling. The bunkers were built near the outer hull for additional protection; however, their proximity to the ammunition magazines created a possible fire hazard.

The armor and main battery were both larger than any other ship had in the fleet. The huge 13-inch guns were not centered on the ships, so when they were pointed to port or starboard, the vessel listed to that side, limiting their maximum elevation. This also threw the hull armor belt off-kilter, although the problem was fixed by adding counterweights to the gun turret's back walls. The ships were also prone to excessive roll until all three of them were fitted with bilge keels, a fin of metal attached to the side of the hull that stabilized the vessel.

The three ships all served their country gallantly. Both the *Indiana* and the *Massachusetts* fought in the Spanish-American War. During World War I, the *Indiana* and the *Massachusetts* were used as target ships for the Navy and were sunk.

Although retired in 1924, the *Oregon* was offered to the Navy after the attack on Pearl Harbor. The offer was refused, so it was stripped in 1943 and converted into a floating ammunition magazine. The battleship was scrapped in Japan in 1956, with its mast on permanent display in Portland, Oregon.

Statistics (the following are for the *Oregon*, but they apply to each battleship):

Cost (in 1891 dollars): $3,180,000

Power: 4 double-ended and 2 single-ended cylindrical boilers

Propulsion: Vertical triple-expansion engines generating 11,111 horsepower

Length: 348 feet

Beam: 69.35 feet

Mast: 1 military rig

Displacement: 10,288 tons

Top speed: 16.79 knots (approximately 20.15 miles per hour)

Crew: 473 total—32 officers and 441 enlisted men

Armor: 18 inches on the hull, 6–17 inches on the turrets

Armament: Four 13-inch guns, eight 8-inch guns, four 6-inch guns, twenty 6-pound guns, six 1-pound guns, two Colt Gatling Guns (for landing parties), one 3-inch field gun (for landing parties), 3 Whitehead torpedo tubes

Coal bunker capacity: 1,594 tons

Range: 5,500 nautical miles

Date deployed: July 15, 1896

The USS *Holland:* A Practical Submarine

As nations raced to outdo each other on the water, another competition was going on for control underneath the water. The French were using compressed air both for propulsion and to expel ballast water, and they had created the first electric power systems in submarines. British engineer Robert Whitehead had perfected the first self-powered torpedo by 1870, with a speed of 7 knots and a range of 700 yards. In Sweden, inventor Torsten Nordenfelt built the first internal torpedo tube.

In America, inventor John P. Holland was also experimenting with submarines in the mid-1870s. He and another inventor, Simon Lake, were competing to create the first submarine used by the U.S. Navy. When the dust settled in 1900, the *Holland* had won the day.

The *Holland* combined several now-standard components in one sleek design. It had two propulsion systems—a gasoline engine for surface running and a rechargeable electric system for underwater use. With a fixed longitudinal center of gravity, created by keeping the main ballast tanks filled at all times, Holland's submarine rose and dove at an angle using its stern-mounted diving planes. It also had a main ballast system, which was used to dive and rise, and a secondary ballast system, used to compensate for different loads and water densities. Its major flaw was that there was no way to see outside while submerged; this was not be remedied until the development of the periscope in 1902.

After more than two years of tests, the Navy purchased and commissioned the USS *Holland* in 1900. It was decommissioned in 1910. Although the *Holland* never saw military action, it formed the basis for virtually all American submarines of the next 30 years.

Statistics:

Propulsion: Screw propeller

Engines: 50-horsepower gasoline engine for the surface, battery-powered electric motors for running while submerged

Length: 54 feet

Beam: 11 feet

Height: 10 feet

Displacement: 74 tons

Top speed: 8 knots (approximately 9.6 miles per hour) on the surface, 5 knots (6 miles per hour) submerged

Crew: 6 men

Armament: 1 torpedo tube

Date launched: May 17, 1897

The Destroyer: Greyhound of the Sea

The destroyer class was created to combat the fast torpedo boat used in the Chilean Civil War and the Sino-Japanese War during the late nineteenth century. Looking for an escort ship able to prevent the agile boats from getting in range, the destroyer class was armed with guns for offense and torpedoes to protect it against capital ships.

The first American destroyer, the USS *Bainbridge*, was launched on August 27, 1901. It patrolled and escorted merchant convoys across the Atlantic until the end of World War I. Decommissioned in 1919, it was sold for scrap in 1920.

Destroyers quickly became the escort of choice against enemy submarines during World War I, with the USS *Fanning* even sinking a U-boat. Destroyers escorted 2 million men across the Atlantic without loss of life. In the 1920s, dozens of destroyers were decommissioned or scrapped under naval limitation treaties.

By 1940, the program was underway again, with a new command unit—Destroyers, Atlantic Squadron, U.S. Fleet—patrolling the Atlantic Ocean. When the U.S. entered World War II, its destroyers once again did battle with U-boats (see Chapter 13) in the Atlantic Ocean, fought Japanese warships in the Pacific, and escorted millions of tons of convoys in both war theaters.

In the past half century, destroyers have served in conflicts from the Far East to the Persian Gulf, providing escort, antisubmarine, and fire support duties. With designs such as the *Arleigh Burke* and the future DD (X) class, this swift, multimission ship will remain a valuable part of the modern Navy for many years to come.

Statistics (for the USS *Bainbridge*):

Classification: Destroyer (DD-1)

Power: 2 vertical inverted triple-expansion engines generating 8,000 horsepower

Propulsion: Twin screw propellers

Length: 420 feet

Beam: 24 feet

Draft: 10 feet

Displacement: 420 tons

Top speed: 29 knots (approximately 34.8 miles per hour)

Crew: 73 total—4 officers, 69 enlisted personnel

Armament: Five 6-pound guns, two 3-inch guns, two 18-inch submerged torpedo tubes

Date commissioned: November 24, 1902

The *Michigan* (BB-26) and *South Carolina* (BB-27): The First U.S. Dreadnoughts

The *South Carolina* class of battleship came into being in the roiling wake of the British ship the *Dreadnought,* launched in 1906. Plans for a U.S. version of the big-gun platform were done on a smaller scale. Although roughly the same dimensions as the *Connecticut*-class battleships that preceded it, these new ships' main battery of eight 12-inch guns put them in a league with the new warships built around the world. The *Michigan* and her sister ship, the *South Carolina,* mounted one main turret on the deck and then a second one over and behind the first, enabling a devastating broadside to be fired and making the gunnery systems more efficient than the *Dreadnought*'s itself.

Active for only about 11 years, their service records were unremarkable. Both vessels served in the Western Hemisphere during World War I, with the *Michigan* assisting in the incident at Vera Cruz in 1914. The *South Carolina* partially escorted a convoy into the Atlantic and helped bring more than 4,000 American servicemen home from France.

Decommissioned in accordance with the new naval limitations treaty, the *Michigan* in December 1921, and the *South Carolina* in February 1922, the two vessels were sold for scrap in 1924.

Statistics (for the *South Carolina* class of battleship):

Classification: Battleship: BB-26 (*South Carolina*), BB-27 (*Michigan*)

Power: 2 triple-expansion reciprocating steam engines generating 16,500 horsepower

Propulsion: Twin screw propellers

Length: 453 feet

Beam: 80 feet

Draft: 24.5 feet

Mast: 2 military masts, no sails provided

Displacement: 16,000 tons

Top speed: 18.5 knots (approximately 22.2 miles per hour)

Crew: 869 total—51 officers, 818 enlisted men

Armor: Hull: 11 inches, turrets: 12 inches, deck: 3 inches, conning tower: 12 inches

Armament: Eight 12-inch guns, twenty-two single-mounted 3-inch guns, four 1-pound guns, two .30–caliber machine guns, two 21-inch submerged torpedo tubes

Fuel capacity: 2,380 tons

Dates commissioned: January 1910 (*Michigan*) March 1910 (*South Carolina*)

USS *Lexington* (CV-2) "Lady Lex" and USS *Saratoga* (CV-3): The First Aircraft Carriers

Both carriers incorporated the latest designs and construction, including the "island" system of locating all above-deck buildings in the center of the ship on the starboard side and providing a stack to vent the smoke from the engines away from the flight deck. The elevators used to haul planes were hydraulic plunger systems capable of moving a plane on deck every four minutes. A foam fire-prevention system and secondary sprinkler system were installed. The carriers were large enough to hold 81 aircraft, almost twice the size of the British or Japanese carriers.

The *Lexington* joined the Battle Fleet in San Pedro, California, until 1941, when it transferred to Hawaii. When Pearl Harbor was attacked (see Chapter 13), the *Lexington* met with the *Enterprise* task force to search for the enemy.

In January 1942, the *Lexington* headed for the Coral Sea, where it's fighters shot down 17 of 18 attacking enemy planes on February 20. On May 8, 1942, the *Lexington* was hit and eventually sank during the Battle of the Coral Sea (see Chapter 13).

The *Saratoga* also joined the battle fleet at San Pedro and went on to see tours of duty in both the Pacific and Atlantic oceans. At San Diego when the U.S. declared war, the *Saratoga* was ordered to relieve the Marines on Wake Island, but it was recalled beforehand.

On January 11, 1942, the *Saratoga* was hit by a Japanese submarine torpedo off Hawaii, which put it out of action until May. It fought at Guadalcanal (see Chapter 13), at the Solomon Islands, at the Marshall Islands, and in Sumatra and Java during the last days of the war.

Statistics (for the USS *Lexington* and USS *Saratoga*):

Cost: *Lexington:* $45,952,644.83, *Saratoga:* $43,856,492.59

Classification: Fleet carrier, *Lexington* class

Propulsion: 16 boilers powering engines generating 180,000 horsepower

Length: 888 feet

Beam: 106 feet

Draft: 32 feet

Displacement: 33,000 tons

Top speed: 34 knots (approximately 41 miles per hour)
Crew: *Lexington:* 2,122, *Saratoga:* 2,111
Armament: Eight 8-inch guns, twelve 5-inch guns, four 6-pound guns
Aircraft capacity: 81
Date commissioned: *Lexington:* December 14, 1927; *Saratoga:* November 16, 1927

USS *Yorktown* (CV-5) and USS *Enterprise* (CV-6): The Next Generation of Aircraft Carrier

After the 14,500-ton carrier the *Ranger* was launched, the Navy decreed that all future aircraft carriers would displace a minimum of 20,000 tons, have a maximum speed of 32.5 knots, and have underwater subdivisions for damage control, a protective horizontal deck over magazine stores and fuel tanks, more plane storage, four fast elevators, complete ordinance-handling facilities, two launch decks, and improved antiaircraft defenses. The *Yorktown* and the *Enterprise* carried many of these improvements and refined carrier tactics before World War II.

At Norfolk when Pearl Harbor occurred, the *Yorktown* was assigned to the Pacific Fleet and escorted Marines sent to reinforce American Samoa. From there, it traveled to the Gilbert Islands. Its first major engagement was the Battle of the Coral Sea, where it took a bomb hit that killed 66 men. After just three days in Hawaii for repairs, the carrier went to reinforce the fleet at Midway, where it took heavy damage and sank.

When the U.S. declared war on Japan, the *Enterprise* was in the Pacific, having just delivered a Marine fighter squadron to Wake Island. The *Enterprise* participated in most of the major engagements in the Pacific, include General Doolittle's raid on Japan, Midway, the Guadalcanal campaign, the assault on Truk in the Caroline Islands, the Battle of the Philippine Sea, the Battle of Leyte Gulf, and the Marine landing at Iwo Jima. The ship received the Presidential Unit Citation, the Navy Unit Commendation, and an incredible 20 battle stars for its valiant and steadfast service during World War II, making it the most decorated ship of the war. Decommissioned in 1947, the *Enterprise* was sold on July 1, 1958.

Statistics (for the USS *Yorktown* and USS *Enterprise*):
Classification: Fleet carrier, *Yorktown* class
Propulsion: Geared turbine engines on 4 screws generating 120,000 horsepower
Length: 809 feet
Beam: 83 feet

Draft: 28 feet
Displacement: 19,800 tons
Top speed: 34 knots (approximately 41 miles per hour)
Crew: *Yorktown:* 2,919, *Enterprise:* 2,919
Armament: Eight 5-inch guns, 22 .50–caliber machine guns
Aircraft capacity: 85
Date commissioned: *Yorktown:* September 30, 1937; *Enterprise:* May 12, 1938

The *Gato* Class Submarine: Death from Below

Although often overlooked in favor of the large-scale surface battles, U.S. submarines played an important role in the Pacific during World War II. At first submersibles were equipped with faulty torpedoes that ran too low, passing under their targets; when they did impact, they often didn't detonate due to faulty design. But when the subs got weapons that worked and the latest in sonar systems, they were a formidable force indeed.

In 1944 alone, Navy subs sank more than 600 Japanese ships totaling 2.7 million tons, more than in the previous three years combined. The submarine fleet accounted for 55 percent of the Japanese merchant vessels sunk during the war and more than a quarter of the warships, including the biggest aircraft carrier ever built up to that point, the *Shinano,* which was torpedoed on its maiden voyage. Submarines were also responsible for saving the lives of more than 500 downed airmen, including one Navy pilot named George Bush, who later became the president of the United States.

The backbone of the fleet was the *Gato* class, named after the first submarine that was completed. The *Gato* subs were fast and powerful and, with a cruising time of more than two months, could patrol longer than most submarines. After the war, many *Gato* subs operated well into the 1960s until they were replaced by nuclear submarines.

Statistics:
Propulsion: Twin shaft-driven propellers
Engines: 4 diesel motors producing 5,400 horsepower surface running, 2 main batteries powering four electric motors for submerged running
Length: 311 feet
Beam: 27 feet
Draft: 15 feet
Displacement: 2,025 tons surfaced, 2,424 tons submerged

Top speed: 20.5 knots (approximately 24.6 miles per hour) on the surface, 8.75 knots (10.5 miles per hour) submerged
Crew: 10 officers, 70 sailors
Armament: Six 21-inch bow torpedo tubes, four 21-inch stern torpedo tubes, one 3-inch deck gun, one .50–caliber deck gun
Maximum dive depth: 300 feet
Submerged endurance: 48 hours at 2 knots
Range: 11,000 miles at 10 knots
Maximum cruise time: 75 days

The USS *Forrestal:* The First Supercarrier

Named for the first secretary of defense, the *Forrestal* combed all the lessons learned about carriers from pre–World War II to the present. It was the first ship built with an angled flight deck, enabling planes to land and take off at the same time. It also had four new steam catapults and four deck elevators to swiftly move planes on and off the deck.

Its first year was spent in intensive training operations for sailors and pilots on using the ship's advanced technology. From there it sailed to the Mediterranean, where it put on demonstrations of its abilities. From 1958 to 1966, the *Forrestal* alternated tours between the Atlantic and Mediterranean squadrons. During this time, the carrier made history when a C-130F Hercules cargo plane landed on its deck, the largest plane to ever use a carrier.

In June 1967, the *Forrestal* headed for Vietnam to support the military action with air strikes. The next month, while launching A-4 Skyhawks, an ordnance accident ignited jet fuel and caused a raging inferno on the flight deck, killing 134 crewmen and injuring 62, and extensively damaging the carrier. The ship was repaired and returned to the Mediterranean the next year, where it stayed until 1975. It next participated in several military maneuvers for the Navy and NATO, including one in 1978 that took the carrier 150 miles south of Iceland to drill in severe weather.

In 1983, the carrier was refitted to extend its life for another two decades. It served in various tours near Libya, Turkey, and the Suez Canal. The *Forrestal*'s last action was in Desert Storm. Afterward, it became the Navy's training carrier until its decommissioning on September 11, 1993.

APPENDIX C: FAMOUS SHIPS OF THE UNITED STATES

Statistics:
Classification: Fleet carrier, *Forrestal* class
Propulsion: 8 boilers, 4 geared steam turbine engines on 4 screws generating 260,000 horsepower
Length: 1,046 feet
Width: 252 feet
Beam: 129 feet
Draft: 31 feet
Displacement: 60,000 tons, 79,300 tons full load
Top speed: 33 knots (approximately 40 miles per hour)
Crew: 3,019—flight crew: 2,480
Armament: Eight 5-inch guns
Aircraft capacity: 85
Date commissioned: October 1, 1955

The USS *Nautilus:* The First Nuclear Submarine

The Navy took its first voyage into the nuclear age with the *Nautilus.* The world's first nuclear submarine was begun on June 14, 1952. It was christened by Mamie Eisenhower and launched on January 21, 1954, and it began its first cruise powered by nuclear energy on January 17, 1955.

With its nuclear power plant providing energy for the ship's systems, including clean water and carbon dioxide scrubbers, the *Nautilus* was the world's first true submarine because it did not have to surface every few days to recharge batteries. Over the next few years, the submarine broke all underwater speed and endurance records. On July 23, 1958, the submarine left Pearl Harbor to make history again; 12 days later, it became the first vessel to sail under the North Pole.

In 1959, the fuel core was recharged. Then the submarine sailed to the Mediterranean, becoming the first nuclear-powered ship to serve with the Sixth Fleet. In the spring of 1966, the *Nautilus* logged its three hundred thousandth mile traveled. Over the next 12 years, it served in testing programs while new classes of submarines were being built.

The *Nautilus* was decommissioned on March 3, 1980, after 25 years and almost 500,000 miles covered in the world's oceans. Designated a National Historic Landmark in 1982, it is currently an interactive museum ship in Groton, Connecticut.

Statistics:
Cost: $65 million
Classification: SSN-571, *Nautilus* class
Propulsion: Twin shaft-driven propellers
Engine: S2W (Submarine, Model 2, Westinghouse) pressurized-water nuclear reactor
Length: 324 feet
Beam: 28 feet
Draft: 22 feet
Displacement: 3533 tons surfaced, 4,092 tons submerged.
Top speed: 22 knots (approximately 26.4 miles per hour) on the surface, 25 knots (30 miles per hour) submerged
Crew: 13 officers, 92 enlisted men
Armament: Six 21-inch bow torpedo tubes
Maximum dive depth: 700 feet
Range: 100,000+ miles
Date commissioned: September 30, 1954

The *Los Angeles* Class (SSN): The Next Generation of Submarines

The *Los Angeles* class of nuclear-powered submarine was developed in response to general concerns over the new Soviet submarines, particularly the November and Victor classes. Adm. Hyman Rickover pushed the funding through for a high-speed (35 knots) attack submarine to gradually replace the older *Sturgeon* class. Because Admiral Rickover wanted more speed, diving depth was reduced to 950 feet (the *Sturgeon* class could go about 1250 feet). But the first submarine, the *Los Angeles*, launched on April 6, 1974, satisfied his requirements and was a new class of fast, quiet, more-than-capable attack submarine.

In the 1980s, the *Los Angeles* class was upgraded to what is called Flight II, with improved sonar and the Vertical Launch System for Tomahawk Cruise Missiles installed, as well as a new antisonar coating to reduce signature and noise even further. The fuel core was also redesigned to keep the high speed despite the other improvements.

The *Los Angeles* hosted President Jimmy Carter in 1977 to demonstrate the new submarine's capabilities. It was then assigned to the Mediterranean squadron, where it earned the first of four Meritorious Unit Citations. It served for the next 15 years in the Pacific and Indian oceans. In 1992, the submarine reported to Pearl Harbor and was given the first Engineered Refueling Overhaul of a nuclear submarine, upgrading its sonar system, fire control, and reactor control equipment. In March 1995, the improved *Los Angeles* returned to duty and was assigned to Pearl Harbor.

Statistics:

Propulsion: 1 shaft-driven propeller

Engines: 1 SG6 nuclear reactor driving geared steam turbines producing 35,000 horsepower

Length: 360 feet

Beam: 33 feet

Draft: 32 feet

Displacement: 6,080 tons surfaced, 6,925 tons submerged

Top speed: 35 knots (approximately 42 miles per hour)

Crew: 14 officers, 127 sailors

Armament (688I class): Four 21-inch torpedo tubes, 12 VLS launch tubes for Harpoon and Tomahawk missiles

Maximum dive depth: 950 feet

The USS *Iowa* (BB-61), *New Jersey* (BB-62), *Missouri* (BB-63), and *Wisconsin* (BB-64): Giants of the Fleet

The next class of dreadnought battleship, a huge warship with nine 16-inch guns, was begun in 1940 and completed during World War II. After the war, fleets around the world scrapped their battleships, but the U.S. Navy decided to keep four in reserve. They were all reactivated for the Korean Conflict and then mothballed again after the war. The *New Jersey* served as part of the fleet in Vietnam but returned to inactive status in 1969.

With the construction of the Soviet *Kirov*-class battleships, the *Iowa class* warships were updated and reactivated. The *New Jersey* led the way in 1982, with its tour of duty taking it from El Salvador to Lebanon in under a year.

The other three ships followed after a refit that included new electronics and living quarters, a converted fuel system, a helicopter landing pad, and upgraded weapons systems. The battleships' defenses now include both Harpoon and Tomahawk cruise missile launchers, giving the venerable ships a new multi-strike capability.

In 1989, the *Iowa* suffered a mysterious internal explosion that killed 47 crewmembers and helped result in its decommission, along with the *New*

Jersey. The *Missouri* and the *Wisconsin* remained on duty and participated in Operation Desert Storm. Since then, all of these mighty giants have been decommissioned, with their future fate in the Navy undecided.

Statistics (for the *Iowa,* but they apply to each battleship):

Classification: *Iowa*-class battleship

Power: Eight 3-drum boilers, 4 sets of geared turbines generating 212,000 horsepower

Propulsion: Two 17-foot inboard propellers, two 18-foot outboard propellers

Length: 887 feet

Beam: 108 feet

Displacement: 43,900 tons, 57,200 tons fully loaded

Top speed: 33 knots (approximately 39.6 miles per hour)

Crew (as of 1983): 1,653 total—74 officers, 1,579 enlisted men

Armor: Hull: 12 inches, main deck: 1.5 inches, turret face: 20 inches, turret side: 9.5 inches, conning tower: 17.5 inches

Armament (in 1983): Nine 16-inch Mark 7 guns in three triple turrets, twelve 5-inch Mark 12 guns, four 20-mm Phalanx CIWS antiaircraft/missile guns, thirty-two BGM-109 Tomahawk cruise missiles, 16 RGM-84 Harpoon antiship missiles

Range (in 1945): 18,000 nautical miles at 12 knots

Date deployed: February 22, 1943

The *Arleigh Burke* Class (DDG): A Destroyer for a New Age

In 1980, a new class of destroyer was created to take advantage of the improved *Aegis* combat system, an integrated tracking weapon system using the AN/SPY-1B radar and satellite information that can identify more than 100 individual targets and guide a cruise missile to any one of them. This new destroyer would be equally capable against air, surface ship, and submarine threats.

Previous *Aegis* ships were modeled on the *Spruance* class, but this new ship would also have a hull designed for a smaller infrared and radar signature, and the Vertical Launch System that has become standard issue for the destroyer class. In 2002, the class is scheduled for another upgrade to the expandable *Aegis* system, installing new radar designed for a coastal environment and improved against electronic countermeasures.

In 1991, the DDG-51 *Arleigh Burke* was the first of its class deployed. With its cruise missile payload, its antimissile guns, including the computer-guided

MK 34 Gun Weapon System (GWS) and antiship or antisubmarine torpedoes, the *Burke* is among the most powerful ships ever built by the Navy. After a minor engineering overhaul, the *Arleigh Burke* was assigned to the USS *Harry S. Truman* battle group in the Persian Gulf in 2001. Currently, it is stationed in Norfolk, Virginia.

Statistics:

Classification: Destroyer

Propulsion: 4 General Electric LM 2500 gas turbines, with a total output of 134,400 horsepower

Length: 505 feet

Beam: 67 feet

Draft: 30 feet

Displacement: 8,300 tons full load

Top speed: 30+ knots (approximately 36 miles per hour)

Crew: 23 officers, 24 chief petty officers, and 291 enlisted men

Armament: 2 MK 41 Vertical Launching Systems for Standard missiles, 56 Tomahawk and 8 Harpoon missiles, 1 MK 45 5-inch gun, 2 Phalanx CIWS antimissile systems, 2 triple-tube MK 46 torpedo launchers

Date launched: September 16 1989

Date commissioned: July 4, 1991

The USS *John C. Stennis* (CVN-74): The Modern Aircraft Carrier

The latest version of the *Nimitz*-class aircraft carrier is the *John C. Stennis*, which incorporates the latest innovations developed since the original *Nimitz* carrier was completed in 1975.

Named for a United States senator, the *John C. Stennis* carries eight to nine aircraft squadrons, consisting of the F/A-18 Hornet, F-14 Tomcat, the EA-6B Prowler, the S-3 Viking, the E-2C Hawkeye, and the SH-60 Seahawk. In January 1997, the carrier received the first F/A-18 E/F Super Hornet on its deck, the first carrier landing by the new fighter plane.

The *John C. Stennis* is fully equipped for extended duty at sea and has major aircraft repair facilities, including a maintenance department, a micro-miniature electronics repair shop, already on board. The carrier carries approximately 3 million gallons of fuel for its aircraft. With four aircraft elevators and four steam catapults, it can launch dozens of planes as quickly as needed.

Since its launch in 1993, the carrier has served as the centerpiece of the *John C. Stennis* battle group, which also contains two missile cruisers, one antiaircraft missile destroyer, on antisubmarine warfare destroyer, one antiaircraft warfare frigate, one fast combat support ship (AOE), and two nuclear attack submarines. The group has served in the Persian Gulf during Operation Southern Watch and recently returned from providing support to American forces in Operation Enduring Freedom. It is stationed at San Diego, California, and was the aircraft carrier responsible for protection of the West Coast after September 11.

Statistics:

Classification: Nuclear-powered carrier, *Nimitz* class

Propulsion: 2 nuclear reactors powering 4 engines on 4 screws generating 130,000 horsepower

Length: 1,092 feet

Beam: 134 feet

Draft: 38 feet

Displacement: 100,000 tons with full load

Top speed: 35 knots (approximately 42 miles per hour)

Crew: Ship crew: 3,200, air crew: 2,480

Armament: 3 MK 29 Sea Sparrow missile launchers, 4 MK 15 20-mm Phalanx CIWS

Aircraft capacity: 85

Date commissioned: December 9, 1995

Projected service life: 50 years

APPENDIX D

SECRETARIES OF THE NAVY

Benjamin Stoddert
1798–1801

Robert Smith
1801–1809

Paul Hamilton
1809–1812

William Jones
1813–1814

Benjamin W.
Crowninshield
1815–1818

Smith Thompson
1819–1823

Samuel Southard
1823–1829

John Branch
1829–1831

Levi Woodbury
1831–1834

Mahlon Dickerson
1834–1838

James K. Paulding
1838–1841

George E. Badger
1841

Abel P. Upshur
1841–1843

David Henshaw
1843–1844

Thomas W. Gilmer
1844

John Y. Mason
1844–1845

George Bancroft
1845–1846

John Y. Mason
1846–1849

William B. Preston
1849–1850

William A. Graham
1850–1852

John P. Kennedy
1852–1853

James C. Dobbin
1853–1857

Isaac Toucey
1857–1861

Gideon Welles
1861–1869

Adolph E. Borie
1869

George M. Robeson
1869–1877

Richard W.
Thompson
1877–1880

Nathan Goff Jr.
1881

William H. Hunt
1881–1882

William E. Chandler
1882–1885

William C. Whitney
1885–1889

Benjamin F. Tracy
1889–1893

Hilary A. Herbert
1893–1897

John D. Long
1897–1902

William H. Moody
1902–1904

Paul Morton
1904–1905

Charles J. Bonaparte
1905–1906

Victor H. Metcalf
1906–1908

Truman H. Newberry
1908–1909

George von L. Meyer
1909–1913

Josephus Daniels
1913–1921

Edwin Denby
1921–1924

Curtis D. Wilbur
1924–1929

Charles F. Adams
1929–1933

Claude A. Swanson
1933–1939

Charles Edison
1940

Frank Knox
1940–1944

James Forrestal
1944–1947

John L. Sullivan
1947–1949

Francis P. Matthews
1949–1951

Dan A. Kimball
1951–1953

Robert B. Anderson
1953–1954

Charles S. Thomas
1954–1957

Thomas S. Gates
1957–1959

William B.Franke
1959–1961

John B. Connally Jr.
1961

Fred Korth
1962–1963

Paul B. Fay (acting)
1963

Paul H. Nitze
1963–1967

Charles F. Baird (acting)
1967

Paul R. Ignatius
1967–1969

John H. Chafee
1969–1972

John W. Warner
1972–1974

J. William Middendorf
1974–1977

W. Graham Claytor Jr.
1977–1979

Edward Hidalgo
1979–1981

John Lehman
1981–1987

James H. Webb
1987–1988

William L. Ball
1988–1989

Henry L. Garrett III
1989–1992

Daniel Howard (acting)
1992

Sean O'Keefe
1992–1993

Adm. Frank B. Kelso, II
(acting)
1993

John H. Dalton
1993–1998

Richard Danzig
1998–2001

Robert B. Pirie Jr.
(acting)
2001

Gordon R. England
2001–present

CHIEFS OF NAVAL OPERATIONS

Adm. William S. Benson
1915–1919

Adm. Robert E. Coontz
1919–1923

Adm. Edward W. Eberle
1923–1927

Adm. Charles F. Hughes
1927–1930

Adm. William V. Pratt
1930–1933

Adm. William H. Standley
1933–1937

Adm. William D. Leahy
1937–1939

Adm. Harold R. Stark
1939–1942

Fleet Adm. Ernest J. King
1942–1945

Fleet Adm. Chester W. Nimitz
1945–1947

Adm. Louis E. Denfeld
1947–1949

Adm. Forrest P. Sherman
1949–1951

Adm. William M. Fechteler
1951–1953

Adm. Robert B. Carney
1953–1955

Adm. Arleigh A. Burke
1955–1961

Adm. George W. Anderson Jr.
1961–1963

Adm. David L. McDonald
1963–1967

Adm. Thomas H. Moorer
1967–1970

Adm. Elmo R. Zumwalt
1970–1974

Adm. James L. Holloway III
1974–1978

Adm. Thomas B. Hayward
1978–1982

Adm. James D. Watkins
1982–1986

Adm. Carlisle A. H. Trost
1986–1990

Adm. Frank B. Kelso III
1990–1994

Adm. Jeremy M. Boorda
1994–1996

Adm. Jay L. Johnson
1996–2000

Adm. Vern Clark
2000–present

APPENDIX F

SELECTED BIBLIOGRAPHY

Bachrach, Deborah. *The Spanish American War.* San Diego, California: Lucent Books, Inc., 1991.

Beach, Edward L. *The United States Navy: 200 Years.* New York: Henry Holt and Company, 1986.

Beier, Betsy and Nathaniel Marunas. *Battleships.* New York: Michael Friedman Publishing Group, Inc., 2001.

Brown, Ashley and Jonathan Reed, ed. *The Navy.* Harrisburg, Pennsylvania: The National Historical Society, 1989.

Chambers, John Whiteclay II. *The Oxford Companion to American Military History.* New York: Oxford University Press, 1999.

Clancy, Tom. *Carrier: A Guided Tour of an Aircraft Carrier.* New York: Berkley Books, 1999.

———. *Submarine: A Guided Tour Inside a Nuclear Warship* (revised edition). New York: Berkley Books, 2002.

Fowler, William M. Jr. *Under Two Flags: The American Navy in the Civil War.* New York: W. W. Norton & Company, 1990.

Gailey, Harry A. *War in the Pacific: From Pearl Harbor to Tokyo Bay*. Novato, California: Presidio Press, 1995.

The Grolier Library of World War I. *The Causes of the War*. Danbury, Connecticut: Grolier Educational, 1997.

1914: The Race to the Sea. Danbury, Connecticut: Grolier Educational, 1997.

1917: The US Enters the War. Danbury, Connecticut: Grolier Educational, 1997.

The Aftermath of the War, Danbury, Connecticut: Grolier Educational, 1997.

Gruppe, Henry. *The Frigates*. Alexandria, Virginia: Time Life Books, 1979.

Hagan, Kenneth J. *This People's Navy: The Making of American Sea Power*. New York: The Free Press, 1991.

Harris, Brayton. *The Navy Times Book of Submarines: A Political, Social, and Military History*. New York: Berkley Books, 2001.

Hearn, Chester G. *An Illustrated History of the United States Navy*. London: Salamander Books, L2002.

Hoehling, A. A. *Damn the Torpedoes!: Naval Incidents of the Civil War*. Winston-Salem, North Carolina: John F. Blair, 1989.

Honan, William H. *Fire When Ready, Gridley!* New York: St Martin's Press, 1993.

Howarth, Stephen. *To Shining Sea: A History of the United States Navy 1775–1991*. New York: Random House, 1991.

Jordan, John. *The New Illustrated Guide to the Modern US Navy*. London: Salamander Books, 1992.

APPENDIX F: SELECTED BIBLIOGRAPHY

Kaplan, Philip. *Fly Navy: Naval Aviators and Carrier Aviation—A History.* London: MetroBooks, 2001.

Keegan, John. *The First World War.* New York: Alfred A. Knopf, 1999.

Kunhardt, Philip B. Jr., Philip B. Kunhardt III, and Peter W. Kunhardt. *The American President.* New York: Riverhead Books, 1999.

Layton, Edwin T., and Roger Pineau. *"And I Was There": Pearl Harbor and Midway—Breaking the Secrets.* Old Saybrook: Konecky & Konecky, 1985.

Lehman, John. *On Seas of Glory: Heroic Men, Great Ships, and Epic Battles of the American Navy.* New York: The Free Press, 2001.

Leckie, Robert. *The Wars of America.* Edison, New Jersey: Castle Books, 1998.

Man, John. *The War to End Wars 1914–1918.* Pleasantville, New York: The Reader's Digest Association, Inc., 2000.

Marrin, Albert. *The Spanish American War.* New York: Atheneum, 1991.

Marvel, William, ed. *The Monitor Chronicles.* New York: Simon & Schuster, 2000.

Musicant, Ivan. *Divided Waters: The Naval History of the Civil War.* New York: HarperCollins, 1995.

Nardo, Don. *The Mexican-American War.* San Diego, California: Lucent Books, Inc., 1999.

———. *The War of 1812.* San Diego, California: Lucent Books, Inc., 1999.

Popular Science Books. *21st Century Soldier: The Weaponry, Gear, and Technology of the New Century.* New York: Time, Inc., Home Entertainment, 2002.

Reilly, John C. Jr. *United States Navy Destroyers of World War II.* Poole, Dorset: Blandford Press, 1983.

Strachan, Hew. *The Oxford Illustrated History of the First World War.* Oxford, New York: Oxford University Press, 1998.

Sulzberger, C. L. and Stephen E. Ambrose. *American Heritage New History of World War II.* Middlesex: Viking, 1997.

Traxel, David. *1898: The Birth of the American Century.* New York: Alfred A. Knopf, 1998.

Van der Vat, Dan. *The Pacific Campaign: WW II: The US–Japanese Naval War 1941–1945.* New York: Simon & Schuster, 1991.

Winter, Jay and Blaine Baggett. *The Great War: And the Shaping of the 20th Century.* New York: Penguin Books USA, Inc., 1996.

Woog, Adam. *The 1900s: A Cultural History of the United States: Through the Decades.* San Diego, California: Lucent Books, Inc., 1999.

INDEX

X-Y-Z